ON WINE

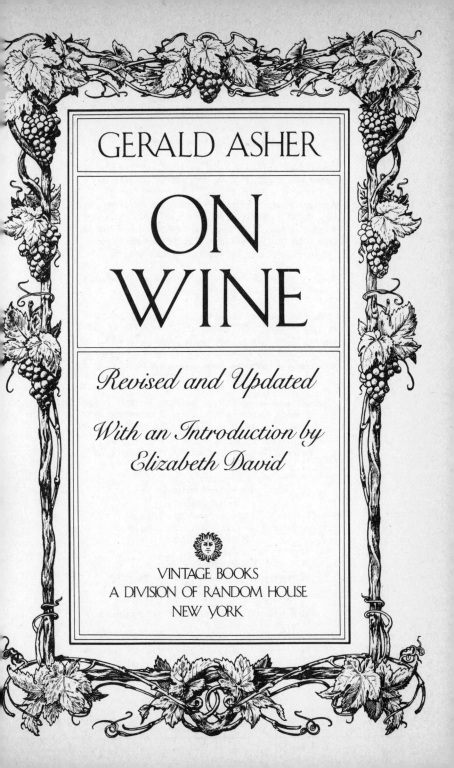

GERALD ASHER

ON WINE

Revised and Updated

With an Introduction by
Elizabeth David

VINTAGE BOOKS
A DIVISION OF RANDOM HOUSE
NEW YORK

Library of Congress Cataloging-in-Publication Data
Asher, Gerald.
On wine.
"Revised and updated."
Includes index.
1. Wine and wine making.   I. Title.
TP548.A79 1986   641.2'22   85-40696
ISBN 0-394-74328-8

Drawings by Paul Sharp
Cartography by Anita Karl and James Kemp
Typography by J. K. Lambert

Cover painting: *Still Life* by Jean Baptiste Simeon Chardin. Courtesy of The National Gallery, London.

FOR MY SONS
Jeremy and Japhet

CONTENTS

MAPS

INTRODUCTION

I READ somewhere recently that one of our more unconventional British wine writers once wrote of a wine that it grasped you by the hand and called you by your first name. Well, however unconventional Gerald Asher may be I don't think talking wines are much in his line—the one in question sounds ominously like the Club Buttonholer—but I do think he's a phenomenon equally unexpected. He's such a compelling talker about wine that even the most uninitiated, including myself, is going to listen and be entertained and learn, and as Gerald—to do my own bit of first-name calling—writes exactly like he talks, anyone who reads this book is going to have a lot of entertainment and enlightenment. It is like this. Should Gerald by any chance be saying—he isn't, I'm just supposing—that a wine has a hint of hyacinths he doesn't even wait for the skeptical look to appear on your face. He explains— this time I quote—that "all wines share at least traces of most of the acids, alcohols and esters occurring in everything from bananas to roses." That's something that may be obvious to wine experts and chemists, but until I learned it from Gerald I didn't appreciate the point, so I've always been exasperated by the violets and truffles of wine analysis. I should add that Gerald seldom resorts to that kind of description, preferring to give information more illuminating and exact. Thus we learn that a wine from vineyards halfway down the higher slopes of the Sancerre hills is likely to be one of the best of the district. A particular combination of soil types contributes to this excellence. These fine points once appreciated, we have at least a clue as to why so many bottles of Sancerre don't come up to expectation and why, when one does, it does. I like that. Isn't it what anybody who has just once or twice experienced a bottle of that enchanting wine at its best and is at last about to renounce the search for more of the same will want to know?

The kind of knowledge to be acquired from this book may well of course end in getting a trifle troublesome and expensive. So I should warn potential readers that it's pretty well crammed with tempting invitations to be off on restless quests for this or that rarity. Here's an unexpected sample. One of the most delicious rosés in the world, it turns out, so far from being the overpriced—and overpraised—Tavel of tradition, is German. It comes from the Glottertal, is made from a combination of Spätburgunder and Ruländer grapes, and is to be sought in and around Freiburg. So. And did you ever before hear of a grape from the Neckar valley called the Trollinger, from which is made another rosé which sounds as if it had been named after the poet Schiller? Well, that's a tease, because Schillerwein means that the wine is iridescent, which I take to mean that it has the shimmer of shot silk or taffeta. Still, it's only the wine of the Heidelberg students, and according to Gerald's account it wouldn't be worth going all that way just to drink like a Heidelberg student. We're warned off that one.

Now it would be most wrong of me to give the impression that this book is entirely or even mainly concerned with such unicorns as the faultless Sancerre or with what Gerald himself calls "other wines," and what one of my old friends in the English wine trade used to call funnies, a term he applied to all table wines that didn't come from Bordeaux, Burgundy, Alsace, or the classic vineyards of Germany. But I do have to explain that when I first knew Gerald Asher in London, in the 1950s, it was chiefly for his flair in finding and importing those "other wines" that he had made his firm's name known, in the restaurant world as well as to a very large list of private customers. Joyfully, we discovered that in Asher Storey's cellars there were not only choice rarities like single-vineyard Burgundies and the legendary white Château Grillet from the Rhône, but also rather more approachable treasures in the shape of a quite extraordinary collection of regional wines, some of them encountered perhaps a couple of times on trips to France or Italy but never hitherto on the English side of the Channel because, the wine trade told us, they didn't travel. Under Gerald's auspices, however, unusual wines like the red Saumur-Champigny of Anjou, sweet, mellow Monbazillac, a red Gamay and a fresh dry white Apremont from the Savoie appeared to travel with notable success. (Irrelevant though it is, I can't resist adding here that if Gerald weren't a wine merchant he would probably be the world's best travel agent, tour arranger, courier and guide.)

A beguiling *vin gris* called Cendré de Novembre from the Jura became a London restaurant favorite, and one memorable day an unknown golden dessert wine, bearing on its label the name Muscat de Beaumes-de-Venise, arrived on my doorstep. At the time that delicious wine was the product of just one single vineyard owner, and had rarely traveled further than the boundaries of its native Provence, let alone overseas. Gerald Asher, dauntless as ever, had brought some to London. I fell in love with that wine. Its rapid disappearance from the Asher Storey cellars, partly, I must own, as the result of an article I wrote about it in a small-circulation political weekly, was the occasion of much lamenting among its small band of addicts, myself not least. Beaumes-de-Venise is a familiar name now, and its wine is exported to America as well as to England, but although I still drink it with pleasure it has never again had quite the impact it did on the day Gerald sent it along and left me to discover it for myself.

This small incident I recount because I think discovery of that kind is in many ways the very essence of Gerald's book. He knows that he, as guide, can only take you so far, explain so much, give you the appropriate amount of technical background, communicate his own pleasure—as witness his joyous accounts of trips to the Beaujolais—or, as the case may be, the reverse. Then, expert guide as he is, he will leave you on your own. About wine, as about most things, you must make up your own mind and formulate your own conclusions, and nobody knows that better than Gerald Asher.

In 1981 I visited San Francisco, where Gerald now lives and works, for the very first time in my life. He was my host, and my chief guide around the city and into the country, to restaurants and to food markets, and of course it was he who initially introduced me to the wines of California which are now one of his major interests. It was an enlightening and very happy experience, and although at the time I don't think that this book was even planned, in my mind I connect it with those weeks in California as much as with France and Italy, and the London of Gerald's early days in the wine trade. It all adds up to such a happy, open-hearted, friendly book—nobody has to worry about the author's formidable knowledge and expertise, it is too discreetly concealed to be more than sensed—that it is hard to believe there can be any need for an introduction. But since I was invited to supply one, it has been my privilege to do so.

—*Elizabeth David*
London, April 1982

PREFACE

WHILE STILL a student in London, concerned with Elizabethan dramatists who had had the misfortune to be contemporaries of Shakespeare, I took a job from five to seven every evening behind the counter of a wine shop. It stood in the raffish pedestrian way between Piccadilly and Curzon Street called Shepherd Market, though better known, before the Street Offences Act, for its shepherdesses. Meat was then still rationed to eight ounces a week, or something equally measly, and red wine, I was assured, provided a necessary alternative source of strength. In the early evening, at least, most sales were half bottles of Beaujolais to solitary ladies.

When I had worked there for less than a week, the manager told me, as I arrived one afternoon, that we had to meet a delicate situation. Without warning to allow appropriate preparation, our Beaujolais supplier had replaced the 1947 vintage. Afraid that the regular customers would check other stores before accepting the 1949, he instructed me to hand each of those I recognized a free half bottle. But first he had me taste it against the last of the 1947 so that I could say, with assurance, that the new vintage was every bit as good, if not better. It was a novel experience, comparing one wine with another, and though I suppose there are more bizarre ways of finding a life's vocation, that's when and how I discovered mine.

I soon migrated from Shepherd Market to Pall Mall, to the offices of a large London wine shipper, where I checked the identification numbers of wooden crates returned for credit against records kept in old-fashioned ledgers. It was work tedious beyond imagining in today's world of disposable cartons and electronic records. The stock clerk at the next desk had the job I envied. He went down to the cellars once a month to reconcile his books with actual bottles. I would hear him discussing problems over the telephone with the cellar manager and reporting the discrepancies to the managing director. It was his habit to vary pronunciation of the wine names according to circumstances, perhaps to avoid misunderstandings. The Vosne-Romanée of the office, for example, became Vozny-Romany when he spoke to the cellars, Pauillac became Polly-Ack, and Pouilly-Fuissé, inevitably, Pussy-Fussy.

The young men in the office were free to try any wines open in the tasting room. I am sure there wasn't an actual ban on women clerks and secretaries doing the same thing, but it was understood that they didn't. By a process I no longer remember, I was put in charge of the tasting room and was later allowed to be a silent participant at the ritual of checking current stocks, appraising new wines, examining returned bottles. But tasting such a wide range of disconnected wines, both healthy and sick, day after day, was exposure rather than education. A normal working session assembles wines so varied, and for such different purposes, that it is difficult to arrive at the general conclusions necessary to build a framework of tasting reference.

The London wine trade was, and is, close. At that time, at the beginning of the 1950s, prominent companies were still family controlled if not family owned. They clustered on and around Mark Lane and Tower Hill, to be near the docks and the Custom House, and in the Pall Mall and St. James's area, within striking distance of the West End's clubs, restaurants, and hotels. A well-organized system of trade training now takes entrants through a methodically graduated series of lectures, tastings, and practical work, culminating in examinations for the professional diploma of Master of Wine. The trainees of my day, however, sponsored by their respective companies, presented themselves each spring, very self-consciously, at the Upper Thames Street building of the Worshipful Company of Vintners, and in the splendor of a paneled hall where five kings had dined together in 1363, were there introduced to the ancient mysteries of wine. On Thursday mornings, I recall, under the auspices of the Wine Trade Club (which had been founded by André Simon and his contemporaries), distinguished members of the trade imparted to us something of their knowledge and experience, guiding us through tastings for which each of us would bring six tulip-shaped nosing glasses in identical cardboard boxes.

"Wine," we were taught, like an article of the faith, "is the alcoholic beverage obtained from the juice of freshly gathered grapes, the fermentation of which has been carried through in the district of origin and according to local tradition and practice." Winemaking, thirty years ago, lacked the sophistication that has since become universal. Stainless steel, cultured yeasts, temperature-controlled fermentation and clarification by centrifuge were not unknown, but they had not imposed the dominant grapy fragrance that brings out similarities in modern wines rather than the bold differences we knew. Technique has now acquired importance beyond soil and grape variety. We find red Graves, made by carbonic maceration, that taste like tannic Beaujolais, and *trocken* Rheingau wines that can easily be mistaken for merely unsuccessful Alsatians. Recently, in La Mancha, south of Madrid, a winemaker told me that a well-known brand of Liebfraumilch was his criterion in making and judging his white Valdepeñas. It is all the inevitable result of marketing wine instead of selling it, I suppose. Once we looked for ways to teach the world how to enjoy wine's variety. Now we teach winemakers the ways of the world.

As each spring series ended, we wrote essays that summarized and discussed what we had learned, and depending on their quality we received Certificates of Attendance, Certificates of Merit, or, with luck, bursaries that paid expenses to one of the wine regions where study, and sometimes work, opportunities were arranged. I benefited from these bursaries, and the extended periods I was able to spend in Spain, France, and Germany over three years provided a foundation for my professional training.

Abroad, I saw the physical connection of wines and vineyards, and began to understand the link between wines and those who produce them, especially in the context of the food they ate and the way they lived. My *optique* of wine, as the French would say, was bound up with it as an expression of people, time, and place. I can debate chemical composition of soils with the best of them, but when carried to excess, as they too often are, such preoccupations are a barrier to pleasure, not an enhancement. At the tables of growers and merchants wines were indeed analyzed, pondered, discussed, and compared, sometimes in practical winemaking terms, but always with natural awareness of what we were, after all, talking about, much as a fruit farmer might talk of the cultivation of pears in the course of enjoying one. There was none of the technical one-upmanship, the brittle display, the squandering of pleasure by pointlessly ferreting out and commenting on every fault, real or imagined, that can spell disaster for a convivial evening.

Though I learned a great deal about wine and the wine trade at this time, no one taught me how to make a sales presentation or even how to write an order, because we took for granted that ours was an occupation for gentlemen and that familiarity with wine allied to friendship, rather than salesmanship (a word that would not have been used), was the key to success. So, partly because it was known as the representatives' grave, used both to test the mettle of new men and to dispose of old, but mostly because I was raised there and was presumed to have the qualification of some local acquaintance, I was dispatched to reveal my newly acquired knowledge to the farmers of East Anglia, propelled there in a small, battered Ford, essential transportation nonetheless described by my managing director as a "perk." In providing it, he felt himself relieved of any obligation to increase my salary in keeping with my responsibilities.

Though close to London, East Anglia was still a rural backwater where rook-filled elm trees swayed tall above wide, flat horizons. Except for Ipswich, a city festooned with bus wires and hoardings, I remember nothing ugly about the busy towns and villages of my "territory." But then they included Cambridge and Norwich; Ely, King's Lynn, and Newmarket; Fakenham, Lavenham, and Bury St. Edmunds. Specially satisfying, because I love the pale blur of an East Anglian seashore, were regular visits to Aldeburgh, Southwold, and Cromer. It was a happy time, and within months I had revived for my employers accounts long considered lost, bringing a respectable volume of increased business.

The wine trade was regarded as a convenient refuge for those of good family who were ill equipped for the intellectual challenge of law or medicine, yet insufficiently rich to be placed in private banking in the City. He who had every right to be modest in his expectations was thus kept from the shame of idleness, but, in the process, depressed the expectations of the rest of us. For nearly five years my "salary" had remained unchanged. Proud of my accomplishments, I asked the managing director if he would review it. He was taken aback. "Young man," he said, turning me down, "if I were to grant an increase, it would merely encourage you to ask again another time. There'd be no holding you."

On those conditions there wasn't, and I decided to set up in business on my own. In addition to customers in East Anglia, I had developed a few accounts in London, among them Ivan Storey's Soup Kitchen on Chandos Place adjacent to Charing Cross Hospital, where Ivan was a staff psychiatrist. He had converted an unprepossessing shop front into a student-chic soup, salad, and omelet bar. Blowups of nineteenth-century etchings hung in surreal combinations above tables and benches designed by Terence Conran, then fresh from design school and very much in his post–Festival of Britain bent-wire and plywood period. The venture was hugely successful. Exhilarated, Ivan rented additional premises on Wilton Place near Knightsbridge, where now stands the new Berkeley Hotel, and there he opened an even larger, smarter Soup Kitchen with a consumption of wine, whether by customers, patients, staff, or friends of staff (distinctions were vague) that was prodigious. When he heard what I intended to do, he offered to join me as a partner: hence, Asher Storey & Company.

Except for the bright yellow cover (I was Beardsley-struck at the time), our first list could hardly have been more conventional or dull. I recognized my mistake, and realized that we needed to offer alternatives to other shippers' wines rather than attempt to duplicate them. Their well-established and prestigious labels were too strong for us to compete with directly. I had always been interested in the "lesser" wines of France and went off in search of them. Unlike Bordeaux and Burgundy, meticulously charted and served by brokers and English-speaking shippers who made overseas trade a simple matter, the tributary valleys of the Loire, the far reaches of the southwest, and the slopes of the Jura and Savoie were at that time unsurveyed, and I had only imprecise references by nineteenth-century writers and uninformative pamphlets to go by. Modern books, after dealing adequately with Champagne, Burgundy, and Bordeaux, tended to lump "other French wines" into a few paragraphs that did little more than acknowledge that there were such things. I learned about them as I went,

and having decided for myself what *was* the essential character of
Jurançon, of Irancy, of Jasnières, of Apremont, of whatever, I
had to choose, in each case, the wine that showed that character
best, discover which grower was the most reliable, and arrive myself at definitions of "quality" and "value" in wines isolated from
the mainstream of the trade even within France. (The French are
the most parochial of wine drinkers: few in the Rhône Valley have
tasted Bordeaux; Alsatians do not drink Loire wine; Burgundians
have no curiosity about the wines of Dordogne or Pyrenees.)
Some of the growers had lists of private customers, including a
few in Paris who ordered a case from time to time as a reminder,
perhaps, of a summer vacation or as a sentimental attachment to
their native region. But most sold their wines to local restaurateurs,
and it was through them that I found my most valuable sources.

Just as my later move to California revealed unexpected aspects
of European wines, so my involvement with these "lesser" wines,
set deep in the fabric of rural French life, gave me an uncommon
perspective of the classic wines in which I had been trained. Asher
Storey and its retail side, Wine Vaults, grew, and though we maintained an emphasis on lesser-known French wines (to this day,
from what is said, one might be forgiven for imagining that I
invented them), we needed those classic wines, too. At that period,
Burgundy and Bordeaux were shipped to England mainly through
the established *négoçiants*. There was little estate-bottled Burgundy
imported, surprisingly, and wines of the small, unclassified vineyards of Bordeaux were mostly bottled and sold under the labels
of major shippers. But in my search for the lesser wines I had
formed habits hard to break. In particular, I was used to buying
only in growers' cellars, picking out what I wanted barrel by
barrel. I approached the great regions in the same way, tramping
through *chai* and *cave*, asking the questions I would have asked
in Lot or Languedoc. The growers responded with warmth and
enthusiasm, and our mutual respect became the basis of friend-
ships that have endured.

Since 1967, when we had first received inquiries for our more
esoteric French wines, I had been visiting the United States twice
a year to sell wines for direct shipment from France. Taking the
view that I was selling "British expertise," the British Embassy in
Washington generously sponsored me by providing the chancery
rotunda for the first tasting of our wines. In 1971 I moved to the

United States permanently, leaving a large, old-fashioned house in an overgrown garden near London for a small city apartment high above Manhattan in order to assume responsibility for imported wine sales at Austin, Nichols & Company.

Austin, Nichols were then preeminent in the United States for their unequaled stocks of Bordeaux classified growths. In London, Bordeaux classified growths had played a minor role for me; indeed, my attachment to lesser-known wines had given me somewhat the reputation of an iconoclast. But in New York, to my surprise and amusement, the importance of Austin, Nichols' Bordeaux business was such that I was an instant pillar of the wine establishment.

There were other, less amusing, surprises. If in England the wine trade is a gentlemen's occupation, the "industry" is hardly thought of that way in the United States. I had to supply mug shot, fingerprints, and personal history to the Bureau of Alcohol, Tobacco and Firearms, whose representatives visited friends and acquaintances in the course of their inquiries. It was clear that I was to consider myself henceforth a potential criminal, at very least. Indeed, I was soon to realize that the laws relating to the sale of wine—irrational, demeaning, and absurdly varied from state to state—make certain that everyone involved with the wine and spirit trade of this country will at some time, knowingly or unknowingly, commit an offense. As Bernard Rudofsky, in *Notes and Footnotes on the Lost Art of Living*, comments wryly, "If Jesus Christ should want to visit this country, he certainly would have to mend his ways. A repetition of the multiplication of bread might be greeted with hosannas, but a miracle of changing water into wine would land him in jail in the holier of the states."

State regulations are unbelievably complicated and messy. They add unnecessary costs to the simple distribution of wine, and in many states they seriously restrict the choice of what might reasonably be enjoyed within the bounds of law. For years North Carolina "protected" its residents from fine old Bordeaux because of a state regulation requiring chemical analysis of any wine to be offered for sale. This meant that if we, or any other importer, had a small quantity of, say, Cheval Blanc 1947, none would be offered to the Tarheel State; we were not about to dispatch even one precious bottle to the pipettes and test tubes of a Raleigh laboratory. And the state of Washington still requires chemical analysis of any wine to be sold above the Columbia River.

Winemakers of the world disregard the offensive implication but are cynical about the whole wasteful process. They know that once a wine is "approved," subsequent shipments, even if from later, and therefore different, bottlings, or from later vintages, are not subject to reanalysis. Until quite recently, Michigan subjected all trial bottles to a taste test in the laboratory, as well as chemical analysis. The qualifications a technician might need to fulfill the role of arbiter of what could, and what could not, please the palates of an entire, populous, and sophisticated state would be hard to describe, let alone find, combined, in one mere mortal. The industry suffers this rigmarole quietly as part of the fiscal and emotional cost of doing business, reluctant to disturb relations with state officials, most of whom do their best to make the unworkable workable. Change is unlikely: it can come only through legislation, and the subject is too sensitive for most politicians. They see in it little chance of political advantage to offset the probable political risk.

By representing Austin, Nichols on the Wine Committee (and later on the Champagne Committee) of the National Association of Beverage Importers in New York, I learned a great deal about the structure of the industry and the personalities involved. While absorbing so much that was new, I regretted only that my work as an importer left largely undisturbed my ignorance of American wine.

I had already met California wine under the most propitious of circumstances. In 1967, on my first visit to San Francisco, I had been invited, through a friend's introduction, to a dinner in Pacific Heights where I was served Château Latour 1955 alongside Inglenook Cabernet Sauvignon 1954. Had I nurtured any condescending prejudice, it would have been dispelled. On my return in 1968 I visited the Napa Valley and met Robert Mondavi, then as now overflowing with enthusiasm, and Joe Heitz, calmly matter-of-fact about his wine but as proud as he had a right to be.

Later, when I had moved to New York, I continued to spend a day or two in Napa or Sonoma whenever I visited the West Coast. In a burst of activity, vineyards were spreading in all directions. That included Monterey County, where, early in 1974, a project between a San Francisco corporation and a new vineyard and winery was being formed. The purpose of the joint venture was to develop a range of quality wines that would help bring recognition to a new area, and I was invited to California to direct it, a challenge too exciting to refuse. I stayed with it for two years and earned my education in California wine the hard way.

Since then my work has expanded to embrace, once again, European wines as well as our own, and I am sometimes in the odd position of explaining France to California and vice versa. Shuttling from one to the other, I see the mutual influence: wines from California's newer wineries acquiring the grace to accompany food rather than merely the heft to engage in county-fair combat, and French wines becoming less prone to winemaking accidents.

There are days, of course, when I feel twinges of conscience at having deserted my literary muse to follow Dionysus, but if wine is, indeed, "begetter of all arts," I tell myself that perhaps I have served her better this way.

ACKNOWLEDGMENTS

SO MUCH is owed to so many that it becomes impossible to acknowledge every debt. From almost everyone I have met, every book I have read, and every wine I have tasted, I have learned something that I hope to have passed on in these pages. I owe special thanks to Jane Montant of *Gourmet*, who first asked me to write these essays; to Robert Lescher, who encouraged me to assemble this book; and to Ed Hinger, who plied me with wine while I did it.

ON WINE

Guessing Games

I NEVER ASK a guest to identify a wine—it can too easily wreck friendship and cause indigestion—though I often leave a wine incognito until everyone has had a chance to form an opinion of it. Some years ago, a guest who knows his stuff started to identify a wine I had just poured for lunch with the words, "Well, it's a Burgundy, that much is clear." Afraid he would pursue this line of discovery and have more words to eat than he might have stomach for, I quickly pointed out that the wine was, in fact, from Bordeaux. Completely unruffled, he put down his glass and said, "Oh. In *that* case, it's La Lagune '61." And, of course, he was right.

Less adroit at a dinner in New York, I tangled with a Pétrus 1964. In the circumstances of the dinner (something one should never be influenced by), I was predisposed to expect a mature California Cabernet, read all the signs the wine gave me as miles instead of kilometers, and managed to get myself hopelessly lost. I connected the smoky bouquet and flavor to the gravelly vineyards of Rutherford in the Napa Valley rather than to the gravelly plateau of Pomerol. When (more accurately) I assessed the wine at roughly fifteen years old, a fellow guest, himself a California winemaker, agreed but asked me who could have been making wine in this style *in Napa* in 1964. A Socratic question that, properly considered, should have put me back on track.

What brought both incidents to mind was the comment of a fellow passenger with whom I was chatting on a recent flight home from Denver. When he heard I was in the wine trade, he modestly disclaimed expertise by telling me he couldn't tell Bordeaux from Burgundy. "In fact," he said, "I sometimes confuse French with California." I suppose he thought I was being tactful when I mumbled, "It can happen to anybody."

Before brewers, computers, and quality-control technicians took it over, the London wine trade made a practice of eating rather indifferent cold lunches in each other's offices relieved only by the quality of the wines, good Stilton, and the ritual of "guessing the Port." (To be a better wine merchant in such circumstances, as Talleyrand knew in another context, required mostly a good cook and a battery of saucepans.) Everyone chipped in half a crown— a taxi fare in those days rather than today's price of a daily newspaper—and if no one got it right, the kitty went to a trade charity. Listening to more experienced colleagues exchanging reasons why the wine might be Cockburn's rather than Taylor's, a 1927 rather than a 1934, taught me more about vintage Port than any number of academic tasting-room sessions. The false starts and spoken thoughts of one would spur on another, and a single remark could illuminate for me and make memorable the style of a shipper, the characteristics of a year, the distinctive contribution of a particular vineyard site. There were no far-fetched analogies in such company: words were few and apt.

Roald Dahl's short story "Taste" exaggerates the sort of language we used (at least, I *hope* it does); but as a baroque exposition of such signpost reading and checking of clues against memory, knowledge, and reason, it is as good an account as any. In it a guest displays a sinister combination of aesthetic scholarship and unscrupulous lust, or perhaps the other way round, by concealing his prior knowledge of what he is drinking so that he might give a convincing performance of identifying a wine and thus win possession of his host's horrified young daughter. To arrive at this conclusion too quickly would arouse suspicion; to do so without showing his reasoning, while gaining his immediate objective, might make an equally disquieting impression. He builds to his conclusion slowly, questioning himself on the significance of each whiff and wink in the glass, rejecting the suggestion of one when it clashes with the certainty of another. (Be reassured, those of you who have not yet read the story: Bacchus will not be mocked. In a masterly ending the girl is saved from a fate worse than a poor vintage.)

My favorite story of wine guessing games, told by Peter Sichel about his cousin Charles, distills the ethos of certain wine-trade encounters. Guests at a luncheon in Paris, they were asked to guess the wine. Almost without pausing, Charles identified it as La Tâche 1929, and their host congratulated him. When they left the house, Peter turned to his cousin and asked why he had made such a ludicrous suggestion, adding, "The wine was no more La Tâche than it was 1929. It wasn't even Burgundy."

"I just wanted to see if D——— is really as excessively polite as everyone says he is," said Charles.

Professionals don't, in fact, spend their lives attaching identities to wines; but the more they taste in the course of their work, the greater their ease in naming what is put before them. Some are more skilled than others, naturally, and for obvious reasons most who specialize have areas of particular competence. Just as an art historian looks for the style associated with a place and period—a characteristic brush technique, a master's assurance—so a taster is taught, or teaches himself, what to expect of wines according to when, where, and how they are made.

Approaching a wine professionally, as opposed to drinking it for pleasure, the taster first gets an overall impression by looking, smelling, and tasting, and then he starts to analyze. Usually he is told what the wine is supposed to be, and he measures it against his expectation of a Pommard, a Graves, a Bernkasteler, or whatever. He must know why individual wines taste as they do, not just in terms of their physical composition—more or less tannin, higher or lower acidity—but in terms of the soil, the climate, and the manner in which the grapes were harvested and fermented. Only then can he judge whether a missing component is an accident of weather, a result of winemaking technique, or an indication of something more seriously amiss. Understanding "what makes a wine taste how" is the basis of identifying an unknown. Each grape variety gives wine distinctive characteristics; the soil in which it is grown and the climate (even the weather of a particular growing season) will influence the style in a predictable way. Picking up the varietal characteristics and "reading" the style is how the taster traces the wine to its origin, including the year it was grown. From first impressions he develops a hypothesis that he tests and modifies against each subsequent clue he finds in smelling and tasting the wine.

On rare occasions, if a wine is very familiar, one can tell by the first look, smell, and taste, but the chances of such instant recognition are remote. In the early 1960s, when Booth's Distilleries in London closed down their wholesale wine department, I bought a few cases of half bottles of Château de Rayne-Vigneau 1923, a Sauternes that was drying slightly but that made a perfect ending to many of our twice-weekly office lunches. Kenneth Bell, who had recently opened his restaurant at Thornbury Castle near Bristol, must have bought some too. When I had consumed so much Rayne-Vigneau so often and for so long that I could have identified it from the smell of an emptied glass, he brought to my table one evening a mysteriously swathed half bottle and promised me a reward of any wine in his cellar (quite a collection at that time) if I could guess the vintage and vineyard of the sweet white wine he poured for me. Identifying sweet white wines, especially older ones, is notoriously difficult. The sugar dominates everything and tends to block out or overwhelm the other clues. Very sweet, late-picked Johannisberg Rieslings from California are almost indistinguishable from German Trockenbeerenauslesen with histories as long and as complicated as that of Alberich's ring for this reason.

Anyway, as luck would have it, Bell had landed on a tiny area of what was, at that time, my particular competence. Unfortunately, I lacked the theatrical talent of the central character of Roald Dahl's story and blurted out the vintage and vineyard so precipitately that Bell's suspicions were aroused. To protect my honor I felt obliged to explain. Worse, I then felt obliged to refuse to despoil him of his best bottle by taking advantage of a coincidence.

Normally, however, the wine reveals itself more slowly. Most tasters try to decide first what grape, or family of grapes, it was made from. Even when the characteristic of a particular grape is low-key, like a Gamay, or possibly neutral, like one of the several white grapes used in the south of France, it is still the dominant factor. If the wine is European, the grape variety points to where the wine was grown. In France, for example, wines made from Pinot Noir, Gamay, and other early-ripening varieties come from the center and the northeast: Beaujolais, Burgundy, Jura, and Champagne. Wines from Cabernet Sauvignon, Cabernet Franc, Merlot, and related varieties are produced down the Atlantic coast and in the valleys that open to the ocean.

When a wine is young, the grape variety gives a very distinctive aroma, but as it ages the influence of soil on bouquet and flavor emerges more clearly and the varietal aroma fades. The effect of soil on vine and wine probably stems more from water-holding properties than from chemical composition, though chalk and iron do affect the style of wine appreciably. Chalk improves color and boosts alcoholic strength; it intensifies varietal aroma and flavor. Compare, for example, a Sauvignon Blanc wine grown on the chalky hillsides of Sancerre with a Sauvignon Blanc grown on the gravel of Bordeaux or on the sandy hills of California. It is chalk, too, that concentrates the Pinot Noir flavor of Côte d'Or Burgundies, and the scantiness of such terrain in California is one possible reason why we do not do as well with Pinot Noir here as we do with Chardonnay.

The significant difference from clay to sand to gravel, however, is the size of the particles and the water space around them. Sand is planted with varieties that are best adapted to light, fast-maturing wines: Gamay grapes, Muscadet, and others that give delicious, fresh young wines with little prospect of long-term maturing. On clay, grape varieties lose much of their personality and give heavy wines—high in tannin, clumsy, and, in France, usually described as having a *goût de terroir*. (In a recent, published interview the buyer for a major British wine group discussed his reasons for choosing a *non-appellation* Gamay wine from the Loire rather than one from Yugoslavia. He preferred the French wine, he said, because it was grown on light, shattered granite, which didn't overwhelm the low-key style of the Gamay. The Yugoslav wine, on the other hand, though "very good," had a "tannic, more aggressive" style, from the heavy clay on which it was grown. Just as one would expect.) Gravel gives the best Bordeaux wines their balance, finesse, and, in mature wines when soil takes over from grape, a special smoky quality that is reminiscent of hot sealing wax, sometimes of charcoal. If we compare a young Pétrus with a young Mission-Haut-Brion, for example, when the grape in each is still dominant, we can see how the preponderance of Cabernet Sauvignon in La Mission-Haut-Brion contrasts with the Merlot of

Pétrus. But in mature vintages of the same two wines, the contrast of grape variety will have diminished and the emerging influence of their common gravel soils brings them closer together.

Tasting wines side by side, in fact, is more instructive and often more enjoyable than tasting each alone. Points of contrast and similarity bring out more clearly their individual styles, and sometimes make identification easier. By way of illustration, here is an extract from my diary entry of a recent dinner:

Two magnums were decanted to accompany the roast lamb and poured blind for discussion and identification. The first had a more dense color, but both showed visual signs of being twenty to thirty years old—confirmed by the "nose" particularly of the second. We were told both were from Bordeaux. Though they seemed to be late 1940s vintages, they had none of the characteristics of 1945 and were obviously of quality above 1946, 1950, and 1951. At first I thought they could be of the same year, perhaps 1948, but from different areas. Then I inclined to 1947 for the second wine because it showed the wear I've noticed in some 1947s recently. I wasn't sure about the first. It seemed to be a 1949 in scale, but P——— didn't find it rich or long enough for a 1949. I agreed, but thought it bigger than the 1948s I remembered. I remained undecided between the two. We were all agreed that it was a Médoc. Nobody felt very sure what the second wine could be. The majority were pro-Graves, but I could detect no Graves characteristic. I had an open mind on the possibility of its being a Pichon-Baron; it had the flat style I associate with the property. J.B. thought a Saint-Emilion. Finally, the vintage of the first wine was confirmed by our host as 1949 and the second 1947. With certainty of the year, J.B. now felt confident in identifying the second wine as Saint-Emilion, and specifically as Château Canon. He was right on both counts. Knowing the first wine to be a 1949 for sure, I felt that its abrupt finish in such a big year placed it as a Saint-Estèphe. I took a guess at Château Montrose because of their tough style. I was right on the *commune* but wrong on the château: it was Cos d'Estournel, and with a little more time in the glass it opened up to reveal the finesse and fruit that one would, indeed, have expected from Cos.

Bordeaux presents an unusual challenge because every vineyard has its own formula of grape varieties: more Cabernet Sauvignon here, less Merlot there, perhaps some Malbec or Cabernet Franc.

And, depending on the vagaries of the vintage, one or another variety might do better. A wine usually recognized for the softness contributed by a higher proportion of Merlot might, in a year when the Merlot failed to "set," produce a wine of unexpectedly hard style. On the other hand, the spring frosts in 1961 caused havoc in the Médoc and reduced the potential crop—when La Lagune, for example, was just coming into production again after years of replanting and restoration. There the proportion of Merlot had been increased, and the frost, by mischance, increased it further. When still quite young, La Lagune 1961 caused a sensation for its full-blown style—quite unlike that of any other young Médoc. Which takes us back, I think, to where we started.

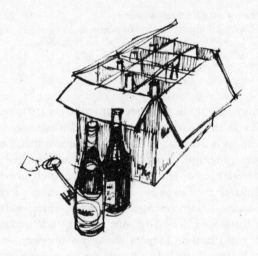

In the Sign
of the Beaujolais

*Every man shall eat in safety
Under his own vine what he plants, and sing
The merry songs of peace to all his neighbours.*

Shakespeare, *Henry VIII*

JOSEPHINE BAKER, so the legend goes, brought her own heat wave to Paris back in the 1920s. The one I found there one June was more than enough for me. As the city became hotter and stickier and my consumption of iced *citrons pressés* reached a stage where I was in danger of sprouting leaf and branch, the thought of the cool hills of the Beaujolais became increasingly irresistible. I longed for a pine-shaded bedroom and the soothing welcome of garden-aired linen sheets. Finally, one evening when the illuminated sign in the Place de l'Opéra showed a temperature in the nineties at midnight, I decided to be off the next morning. Before nine I was on a train to the Beaujolais, to Brouilly, to Château Thivin, the house of Yvonne Geoffray, my self-appointed godmother.

The Beaujolais hills are wide rather than high, the last undulating folds of the Massif Central, softly contoured and generously draped with vineyards. Houses, barns, and courtyards, built for the protection and comfort of man and beast, lie scattered about the hillsides; for this has long been a peaceful region, and there are few villages of feudal style clustered in fear at the foot of a forbidding castle. The men of the Beaujolais built to resist weather rather than baronial mercenaries. Gabriel Chevalier would still find the familiar sights and sound of *Clochemerle* everywhere. New washing machines and tractors permit the villagers yet more time to ponder the attractions—real and imagined—of their neighbors' spouses.

The Mont de Brouilly, a great mound of granitic sand that looms at the very center of the Beaujolais, has on its southern slope the finest *appellation* of all. The Côte de Brouilly, a scant 420 acres, is by some standard of *noblesse oblige* the highest *appellation* of the region. French law imposes a higher minimum quality requirement on its small production than on the broader area of Brouilly surrounding it or, for that matter, on any other wine of the Beaujolais, including Juliénas and Moulin-à-Vent. And Thivin's vineyards, older than the house, are at the very heart of this exceptional slope. For three hundred years, until it passed to the local Abbaye de Saint-Augustin in 1446, the vineyard had been the jealously guarded *domaine* of the canons of neighboring Belleville-sur-Saône. It was they who built the earliest part of the house in 1383, leaving a warren of underground passages and cellars. But most of what is visible today, especially the two low, square towers that support the arched entrance to the narrow courtyard, was built in 1828.

It is a sturdy house, solidly buttressed and somnolent with the perpetual cooing of pigeons in their lofts beneath the tiled roof. It is a snug house; on days when snowflakes fall thick as blotting paper, the iron-gray cold outside is only an added quality, increasing our pleasure as we sit in the warm dining room, hung with fading damask, and drink the last of our wine with *chèvretons*, little goat cheeses of the village. And in summer the house is a carefully shuttered refuge from the day's glaring heat, flung open only to the shady cool of evening and the drowsy night fragrance of the creepers and flowers that threaten to smother it.

Lunch had been delayed to allow for my train, but there was still time for a cold apéritif under the canopy of wisteria in the courtyard. Colette, who used to visit the house in the 1940s, described that wisteria in *Le Fanal Bleu* as a "contorted python, rearing up, and lost in its own foliage." The leaves filter the light, and beneath it all is cool and green and secret.

In the dining room, small iced Cavaillon melons were waiting, each moistened with a few drops of Muscat of Beaumes-de-Venise. We followed them with slices of home-cured ham and the bread that Yvonne buys from a village baker far off in the hills.

"He's the only one who still uses wood to fire his oven," she says. She herself still cooks everything on a wood-burning stove—or sometimes over charred vine cuttings in the fireplace of the dining room itself. "Wood gives a softer heat," she often says to me patiently, with the air of one who is embarrassed to have to explain obvious truths.

With the ham we drank a Pouilly-Fuissé 1974, dry but softly, delicately fruity. We were to continue with duckling, but first, in the French manner, we had a dish of *haricots verts*. The beans had been picked in the garden before dawn. "*Haricots* must be picked before the sun is on them," Yvonne says earnestly, "or the flavor is lost." With the duckling, we were able to enjoy the Château Thivin 1974, an elegant Côte de Brouilly with a perfume of sun-warmed strawberries. The salad was dressed with walnut oil that Yvonne buys freshly milled in Beaujeu; then there was farm *fromage blanc*, serene in a flood of thick cream, and a sweet-sharp ice made from raspberries and blackcurrants.

Oh, how richly one eats in the Beaujolais! Not finicky *haute cuisine*, but generous country food that nourishes a man spiritually as well as physically: rabbits and hares, plump pigeons and Limousin steaks; salads from the gardens, mushrooms from the fields, and chickens from Bresse. The rivers and lakes of the Dombes seem to be crammed with crayfish, pike, and perch; and while *chèvreton* cheeses age, suspended in little wicker cages like bewitched songbirds, ropes of piquant sausages hang looped from dark rafters in cellar and kitchen.

No wonder, then, that the wine of the Beaujolais, too, should be as enlivening to the spirit as it is restoring to the senses. It is not a wine to sip, to contemplate or analyze; it is for quaffing, for brightening the eye and loosening the tongue.

The vineyards of the Beaujolais stretch for about forty-five miles from a little south of Mâcon almost to the gates of Lyon. Never more than nine or ten miles wide, the area covers some sixty villages, only a handful of which are ever identified on the label of a bottle. The *crus* of the Beaujolais, those wines entitled to be sold with a village name—Saint-Amour, Juliénas, and Morgon, for example—are clustered in the northern part of the area. They emerge from the broader *appellation* of Beaujolais-Villages, wines from about thirty villages specified by law but not on the label and, again, all in the north. To the south the wine is either just Beaujolais or Beaujolais Supérieur, the latter name applied to plain Beaujolais when the sugar level in the grapes is above a prescribed minimum level and the yield per acre below a prescribed maximum. There is another, more subtle, distinction between the *crus* and Villages on the one hand and the plain wines of Beaujolais—Supérieur or not—on the other. In vineyards producing the latter, the grower may train his vines along wires in what is known universally as the Guyot method of pruning. But in those vineyards planted for the higher *appellations* the vines must be unsupported, pruned by the gobelet method like a stumpy fist of fingers—a natural way to force on the *vigneron* restraint of growth and limited fruiting.

Grape vines are reproduced from cuttings, and by selecting for specific qualities in his vines a grower can gradually change the strain in his vineyard, compared with that of his neighbor. Over many generations—of vines and men—these distinctions can become quite marked and might even appear to be separate varieties. Each strain is called a "clone."

All Beaujolais wines are made from Gamay vines, a variety with a bewildering proliferation of clones. For a start, the clones principally used in the Beaujolais are different from those used to produce the lesser Burgundies of the Côte d'Or. We frequently read and hear exclamations of wonder that the lowly Gamay of the Côte d'Or (where only Pinot Noir is used for fine wines) once translated to the Beaujolais hills miraculously produces better wine. But it is, in fact, a matter of different clones matched to the different conditions of the Beaujolais. Only clones of the Gamay Noir *à jus blanc*, black-skinned but with clear pulp, give quality wine. (The clones with pink pulp, called Gamays *teinturiers*, give coarser wine and are not recommended.) The Gamay Noir *à jus blanc* presents itself in many ways. Sometimes the shoots are stiffly upright, and sometimes they fall in graceful curves; sometimes the bunches are small and sometimes large, even "winged" in the form of a tricorne. Sometimes the bunches are tight and sometimes loose; the individual grape berries are sometimes round, sometimes oval, and sometimes almost oblong. The grape skin will vary in color from deep violet to black and may be thin or thick; and clones vary in their maturity season from early to late. Each grower has his own criteria for selecting among these clones: one might need better flavor, another better color, another better yield. Clones used mainly to increase yield include Gamay Labronde (also called Gamay des Gamays), Gamay Picard, Gamay Malarin (favored because it will put out new shoots if the first are damaged by spring frosts), and Gamay d'Arcenant (very productive but very vulnerable to rot). The three clones used for finest quality—all with relatively low yields—are Gamay Chatillon, Gamay Geoffray (also known as Gamay de Vaux), and Gamay Magny.

To add to the confusion, the clone called Gamay Beaujolais in California is not a Gamay at all and has nothing to do with the Beaujolais. It was introduced here in the nineteenth century, and by constant selection of cuttings toward a desired end the wine produced from it is of Gamay style. The University of California at Davis has recently identified it as a clone of Pinot Noir—not exactly a matter of shame—rather than a clone of Gamay. The plain Gamay introduced to California in the 1930s, and sometimes known as Napa Gamay to distinguish it from the unfortunately misnamed Gamay Beaujolais, is said to be a clone of the true Gamay of the Beaujolais. It is, however, one that has been adapted to our own growing conditions and is, by now, distinct from the clones in France. Professor Galet of the University of Montpellier, a distinguished ampelographer, suggests that even the Napa Gamay is not a true Gamay. Whatever it might be, most California wines labeled Gamay Beaujolais are made from a blend of these two varieties.

In France the choice of Gamay clones for each commune or hillside, whether traditional or personal, probably contributes as much to the style of individual wines as the soil and the particular exposure to the sun. Moulin-à-Vent, Chenas, and Morgon, for example, are known for the heaviness of their wines—a relative term when discussing Beaujolais, I should add. Fleurie and Juliénas are lighter and more flowery, and Brouilly, especially the Côte de Brouilly, is known for its finesse and elegance.

Most Beaujolais wines are made for early drinking, preferably within the twelvemonth of the vintage. But that is neither to say that they *must* be consumed within the twelvemonth nor to deny that some—particularly wines from Morgon and Moulin-à-Vent— often improve with a year or two in bottle. There is little point in holding any Beaujolais for longer than that.

Terms like *nouveau* (new), *primeur* (early), and *de l'année* (of the year) are increasingly bandied about. The date on which new Beaujolais can be released on the market from growers' cellars is controlled in France. Although there has been some pressure to have a "floating" date that could relate to the time of picking, at present the opening date is held rigidly to November 15. On that day the smaller wines that would hardly repay bottling, let alone keeping, were traditionally released in wood to the bistros of nearby Lyon and, in more recent years, to the bistros of Paris. Often this young wine was still working when released, but it was the harbinger of a new crop, and even in its rude qualities there was a link with the mystical cycles of vine and cellar that most Frenchmen crave. *Nouveau* is the undefined, popular way of describing it; *primeur* is the official name for wine released in the first month after the opening date. All *primeur*, then, is *nouveau*; not all *nouveau* (undefined) is *primeur*. Some might think that the practice of releasing Beaujolais *primeur* has been exaggerated of late. Shipping a small cask of still-frothing red wine to Chez Allard in Paris is one thing; stunning it for unsuitable early bottling and shipping it to far-flung continents is another.

De l'année means quite simply wine from the most recent vintage, and it is automatically superseded by the next crop.

Because Beaujolais is now always fruity and is usually drunk quite young, it is best when cool, but not chilled; half an hour or so in the refrigerator is ample time. Fruity red wines can seem excessively so when drunk at room temperature, and young wines, with their greener acidity, need a cooler temperature to keep that acidity in taste balance.

In former days growers would leave the fermenting juice on the skins for a longer period, and they made harder wines as a result. Today they aim for a light, tender style. The wines are also less complex in flavor than they once were. Yvonne Geoffray, with the countrywoman's instinctive response to life around her, complains that the bacteria and yeasts that affect the subtlety of fermentation have changed. "Fifty years ago, the vineyards were tended by horse, hand, and hoe. But now they don't plow so much. The soil is kept clear with herbicides, and that affects the balance of organisms." To be sure that yeasts at Château Thivin remain active, grape-skin residue from the presses is first mixed with earth and then laboriously carted up the hillside to be replaced on the vineyard every year.

In her eight decades, Yvonne Geoffray has seen many changes in the Beaujolais and accepts most of them philosophically. She saw nothing picturesque nor romantic in the old village *lavoir*, fed by an ice-cold hillside spring, where the women once brought their household wash. "They all have washing machines now," she says with evident satisfaction, "and some have dishwashers too."

She regrets television; it ended the neighborliness of her youth. "The winters were so much gayer then. Almost every evening there were *veillées* in different houses—cards, music, and gossip. At least once or twice a year there would be a *méchoui* to roast two or three sheep, and every household would contribute to the cost.

"I loved the village dances," she says, looking down at her hands. "Claude Geoffray"—she refers to her late husband—"first took notice of me at a village dance. Our families were neighbors and had always known each other, but he was older and hadn't paid much attention to me. I was seventeen when he came back from his military service. He asked me to dance.

"Quite soon after, his mother came to see my mother. When I saw she was wearing white gloves I knew her visit was not an ordinary one; it wasn't usual for Madame Geoffray to wear white gloves. She had come to ask if Claude might propose to me." She laughs self-consciously. "He came himself for the answer.

"When we married we had two hectares (about five acres), and eventually we inherited seven or eight more. Good vineyard land is precious, but we had very little money. Over the years we managed to acquire seven or eight more hectares of good, adjacent vineyard land. They were more important to me than bracelets. In those days life was hard for everyone in the Beaujolais. Our wines sold almost exclusively in Lyon, and we were not treated very fairly by the trade there. Claude was the first of the growers to go to Paris to try to get the restaurants there interested in the wines of the Beaujolais. He was always a shy man, and it was not easy for him, but everyone seemed to like him. Theater people and writers started to visit the region, and it was they who really promoted our wines back in the thirties and forties by ordering them in Paris and wherever they went in the world. Now the best Beaujolais goes to Paris, London, even New York. You will find better wines abroad now than in Lyon, even though Lyon is so close."

My visit coincided with an evening reunion of the Confrérie de l'Ordre des Compagnons du Beaujolais. Six hundred of us sat down to dinner in the old *cuverie* at Lacenas, where the Confrérie makes it headquarters. With songs of the Beaujolais on our lips, we attacked jellied roulade of duck stuffed with foie gras, truffles, and pistachio nuts. Before the second dish appeared—a selection of *charcuterie à la mode du Beaujolais* with a vintner's salad—the more energetic guests were already dancing in the aisles, perhaps to make room for the young chickens braised with *morilles*. Cheeses of the area, from goat and cow, were followed by small tarts of strawberries and raspberries. And to make us rejoice, we had, as the menu put it, "*la force de persuasion du vin de Beaujolais*." By French law firemen must be present at every public gathering. Present they were, surveying the scene benignly, hats tipped back, coats unbuttoned, a large glass in hand to sustain each and every one of them. A puff of their breath, I fancied, would do wonders for any fire.

When we left for home in the early hours of the morning, we could hear music drifting across the hills from almost every village we passed. The moon was particularly bright, and we agreed that it was, without doubt, in the seventh house.

Beaune
and the Rest

A<small>N</small> <small>APOCRYPHAL</small> story used to circulate in the London wine trade of the country wine merchant who, instructing his staff in the mysteries of Burgundy, would tell them, "There are two sorts: Beaune, and the rest. We sell Beaune." Substitute Pommard for Beaune, and the situation in the United States is not so very different from that of pre–Common Market England. Nor is it difficult to understand why a wine drinker, faced with the uncharted tangle of Burgundian labels, might settle on one familiar and uncomplicated name.

In fact, there is a basic and easily understood pattern to the labels of Burgundy, even if it is not as neatly apparent as the pyramid of Bordeaux *appellations* that rises from the broad base of Bordeaux Rouge to the five-peaked crown of first growths. The difference is that, where Bordeaux is a hierarchy, Burgundy is a democracy, its qualities and riches widely dispersed. This is a good time to look at Burgundy, to refresh the memory of wines long neglected, and to brush up on less familiar names because prices for well-known wines like Pommard and Pouilly-Fuissé have soared.

The 1975 vintage in Burgundy was small and, for red wines, disastrous. On the eve of the 1976 vintage, stocks were dangerously low, down 40 percent from the previous year. In the Beaujolais,

the growers' cellars were depleted. In Chablis the price of a barrel
(about sixty U.S. gallons), just 700 francs for the 1975 vintage, rose
to 1,200 francs for the 1976—if wine could be found. And in the
Côte d'Or the urgent need of the trade to replenish stocks was
matched by reluctance on the part of the growers to sell. In the
political mood and economic climate of France at the time, a full
cellar was preferable to a large bank balance.

Obviously prices were highest where market pressure was greatest. Pommard has one of the largest productions of any Burgundy
commune, as much as 100,000 cases a year. But in terms of French
consumption, let alone the requirements of the rest of the world,
the quantity is trifling. So much demand for so little wine pushed
the price of even the most ordinary 1976 Pommard to 4,500
francs a barrel. Paradoxically, this affects the prices of Volnay,
Beaune, and all the other internationally known *communes*. They
consider their wines to be as good, and won't accept prices far
behind.

The Côte d'Or—not the *département* of that name but the narrow ribbon of vines that runs from the outskirts of Dijon south to
Santenay—is the heart of viticultural Burgundy, which also en-
compasses Chablis, some eighty miles to the north, the last remnant
of a once huge winegrowing area that stretched from Joigny
(where there is still one small vineyard on the hill behind the
town) to Tonnerre (where the last vineyard was uprooted a bare
fifteen years ago). To the south of Santenay, Burgundy also includes the Côte Chalonnaise, long neglected in this country, and the
Mâconnais; the Beaujolais, though never a part of Burgundy, is
usually considered to be an extension of it viticulturally.

The northern segment of the Côte d'Or, called Côte de Nuits for
its commercial hub, Nuits-Saint-Georges, produces red wines of
deep color, great force, and taut flavor. The Côte de Beaune, to
its south, produces some of the finest white wines in France and
reds that are softer than those of the Côte de Nuits, their flavors
and aroma subtly blurred. I have always thought of these two halves
of the Côte d'Or as the Rembrandt and Rubens of the wine world,
one darkly spiritual, the other light and sensuous.

Reading a wine label from the Côte d'Or is easier if one remembers that Burgundy uses both *commune* (village) and *climat* (vineyard site) names. Over the centuries every parcel of vines has been
delimited and identified with a name that distinguishes its *climat*,

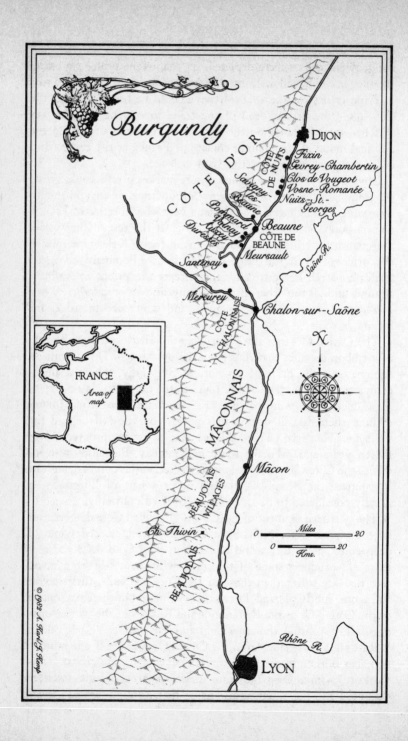

Burgundy

DIJON

CÔTE D'OR

CÔTE DE NUITS

Fixin
Gevrey-Chambertin
Clos de Vougeot
Vosne-Romanée
Nuits-St.-Georges

Savigny-lès-Beaune

Pommard
Volnay
Aubry
Duresses

Beaune
CÔTE DE BEAUNE

Meursault

Santenay

Saône R.

Mercurey

CÔTE CHALONNAISE

Chalon-sur-Saône

N

FRANCE

Area of map

MÂCONNAIS

Mâcon

BEAUJOLAIS VILLAGES

Ch. Thivin

BEAUJOLAIS

Miles
0   20
0   20
Kms.

Rhône R.

LYON

© 1983 A. Karl/J. Kemp

a word that shows an early, perhaps unconscious, understanding of the effect of microclimate at each turn and undulation of the hill on the style and quality of the wine produced.

Sometimes a *climat* is quite large and extends beyond a *commune* border. Les Marconnets, for instance, a *climat* mostly in Beaune, extends into neighboring Savigny. It is possible to find a wine labeled Beaune–Les Marconnets as well as wine labeled Savigny–Les Marconnets. Sometimes the *climat* is so renowned that it is used without reference to the *commune* that contains it. Richebourg, for example, does not usually have any mention of the Vosne-Romanée *commune* on the label.

Climats, though delimited and named, are not the Burgundian equivalents of Bordeaux châteaux. Few are under single ownership. Clos Vougeot, the best known and largest *climat*, though not much more than a hundred acres, is divided among more than sixty proprietors, each of whom makes wine from his own vines in accordance with his own way of thinking. Given the idiosyncrasies of man and nature, *appellation contrôlée* regulations, in such circumstances, can go only so far in imposing conditions for potential quality; they cannot guarantee it, and variations occur even among wines that one might expect to be the same.

Over the years, some simple gradings have developed for the *climats*, and these have been acknowledged and incorporated into the *appellation contrôlée* laws. The finest *climats*, those of such reputation that their names stand alone on the label without reference to *commune*, are designated *grand cru*. Chambertin, Clos Saint-Denis, Musigny, Romanée, and Corton are examples of *grands crus* that have had their names annexed by the respective *communes* within whose borders they lie. This practice reserves, perhaps questionably, some of the glory from the finest vineyard for the wines of the *commune* as a whole. It is the first and most basic trap for Burgundy buyers. By adding Chambertin to its name, the *commune* of Gevrey, in particular, risks a confusion of its communal wine with those of other *grands crus* associated with the Chambertin *climat*. Gevrey-Chambertin is merely the *commune* wine; Charmes-Chambertin, Latricière-Chambertin, Mazis-Chambertin, and others are *grands crus* encircling Chambertin. Morey-Saint-Denis, Chambolle-Musigny, Vosne-Romanée, and Aloxe-Corton are further examples of *commune* names that incorporate reference to a famous *grand cru*. Montrachet, a *grand cru* that lies astraddle the neighboring *communes* of Puligny and Chassagne, has been coopted into both village names.

Behind the *grands crus* in rank, but usually alongside them in the center section, halfway up the slope, where all the finest wines of the Côte d'Or are grown, are the *premiers crus* of each *commune*. On labels their names are always in conjunction with the *commune* name, and the law requires that both names be of equal size; for example, Beaune-Grèves or Volnay-Santenots. Sometimes a wine is blended from two *premiers crus* in the same *commune* and is then labeled, for instance, Volnay Premier Cru without specifying which.

All other unclassified *climat* names may be used or not at the discretion of the grower or bottler. When they are used, the type size may not be larger than half that of the *commune* name; for example, Meursault-Perrières denotes a *premier cru* of Meursault; Pommard, Les Perrières, denotes a wine from an unclassified *climat* of Pommard. One of the first places to look for good value, if not bargains, is among these unclassified *climats*. Most of the owners of sections of the *grands crus* and *premiers crus* have a following, and their wines are inevitably in short supply. The wines of the unclassified *climats*, on the other hand, are generally sold for blending as *commune* wines bottled under shippers' brands. If such a wine is held back, there is probably good reason, and because there is little commercial advantage in using an unknown *climat* name, the mention of it often is the sign of a small grower proud of his ununblended wine. You might find his pride unjustified, of course, but such a wine can occasionally be as good as a more prestigious *premier cru* at a considerably lower price. A grower's name, incidentally, is identified in Burgundy by the term *propriétaire-recoltant*, as opposed to *négoçiant*, which denotes a merchant-shipper.

The second place to look for good value is among the wines of the less fashionable communes of the Côte d'Or. Without the demand enjoyed by the popular names, they have less pressure to produce every possible drop from their vines. The quality of their *commune* wines is often as good as those of any other of the Côte d'Or and at appreciably lower prices, and their *premier crus* can be surprisingly distinguished and delicious. If one likes the wines of Côte de Beaune, a Santenay or Monthélie is a good alternative to Volnay; a red Chassagne-Montrachet (usually a good buy) can be a substitute for Pommard. Savigny-les-Beaune, which has suffered from the shadow of its neighbor, has wine that is described in the lintel stone of an old gateway in the town as *"nourrisant, théologique, et morbifuge."* Be on the lookout, too, for red and white wines from Saint-Romain, nearby. Though light and not recommended for keeping, they are good value.

Shippers' blends from these lesser *communes* are often better balanced than the wines of individual growers, so watch for both. There are fewer overlooked *communes* in the Côte de Nuits, but the wines of Fixin (the *x* in names like Fixin, Aloxe, and Auxey is pronounced like a double *s*) are always undervalued.

Some of the best value in Burgundy is away from the Côte d'Or, however, in the Côte Chalonnaise. The *communes* of Mercurey, Rully, Givry, and Montagny produce wines whose quality has long been acknowledged among French wine merchants. Montagny produces white wines only; Rully, both red and white; the other two, mostly red. Mercurey has the largest production and probably the best red Burgundies outside the Côte d'Or. They are not difficult to find.

From the Mâconnais there is such an abundance of good, reasonably priced white wine that it isn't necessary to pay the present high prices for Pouilly-Fuissé, the best known of them. Most are labeled simply as Mâcon or as Mâcon-Villages, and occasionally a village name is used. Saint-Veran, an *appellation* created in 1971, has not yet achieved the popularity expected for it. It is crisply dry, fresh, and has a fuller flavor than most Pouilly-Fuissé wines. In tasting through these byways of Burgundy, one often wonders what stroke of fortune left some delicious find in the shadow of a more famous neighbor. Obviously not all Burgundies are great or even fine wines, but there are far more than might be expected.

A word on vintages. White wines of the Mâconnais and of the *communes* mentioned on the Côte Chalonnaise are not for long keeping. Since recent years have been reasonably good for white wines, the youngest being offered is generally the one to buy. If one of these wines is more than three or four years old, however, buy it with caution, trying a bottle before risking a case.

One is unlikely to find red wines of the disastrous 1975 vintage from Burgundy. Both 1969 and 1971 produced well-balanced wines that have kept well and are certainly ready for drinking. The wines of 1970 are lighter and might have faded by now, so caution is urged. The vintage of 1972 in Burgundy suffered from the poor reputation of the 1972 crop in Bordeaux; but, in fact, most of the red wines were good and some magnificent. They were expensive at the time, and few are likely to turn up now as bargains. If they do, don't be put off by the vintage. As the result of an enormous crop, 1973 wines were modestly priced and can be good values. Like the 1970s they are light and are not for long keeping; most 1974s have better color and more stamina. The best vintage since then was 1979, a year that gave dense, tannic red wines and impeccably balanced whites. Both 1980 and 1981 have their supporters, but in red wines neither vintage is consistent; both are best approached carefully and with some knowledge or previous experience of the individual grower or merchant (advice generally applicable to Burgundy) or with the counsel of someone who has tasted specifically the wine in question. Alain Roumier, manager of the Comte de Vogue's estate at Chambolle-Musigny, prophesied of recent vintages that a typical 1984 red Burgundy of the Côte d'Or would be like a "well-composed picture that lacked vivacity"; he likened 1983 to "a big-boned woman without curves," and 1982 to a short-distance runner. For white Burgundies, 1982 was a "short" year too, but the 1984s are firm, graceful and well flavored, without the heaviness that marred some 1983s.

Les Trois Glorieuses

Nicolas ROLIN founded the Hospices de Beaune in 1443 and endowed this charity hospital with some fine vineyards. Through the years other pious Burgundians have also bequeathed vineyards to the Hospices, which kept the choicest ones and sold the rest. Today the *domaines* of the Hospices extend over more than a hundred acres of the best grape-growing land in the Côte de Beaune, more than half of it in Beaune itself. (Since 1977 there has been added a small lot from Mazis-Chambertin in the Côte de Nuits.)

The wines from these vineyards are traditionally put up into distinctive *cuvées*, or vats, mostly named for benefactors of the Hospices: Nicolas Rolin (usually the finest), Guigone de Salins, Dames Hospitalières, Brunet, Clos des Avaux, Hugues & Louis Betault, Rousseau-Deslandes, and Maurice Drouhin. With the exception of Clos des Avaux, only village appellations are shown on the label, but all the Beaune wines are from *premier cru* vineyards. Nicolas Rolin is usually composed of wines from Les Grèves, Les Cent-Vignes, and En Genêt; Guigone de Salins, from Bressandes, Les Seurey, and Les Champs-Pimont; and Dames Hospitalières, from Les Bressandes, Les Teurons, Les Grèves, and La Mignotte. For the rest, the connection between a *cuvée* and specific vineyards is not constant. Only the village names and the *cuvée* names remain in permanent relationship. In any scale of quality, the wines of the Hospices de Beaune stand high, but it is open to question whether they really represent the Côte de Beaune at its best. The Pommard of Monsieur Parent and that of Madame de Courcel, for example, are decidedly better than anything the Hospices has to offer; and there are several artisan growers at Savigny who produce wines that are consistently better than the Forneret *cuvée* of the Hospices.

This is not to decry the Hospices, but to put the *cuvées* in proper perspective with other wines from a consumer's point of view. In good years—as was the case in 1966 and 1969—the best *cuvées* of the Hospices are big wines, but they rarely have the finesse and delicacy of flavor one has a right to expect from such august origins. The reason for this seems to lie in the nature and timing of the annual auction at which the wines are sold, always on the third Sunday of November.

It takes influence to obtain a seat in the market hall of Beaune, draped for the occasion with the splendid Flemish tapestries of the Hospices, and there is always a crush of people in the gallery and in a roped-off section at the back. As each lot is offered, a tiny taper is lit, then a second, and bidding continues until both tapers have burned out. Bidding is accomplished more quickly than one might think—perhaps in two or three minutes for each lot. All the *cuvées* are available for tasting in the cellars under the Hospices on the day before the sale, for a charge of a few francs.

But there is pressure on the cellar staff to have wines ready for buyers to taste in this way in November, when sometimes the grapes are picked barely six weeks before. It calls for rapid initial fermentation, with no chance to take the wines straight into a secondary, malolactic fermentation to reduce acidity, now almost universal practice in Burgundy. There are those who believe that long-term development of the wines is sacrificed to short-term presentability.

Furthermore, because the sale and the tasting are the first public viewing of any new vintage of Burgundy, subject to intense publicity, the world is given a less-than-just first impression of the Burgundy vintage as a whole. Psychologically the auction fits in well with postvintage festivities: the three traditional banquets that accompany the sale, Les Trois Glorieuses, have the air of stupendous Thanksgiving dinners. Nevertheless, quality of the wines would improve if the sale were held in January, perhaps to coincide with the Saint Vincent celebrations (Saint Vincent is the patron saint of winegrowers). By that time the wines would have finished the malolactic fermentation and would be tasted in full harmony.

Raising the standard of wines bearing the name of the Hospices would give greater satisfaction and therefore better value, and the prestige would be more appropriate, if some way could be devised to care for the wines and bottle them under the supervision of the Hospices. At present, the wine, once sold, is moved to the cellars of any number of *négociants*, each with his own idea of "raising" the wine until ready for bottling. Thus there is no consistency in a *cuvée* from a single year purchased by different bottlers, and there can be little confidence in the name of the Hospices as a hallmark. If bottled by the Hospices itself, or at least centrally under its direction, these wines could constitute the most important collection of *domaine*-bottled wines in Burgundy. The Hospices funds—still used to support one of the best hospitals in France—would benefit, and so would the wine lover.

Not that I would want to suggest that prices paid at the Hospices auction are depressed; in fact, the contrary is true. Motives of public standing and ostentation, quite apart from charity, combine to exaggerate prices. The amounts paid, when compared with those of earlier years, provide a weathervane for the vintage as a whole. In recent years prices have tended to mount steadily, reflecting not only quality but also increased world demand for Burgundy. The total sale value of the 1972 vintage reached an all-time record of more than 7.5 million francs (about 1.5 million dollars at the rate of exchange at the time), and even 1981, a small crop following a series of weather disasters, yielded more than 6.5 million.

Hospices de Beaune wines are usually sold and distributed through normal trade channels at normal profit margins. But there are exceptions. For instance, a well-known Burgundy shipper, who makes it a point of honor to make the highest bid for a lot, usually returns the wine to the auctioneer for resale so that the Hospices will benefit twice over, and the highest prices paid for outstanding *cuvées* are rarely passed on to the consumer. The top price paid at the 1981 sale, for example, was 46,000 francs a hogshead for the Corton-Charlemagne *cuvée* François de Salins. With normal bottling and shipping costs and standard margins, the wine would have to sell to the consumer in New York at over $100 a bottle. We can be sure that it won't. In this respect, the wine trade of the world makes a gesture to the Hospices de Beaune, following a tradition set by centuries of Burgundians.

The monetary value of the sale at the Hospices is only a part of the benefit. The auction and the associated feasts are the grandest events of the year in the wine world and spread a warmth and luster far beyond the town of Beaune and the borders of France.

Beaune is protected in its entirety by the French state: every steeple, every gateway, and every crooked roof tile is a *monument historique*. On the Sunday of the Hospices sale, Beaune becomes a fairground as well. All day, crowds of small winegrowers from the surrounding villages visit the stands of agricultural machinery and household goods, view the sideshows, and eat *saucissons chauds*. In the chaste elegance of the seventeenth-century Hôtel de Ville, there are booths at which wines from any number of independent growers can be tasted, to be compared with the *cuvées* of the Hospices and to give a broader impression of the vintage.

Yet above all else, this third weekend in November is devoted to Les Trois Glorieuses, each offering a different face of the region. First, on the Saturday evening before the auction, there is a banquet organized by the Confrérie des Chevaliers du Tastevin at Clos de Vougeot. The most "grand" of the three feasts, it is intended to show the international face of Burgundy. The guests are largely ambassadors, ministers, and other distinguished foreign visitors from outside the world of wine.

On Sunday evening, after the auction, a candlelit dinner is held in the huge cellars under the old bastion towers of the town. Several hundred sit down together—mostly wine merchants of Beaune, vineyard owners, and guests.

Chatter reverberates on stone, so the silence when everyone is at last seated and the lights are extinguished is all the more dramatic. Suddenly, from a small doorway, dozens of young men who are to wait on table file into the vast cellars, each carrying a lighted candle. It is simple but effective. Courses and wines are presented with impeccable flourish and well-rehearsed precision, but there is no inappropriate solemnity. Despite numbers, there is a great family feeling, and everyone joins in the singing of the *ban bourguignon* between courses. Perhaps the tradition of boisterously waving hands in the air to the beat of the music was to show a medieval assembly that fingers could be trusted in the sauce?

The food is superb and abundant. My menu from the 1967 dinner shows that we started with a *consommé Celestine* and then drank Beaune Blanc 1964 with a partridge tart, followed by a *suprême de saumon à la norvégienne* with Puligny-Montrachet Clos du Cailleret 1964. Diners regained their breath on a *salmis* of wild duck with a Pommard *cuvée* Dames de la Charité 1964 of the Hospices de Beaune. Then there was a *côte de charolais* accompanied by 1962 Corton in magnums, which we continued to drink with a selection of cheeses. A Champagne Brut 1961 was served with an enormous frosted cake (I can never understand why the French, logical in all else, drink dry Champagne with sweet dishes), and we toyed with petits fours, coffee, and *prunelle de Bourgogne* —the white brandy distilled from the little Burgundy plums—into the small hours. As well as the wines officially accompanying each course, the menu listed twenty-six others, which were presented by growers and merchants and were available, on request, as extra or alternative choices.

Monday morning comes too soon if the Dîner aux Chandelles has been preceded by the Chevaliers du Tastevin banquet at Clos de Vougeot. But gastronomically undaunted, we set off to Meursault for La Paulée. No one knows the origin of the Rabelaisian luncheon that concludes Les Trois Glorieuses. Essentially it is a vineyard workers' banquet, presenting the third and most basic of the three faces of Burgundy. Each guest brings his own bottle, which is to say that each brings several, and there is a great deal of sipping and sampling of one another's wines in an atmosphere of *fête champêtre*. Most of the participants are from the town of Meursault and the surrounding area.

In 1967 I was the guest of Berthe Morey, and we drank Meursault and Volnay from her vineyards. A *jambon persillé*, specialty of the region, was followed by *pâté en croûte* and a glorious *pochouse verdunoise*, a stew of delicate river fish in white wine, savory with garlic. We witnessed the ceremony of marrying *pochouse*—from the other side of the river Saône—with the white wine of Meursault. "*Je vous annonce gastronomiquement mariés*," sang out the mayor of Meursault to the fish cauldron and the bottle, and we all agreed. At least, no one could think of any reason why the two should not be joined in gastronomic matrimony. Then a huge boar was carried round the hall in triumph, head and bristles replaced for decoration. (I was provoked to rather ungastronomic thought, I must confess.)

After La Paulée, the growers throw open their cellars and expect their neighbors to come and taste. Nobody feels very much like eating supper that night.

Champagne: The Brilliant Image

W HEN SIR EDWARD BARRY of the Royal College of Physicians in London published his *Observations, Historical, Critical and Medical on the Wines of the Ancients and the Analogy Between them and Modern Wines* in 1775, England was reeling from the excessive indulgence in Port wine that had resulted from the 1703 Methuen treaty with Portugal. "High politics and high tariff," as H. Warner Allen has put it, "had almost extinguished the importation of French wines." Few of those still entering the country were worthy of attention, according to Sir Edward, but he excepted wines from Champagne. By "Champagne," however, he expected his reader to understand the still wine of that region, not the upstart "sparkling, frothy Champagne," which he dismissed as a "depraved taste" passing out of fashion.

Known as *vin d'Ay*, an allusion to the small town of Ay in the valley of the Marne, east of Paris, where some of the finest Champagne vineyards are still to be found, Champagne was originally a still, light red wine, well reputed even before the Middle Ages, and consumed at the sixteenth-century court of Henri IV of France, along with others that were of easy access to the capital. However, the King's Chancellor at the time, Nicholas de Brulart, was himself proprietor of immense vineyards at Sillery-en-Champagne, just northeast of Ay on what is now known as the Montagne de Reims (though hardly a mountain). It would be unworldly to be surprised that Brulart might want the satisfaction of seeing the court enjoy wine from his estates. Such was his influence that its most discreet exercise (with suspiciously partisan endorsement from the court physicians) was enough to ensure social (and therefore commercial) success. Though a distinction had previously been maintained between the wines of Ay from the valley of the Marne and wines from the Montagne de Reims, at about that time, in deference to Brulart's Sillery-en-Champagne, *all* wines from the region became known as Champagne, thereby gently and profitably engaging the ancient reputation of the wines of Ay to the interests of the Brulart family.

Brulart knew, as we would say, his market. Determined to satisfy the taste of an aristocratic clientele, he encouraged his growers to preserve refinement and freshness of flavor above all else. Growers were urged, for example, to pick no later than ten o'clock in the morning so that grapes might be brought cool to the cellars for crushing. Winemakers were commended to separate juice from the black grape skins as quickly as possible, not in order to avoid color (though eventually wine of palest color became most prized) but to attain the most delicate style possible. As a result, Champagne destined for court palates ceased to be light red; by the late seventeenth century, it had barely a tint of straw-pink and was known as *vin gris*.

To preserve its elusive, fresh flavor, the wine was dispatched in barrels as soon as winter cold had helped it fall bright of sediment, and, on arrival, was promptly drawn off into tightly sealed glass flagons. Northern wines, especially when harvested late before an early winter, were characteristically fizzy when young; for although the connection between grape sugar and alcohol was recognized, there was no real understanding of fermentation before Pasteur, and there were then no means of gauging that all sugar had been converted. Invariably, fermentations that stuck as temperatures fell would start again only in warm spring weather, and since, in those days, most wine was drunk within a year of the vintage, a bubble or two remaining from revived fermentation, "winking at the brim," must have been taken for granted. No doubt that was why the usual closure of bottle or crock was not a tight-fitting cork, as today, but a piece of cloth or a film of olive oil that would allow gas to escape.

The gas formed in the tightly sealed flagons of Champagne, however, foamed and sparkled when released, enchanting the French court. Refined sugar to assist continued fermentation in the bottle was widely available by this period, but, without control of the actual bottling, the growers could not be certain if a barrel of wine, once shipped, would froth or not. In 1724 they appealed to the government for the right to ship their *vin gris de Champagne* in bottles instead of barrels, the better to ensure and control the sparkle. With permission finally given in 1728, and the development of the St. Gobain glassworks to provide the vast numbers of bottles that would be required, real sparkling Champagne, if not quite as we know it today, was born.

Its success was absolute. Voltaire, in 1756, referred to it as "the brilliant image of France," though by modern standards it was still an unpredictable, rather primitive, cloudy wine. It was not until the early nineteenth century (perhaps just in time to avoid that fall from grace predicted by Sir Edward Barry) that experiment led to discovery of the precise pressure of carbonic acid gas generated through fermentation of a given measure of sugar, and Madame Clicquot (founder, with her departed husband, of the Champagne house that still bears her name) devised a way to remove the *débris* of fermentation from the bottle without the pent-up sparkle escaping. Inverted in holes set in a sloping table, the bottles of wine were shaken and gradually twisted from an oblique to an upright position, coaxing the sediment to settle on the cork itself. Then, with one deft movement removing the restraining wire, both cork and *débris* were thrust together from the bottle by the pressure of gas, and a new cork inserted and secured so swiftly that almost no wine or sparkle was lost. (Since then this method, called "riddling" in English, has been improved further by passing the tips of the bottles through a freezing mixture before the disgorging so that the sediment now flies out within a small pellet of ice, the space left in the bottle to be filled with wine carefully adjusted for sweetness to restore balance.) Later, the discoveries of Pasteur on the nature of yeast activity gave Champagne makers all they needed to perfect their technique of controlled, induced, secondary fermentation in the bottle, the essential element of what we call the *méthode champenoise* of making sparkling wines, a *méthode* that would have astounded Dom Perignon, who is credited with having invented it more than a century before.

Dom Perignon, the extraordinarily capable and gifted cellar master of the Abbey at Hautvillers in the valley of the Marne from 1668 to 1715, is properly credited, however, with the idea of blending grapes of disparate origin to arrive at a balance of qualities superior to any that could be found naturally. A worthy successor to those who had developed Champagne's characteristic delicacy of style, he checked all grapes on arrival at the Abbey press house to find the right combinations for his blends *before* fermentation. So sensitive was he to the possibilities of each of the Abbey's vineyards, reported his contemporaries, that to taste a single grape was enough for him to say which vineyard the basket came from, and to decide for which vat it should be reserved. He had not the advantage of the master blenders of today, who can test-blend small quantities of the year's newly fermented wines in the tasting room before assembling their *cuvée*. For him, there was no induced "secondary fermentation" as today, just a continuation of the first into bottle.

At first Champagne was made from black grapes only, but the addition of white grapes revealed both delicacy and sparkle improved, so that in the eighteenth century Pinot Blanc and Chardonnay vines began to appear among the Pinot Noir and Meunier (a distant, humble cousin of the Pinot Noir whose role in making Champagne is rarely acknowledged, although contributing greatly to the soft quality of certain blends). Gradually they found their way along the valley of the Marne and onto the Montagne de Reims, while entire vineyards of them spread over the hillsides south of the river, earning the region the name Côte des Blancs, by which it is still known.

For all this time, of course, and, indeed, until the highly controversial changes of the 1860s and 1870s, Champagne was always a sweet wine, hence the tradition in France of serving Champagne with desserts. The problem is that the wine is now more often dry than not, and dry sparkling wine is hardly the most appropriate accompaniment for a rich St.-Honoré. But, as long as there are French birthdays to celebrate, no doubt they will continue to appear in tandem.

The move to dry Champagne started with a shipment of the

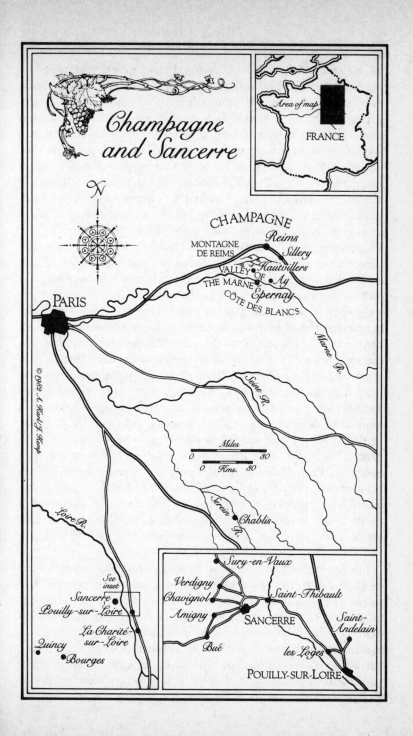

Champagne and Sancerre

FRANCE

Area of map

N

CHAMPAGNE

Reims
MONTAGNE
DE REIMS
Sillery
Hautvillers
VALLEY OF Ay
THE MARNE
Epernay
CÔTE DES BLANCS

PARIS

Marne R.

Seine R.

© 1983 A. Karl/J. Kemp

Miles
0   30
0   Kms.   30

Serein R.

Chablis

Loire R.

See
inset

Sancerre
Pouilly-sur-Loire

La Charité-
sur-Loire

Quincy

Bourges

Sury-en-Vaux

Verdigny
Chavignol
Amigny

Saint-Thibault

SANCERRE

Saint-
Andelain

Bué

les Loges

POUILLY-SUR-LOIRE

1846 vintage of Perrier-Jouët to London, an experiment, urged by the firm's British representative, that failed dismally. In 1860, however, several houses, including Clicquot, sent to London Champagnes of the 1857 vintage that were drier—and more mature—than usual. The extra maturing, crucial to the balance of the wines, was of great economic consequence to the Champagne houses. Patrick Forbes explains in his book *Champagne: The Wine, the Land and the People* that the sweetness added to the disgorged bottles just before shipping "masked the tartness of a young Champagne and enabled the makers to sell the majority of their wines two years, sometimes one year, after they were made; a 'dry' Champagne would need to age for at least three years in the cellars before its rough edges were rounded off, and this would involve an increase not only in the size of the cellars but in overhead and locked-up capital as well." This time the market responded enthusiastically, and although some houses (especially Roederer, who announced that "there would be no bowing to the dry Baal" in *their* cellars) held out until the 1874 vintage—the first that was almost universally shipped dry to England—the change was rapid and opposition faded when the Champagne producers saw the expansion that followed. By 1865, within five years of that first introduction of a dry style, sales of Champagne abroad had more than doubled to 10 million bottles a year, and by the close of the century that number had more than doubled again. Champagne, no longer a dessert wine, competing for attention with Sauternes, Port, Madeira, and the rich, mahogany-colored sherries beloved of the period, had created an unassailable niche of its own. Saintsbury, grudgingly accepting the change in his *Notes on a Cellar Book*, nevertheless commented that dry Champagnes were apt to lose their flavor, and regretted the passing of "the rich and full-flavored variety as an alternative."

But by then Champagne had become something beyond wine itself, and even the *sound* of a cork popping would provoke animated gaiety and cosmic expectation at almost all social levels. Sometimes, of course, the gaiety could be extravagantly misplaced. Maurice Healy describes, in *Stay Me With Flagons*, the visit of a small opera company to his Irish hometown of Cork some eighty years ago, for whom the Lord Mayor of the city, in private life a wine merchant, decided to give a Champagne reception by way of a civic welcome. Secure in his seat, waiting for the opening per-

formance of *La Traviata* to begin, Healy could hear that the Lord
Mayor's hospitality, started some hours earlier, had been transferred
onto the stage.

A creditable performance of the overture took place, and the curtain
rose upon the revel of the first act. The cast was dressed in eighteenth
century costumes, but [the Lord Mayor's] waiters lent a modern note,
and continued to uncork Champagne with an assiduity and a hospitality
that filled me with direful presages. Never was the drinking song rendered with greater gusto; the chorus splashed Champagne in every
direction, and the principals sang with the chorus. Mr. G. Hilton St.
Just, no mean tenor, was in excellent voice; and I felt that for once, if
I was not getting exactly what Verdi had intended, I was undoubtedly
enjoying the authentic atmosphere which Dumas had meant to create.
The volatile wine carried the company through the first act with tre-
mendous *élan*; but when the curtain rose for the second it soon became
evident that there was something rotten in the state of Denmark. When
Alfredo's father came to reason with his son, the latter sat down at a
table and buried his face in his hands; at the end of each line of the
Di provenza he lifted it, glared at his father, and buried it again; occasionally a sob of emotion (which looked uncommonly like a hiccup)
shook his body. Meantime his father, who enjoyed a powerful bass-
baritone, kept alternating between hissed pianissimi and thundered
fortissimi. By this time there was no restraining the gallery. "Tis great
stuff Gussie's been giving 'em," cried one voice, and fifty others joined
in a chorus of not unfriendly chaff, which did not affect the performers
in the slightest. The opera finished triumphantly, Mr. St. Just's final
"O, Violetta!" being a magnificent degeneration from a musical note
into a hysterical sobbing.

Undoubtedly, the popularity of dry Champagne made the
producers exceedingly rich, but, more important, it restored a
taste for delicacy, the origin of Champagne's success too often lost,
subsequently, in a froth of sweet bubbles. Without a mask of
sugar, style and quality were again plainly evident, and as luck
would have it there followed a series of Champagne vintages of
unparalleled splendor. Charles Walter Berry, of Berry Bros. and
Rudd, the London wine merchants, described a dinner with the
head of Perrier-Jouët in 1934 when the 1892, one of the greatest
of them all, was served. "It was so wonderful," he recorded in his
diary, "that the horrid commercial instinct was difficult to quieten.
I wondered if there were any for sale, I dared not ask, being a

guest at the table . . . also I felt there could only be a very small quantity remaining in Monsieur Budin's private cellar for use on special occasions."

But eventually he found a way to draw out his host, and was surprised to learn that what remained of the wine did not belong to Monsieur Budin but to his brother-in-law, who, lying at that very moment dangerously ill, would perhaps "never drink the sixty bottles that remain to him." Berry kept discreet silence, but on parting, he plucked up courage and whispered, while tenderly pressing Budin's hand, "Wouldn't it be a charitable thing if I offered to buy that 1892 Perrier-Jouët . . . and thus put a temptation out of the way of your invalid brother-in-law?" We shall never know whether Monsieur Budin's acquiescence came in a surge of gratitude for such generous concern or in a paralyzing shock of disbelief, but we do know that Berry took the remaining stock of 1892 away with him. A few years ago, in San Francisco, I had an unexpected opportunity to taste it. Alas, I held in my glass only the brown ghost of former magnificence.

Most vintage Champagnes, and it was probably as true then as it is today, are at their best from six to ten years from the vintage date, though exceptional wines can age superbly for fifty years or more, losing sparkle but not vivacity. On the evening when we mourned the 1892 Perrier-Jouët we were lucky enough to have a bottle of 1926 Roederer to console us. Its color was clear gold, and though greatly diminished, it offered a bouquet and flavor of toasted almonds that we were catching just this side of being maderized. But the oldest Champagnes that I have drunk for other than intellectual pleasure have been the 1929s. Even in the past year or two, I have found 1929 Bollinger (in magnum) full flavored and fresh. Recently, a bottle of 1929 Roederer, though darkened in color, was equally fresh on the palate, with an unusual bouquet of vanilla biscuits.

If old Champagne is an acquired taste, pink Champagne need not be. It is a pity that the color carries with it suggestions of frivolity, because a well-made pink Champagne is not just Champagne of a different hue. Some houses make their pink *cuvée* by adding to the blend a little Bouzy (there are growers on this south-facing slope who still make their Pinot Noir into a red wine in favorable years). But others trouble to make a specifically pink wine—leaving juice and skins together just long enough for the pink color to take before separating them and then putting the resultant wine through the usual blending and secondary fermentation process. Along with the color the wine absorbs flavor from the skins, which gives a different balance and style to the wine. The rosé of the growers' cooperative at Mailly has the added interest (and distinctive characteristic) of being made entirely from Mailly *commune* grapes, but it is difficult to find in the United States. Charles Heidsieck offers one that confirms their full-bodied, deeply flavored house style; and Ruinart, the oldest Champagne house, founded by Dom Perignon's assistant, makes a pink vintage Champagne that develops richly complex character in bottle.

The great Champagne houses, of course, take pains with all their vintage wines to ensure such development. (It is assumed that nonvintage wines, by and large, will be consumed soon after release, as they should be.) The mature style that each house aims for has evolved over the years, and though sometimes a result of geographic happenstance (houses with larger vineyard holdings on the Côte des Blancs, in particular, are likely to use their position to make lighter, more elegant wines), usually it is the result of a past personal preference, refined and established by succeeding generations. Pol Roger, for example, blending for a dry, elegant style, uses 60 percent Pinot Noir and 40 percent Chardonnay, thereby increasing slightly the amount of white grapes over the standard blend in Champagne of two-thirds red and one-third white. Roederer, blending for a more complex, fuller style, uses a third Pinot Noir from the Montagne de Reims and a third from vineyards in the valley of the Marne; the other third is made up of white Chardonnay grapes. Piper-Heidsieck does not aim for such a full-bodied style as Roederer.

Mumm looks for "character," taking red grapes from the valley and from the Montagne de Reims in the manner of Roederer. But Mumm introduces some Meunier with the Pinot Noir and uses a slightly higher proportion of white grapes to tone down and lighten their blend. Taittinger blends for a light, delicate style in the tradition of early Champagnes, and has made a specialty of Blanc de Blancs, made, of course, from 100 percent white grapes.

Krug is one of the few firms that still ferment their wines in oak casks. Others use stainless steel for the first fermentation, though Bollinger ferments two thirds in old barrels (new barrels are used first to ferment second pressings, which are then sold to others in bulk) and one third in stainless steel. Fermentation in wood plus a high proportion of Pinot Noir (mostly from the firm's own vineyards on the Montagne de Reims) combine to give Bollinger vintage wines their characteristic body. The best of them are reserved for Bollinger's RD (recently disgorged) Champagne that is allowed to remain with its bottled sediment for eight to ten years. The richness of flavor that results is extraordinarily delicious. In fact, the length of time that wine and sediment remain together before disgorging plays at least as great a role in the development of flavor as the choice of grapes and the method of fermentation.

Recently, Krug has decided to concentrate on production of its Grande Cuvée, which will eventually represent at least three quarters of the firm's total output. Using a blend that will vary from year to year, and which will incorporate wines from several vintages for consistency of style, the wine will be based on roughly half white grapes and half red, of which about half will be Meunier for "charm and fruitiness," as Rémi Krug put it to me. Since it will be aged on the sediment over a six-year cycle, Grande Cuvée should need little sweetening.

Moët et Chandon, by far the largest of the Grande Marque Champagne producers, follows a blend for its California wine that is not too dissimilar from the proportions the firm uses in France. Edmond Maudière, responsible for the *cuvées* in both places, uses 60 percent Pinot Noir, 25 percent Chardonnay, and 15 percent Pinot Blanc at Domaine Chandon. In California, where the problem is one of maintaining the acidity rather than modifying it, there is no need for Meunier. On the other hand, picking of California Pinot Noir and Chardonnay for the Champagne vats must start two or more weeks before the general harvest to obtain the crisp acidity essential for the *prise de mousse*.

Most Champagnes today are fermented to give a pressure of sparkle equivalent to about six atmospheres. *Crémant* Champagne, increasingly rare, is fermented to only four atmospheres, however, and therefore seems softer to the palate even when quite dry. Most Blanc de Blancs, even when not described as *crémant*, are usually made with less pressure, too, to enhance the soft elegance of their style.

A vintage Champagne is best appreciated as a preamble to a fine dinner: by stimulating both palate and mind, it helps focus on wines to follow. As accompaniment to the toasts and good wishes that accompany our triumphs, great and small, and mark the passage of our lives, it has no equal, despite Hemingway's perplexity that "anyone would want to mix emotions with a wine like that." But above all, and who knows by what magic, a fine vintage Champagne makes any one of us feel younger, better looking, and wittier. And whatever Sir Edward Barry thought, I'm all for such depravity.

Vouvray: Wine of the Belle Epoque

VOUVRAY, a cluster of houses by the Loire, a few miles east of Tours, would be unremarkable were it not for the wine that bears its name. Centuries ago Rabelais described that wine as tasting of taffeta, and it remains one of the most appealing in the world. When it is young, its fresh bite brings zest to a soft, natural sweetness, like the crisp taste of a newly picked apple; when it is well aged, and especially when it is made in a year when the grapes had been left to hang late into November, its bouquet and flavor can be of incomparable range.

The four thousand acres of vines that produce Vouvray spread into and over seven other villages and hamlets as well. Sainte-Radegonde, Rochecorbon, Vernou, Noizay, Chançay, Reugny, and Parçay-Maslay carry in their High Gothic names an echo of pious knights and illuminated vellum. They spread around Vouvray like ribs in a fan of the chalky tufa rock that blankets Touraine and breaks into valleys and clefts that open to each other and to the Loire. The slopes and cliffs are of such modest elevation that they seem little more than the twists of an undulating landscape. Here and there a cottage façade, flat against the rock face, appears to be a stage set or an optical illusion until one realizes that its rooms have been gouged from the cliff behind it, with chimneys incongruously puffing smoke among the vines on the plateau above. Acres of other tunnels and vaults extend even farther into the tufa, for what were begun as galleried quarries to build the city of Tours remain in use as working wine cellars.

Tufa rock, porous and crumbly until exposed to air, is penetrated easily by both water and vine roots. Like well-drained gravel or sand it allows a warm surface environment that helps ripen the Chenin Blanc fully while the long, temperate summers of Touraine protect the grapes' natural acidity. Wire-trained but *gobelet* pruned, so that in winter the vines look like rows of stubby clenched fists, Chenin Blanc is here at the limit of its climatic adaptability. It ripens late—picking rarely starts before the last week in October—to give juice that, uncommonly, is both rich in sugar and high in acidity.

It is this unusual balance of ripe grape sugar and clean, tart acids inherent in the grapes of Vouvray that brings together a soft fullness and an etched flavor that are characteristic of the wine they give. Paul de Cassagnac, whose 1930 classic, *French Wines*, guided a post-Prohibition generation, marveled that Vouvray could be both sweet and dry simultaneously. "The sweetness," he said, "exists in the wine, not as a heavy charge, but as a light transparent veil which allows all the charm to appear and the complete and delicate aroma to be freely liberated." In essence the appeal of Vouvray lies in its sweet-tart character, dry enough to be refreshing, gentle enough to be universally flattering. The natural sweetness gives the wine fullness that sustains it against creamy sauces, and the acidity ensures that it never cloys. My favorite veal *escalope* dish, with a pan juice, white wine, cream, and mushroom sauce, is at its best, I think, with a not-too-dry Vouvray.

According to legend, the vineyards of Touraine began from a single vine shoot brought in the fourth century by Saint Martin, who had carried it in a bone from his native village near what is now the Yugoslav-Austrian border. (It is also popularly believed in Touraine that the depredations of Saint Martin's ass among the vines the Saint had planted taught growers the virtues of pruning.) In fact, the Chenin Blanc vine that produces Vouvray and most other white wines of the Loire originated in neighboring Anjou (some speculate that it might even have started there as a wild vine indigenous to the primeval forests of the region) and was brought to Touraine, and hence to Vouvray, in 1445 by Thomas Bohier, then Lord of Chenonceaux. Planted by him on the hill of Mont Chenin, the vine, though to this day more often referred to by growers there as Pineau de la Loire, thus acquired its new name.

At first it was the Dutch who discovered these new Chenin Blanc wines. They shipped Vouvray to the Netherlands, where often it was discreetly "improved" with a little sweet Spanish wine from Málaga. (The seventeenth-century Dutch were the inventors and masters of the art of wine blending.) They encouraged the growers to extend the vineyards and at one period regularly bought almost the entire production. The wars of Louis XIV and the banishment of Protestants from France that followed the revocation of the Edict of Nantes in 1685 greatly reduced that commerce; Pierre Carreau, an observer of Touraine at the time, wrote in a 1698 memorandum that "loss of business with the Dutch has caused vineyards to drop to a half and a third of their value." Trade picked up in the eighteenth century only to suffer again in the wake of the Napoleonic wars.

Through all these vicissitudes the wine of Vouvray came to be increasingly appreciated for its style, unique among French wines. Easy to enjoy, it became pivotal to afternoon entertaining. Sparkling versions appeared, and when conditions were right the fungus of "noble rot" attacked overripe grapes causing them to shrivel rapidly, concentrating still further both sugar and acid and thereby producing prime dessert wines of such intense flavor and exquisite balance that they seem to age indefinitely. Morning mist from the Loire and the warmth of a late autumn sun were all that were needed.

Louis Orizet, in his book *Les Vins de France*, refers to several occasions when he was lucky enough to drink octogenarian Vouvrays, unfailingly "all smiles through their wrinkles." Some years ago my long morning's tasting with a grower at Rochecorbon ended by his reaching for a bottle of the miraculous 1895, buried in sand in a cellar niche. Its orange-gold color gleamed in the light of the cellar candle; the bouquet and flavor, powerfully fresh, were honeyed and rich with suggestions of impossible tropical fruits; and for the full half hour we sat drinking it the wine neither faded nor in any way lost its astonishing freshness. It is curious that where the brilliance of a rich Sauternes at its peak inevitably descends to a dry and sometimes harsh cacophony, fine mature Vouvray, because of its perfect acid-sweet balance, seems only to become more harmonious and increasingly vibrant.

In the nineteenth century all white wines shipped from Touraine were often sold as Vouvray, and until comparatively recent times the wines now sold as Montlouis, grown on the opposite, south, side of the Loire, were included in the area of production. The modern regulations controlling the *appellation* were fought over for fifteen years until they finally established, in the late 1930s, parameters that restrict vines for Vouvray to the shoulder alone of each slope within the eight named communes; land below is devoted to grains, fruits, and sheep pasture, adding bucolic charm to the landscape. Each slope, because of exposure and variation of terrain, is known for the precise difference of quality and style in the wine it will yield. One, perhaps stonier than the others, will sparingly yield an austere wine that brings backbone to a blend; elsewhere, a measure of sand and clay will bring a fuller, more tender element. Then again, wines from valleys closest to the Loire show in their youth a keen acidity, whereas wines from the valleys of Vaux, Cousse, and La Brenne, in what are called the *arrières côtes* of Chançay, Reugny, and Parçay-Meslay, more often show in their youth a hard finish, with even a hint of bitterness, that also augurs well for aging.

The Vouvray vineyard holdings are small; roughly three hundred growers live from viticulture alone—a considerable number of families for only four thousand acres, especially when one remembers that the total acreage includes a few plots attached to mixed farms as well as those, hardly bigger than a backyard, that serve as weekend occupations. A single, unified holding is rare. No matter how small, each is commonly split up, sometimes into as many as thirty or forty tiny, scattered patches. Unlike Sancerre, however, where a similar situation has been hard to change because growers fear so much the consequences of localized frosts or sudden hailstorms—quite apart from each man's conviction that such dispersion of vines brings balance to his wines—Vouvray has seen some cautious swapping of plots to ease the problems of cultivation.

Even so, set as they are on rolling contours among pasture and orchard, meadow and woodland, the vineyards compose a serendipitous picture that entices Parisians down the new autoroute most weekends of the year. Lunch at Vouvray's Grand Vatel or the cozy Perce Neige in Vernou, a picnic, or, more grandly, a visit to

Barrier's restaurant in Saint-Symphorien is followed by a taste (or two) in a cool and labyrinthine cave before loading a case (or two) in the car.

There was a time when weekly shipments to the bars and cafés of Paris absorbed much of the production, but that demand seems to have disappeared along with the Art Nouveau décor to which a glass of Vouvray, it must be admitted, once added a shimmering dimension. Vouvray is a period wine with an intrinsic style that is not always in accord with present sensibilities. A white wine that needs its modicum of sweetness to be in balance and some age to show its quality meets resistance when the first duties of a modern white wine are to be dry and young. That is why Vouvray is now in danger of becoming to wine, I sometimes think, what Chaucer is to books. His *Canterbury Tales* have been so often edited, adapted, abbreviated, and generally pulled about that, even among those who have read them, few have been allowed their full, vigorous flavor. There are Vouvray growers, including some of the best, who have been intimidated, I suppose, by devotees of a *nouvelle cuisine* that, while inserting irrelevant sugared *sorbets* in a meal and combining raspberry juice with everything, frowns for no good reason on even a gram or two of needed, natural sweetness in a glass of wine. Such growers attempt to edit, adapt, abbreviate, and generally pull their wines about to fit a dry strait-jacket. But Vouvray fermented to complete dryness, I find, is a sorry thing: It is hard when it should be soft, sharp when it should be gentle, boring when it should be beguiling. At dinner recently in a distinguished Touraine restaurant, the only Vouvray on the list, from a grower of impeccable reputation, was made with such painful and unnecessary austerity that to drink it required discipline and gave no pleasure. How I longed for a few empty calories.

Bewildered by this misunderstanding of the very nature of Vouvray, the growers have turned increasingly to the option of using their grapes to make wine by the Champagne method of secondary fermentation in bottle. Production has moved inexorably in this direction so that now almost two thirds of Vouvray appears as sparkling wine. The law allows growers to increase yields and to pick earlier with lower natural sugar for this purpose, and, unfortunately, the subvariety of Chenin Blanc used to provide the intense wines, graceful yet strong, that age forever is making way for more productive strains better suited to the light wines needed for the Champagne process.

By good fortune I was last in Touraine on a lucid spring day punctuated by gusty showers. Hedgerows were still bare except for sporadic droops of catkins, but apricot trees scattered blossom profligately over stone walls whenever the wind blew. I spent a morning tasting my way through 1983s, still in the huge 150-gallon wooden barrels in which they are both fermented and aged, and through a series of 1982s, already in bottle. The 1983s made from grapes that were dehydrated and concentrated by the heat of that September have both high alcohol and high acid and need the traditional residual sugar even more than did the 1982s, which were softened considerably by preharvest rains. When I had selected the wines I needed, the grower and I went together to a local inn for a simple lunch. We had finished eating when he drew from a wrapping of old newspaper a bottle of his 1971 dessert Vouvray. He wiped away the cellar cobwebs with his napkin and drew the cork himself with a screw he had in his pocket. A bouquet of ripe fruits wafted from our glasses as he poured. *"Douce France,"* I thought, as I settled more comfortably in my chair.

Chablis:
Kimmeridgian
in Bloom

IN AUXERRE, some hundred miles from Paris, an ancient Pinot
Noir vineyard is a source of therapy to patients at the psychiatric
hospital and of funds to its bursar. The few acres, a medieval gift
to the Hospice Saint-Germain, are the only vines that remain in
what was once the largest, the most distinguished, and the most
flourishing wine city of France. As late as the twelfth century (and
Auxerre wines were well known at least three hundred years before
that), while Bordeaux and Burgundy were still in obscurity, wines
of Auxerre were described reliably as "the very best, the most
precious." When King John of England had wished to be well
recompensed for a service rendered two of his nobles, a cask of
Auxerre wine was the "gift" he asked for, just as Auxerre wine was
the inevitable choice of the powerful Count of Guines at the memorable feast he prepared for the Archbishop of Reims in 1172. In
1245 a visiting ecclesiastic from Italy wrote that there were "more
vines at Auxerre than at Cremona, Parma, Reggio and Modena combined. The local people harvest no other crop; shipment of their
wines to Paris procures for them everything they need."

The vineyards spread along the banks of the Yonne, of course, to
Irancy, Cravant, Vermenton, Saint-Bris-le-Vineux, and Coulanges-

la-Vineuse (some of the names speak for themselves), other communities accessible to boats that plied the Yonne and the Seine to Paris. About that time, or perhaps a little earlier, the monks of the Chapître de Saint-Martin in Chablis, twelve miles east of Auxerre, and of the Abbey of Pontigny, a few miles to its north, began the cultivation of vineyards on those steep slopes above the Serein—more a stream than a river—that we know today as the *grands crus* and *premiers crus* of Chablis.

The seven *grands crus* are an unbroken block of vines, roughly two hundred acres, in an elbow formed by the angle of a side valley from Fyé to Chablis as it falls to the valley floor. Each section, or *climat*, changes slightly in its tilt and direction of exposure, and, because each is divided among numerous small proprietors, there are many subtle shifts of style among them. Blanchots, perhaps the steepest, faces southeast and Les Clos, almost due south; Valmur, Vaudésir, Les Preuses, Grenouilles, and Bougros extend along the southwestern exposure that faces the Serein flowing below. The *premiers crus*, twenty-nine of them according to the *appellation* law of 1967 but with changes as recent as 1980, spread along the Serein and into the narrow valleys of the streams that feed it, encircling the town of Chablis like the points of a snowflake.

Indeed, in choosing sites for those first vines the monks probably watched, as will any modern grower, for slopes where winter snow first melted. They seem to have been directed by more than such simple observation, however, because their vineyards were planted solely and precisely on those sections of hillside that we now know to coincide with the regular emergence of a layer of Kimmeridgian clay that lies below the Chablis hills. Kimmeridgian—named for the village of Kimmeridge in Dorset, England—is composed of a myriad of fossilized crustaceans laid down in the Jurassic period. It is grayish, calcareous, brittle. What appears at first to be rough-shattered rock is in fact a mass of tiny shells, some minute cockles and others, tightly coiled conchs or winkles no larger than a comma on this page. Again, prompted seemingly by more than instinct, those early growers chose to plant on this unusual and difficult terrain only Chardonnay grapes, even though the successful vineyards clustered near neighboring Auxerre were planted mainly with Pinot Noir for red wine. The result was a white wine of sinewy but silky dryness with a delicacy of perfume and flavor both discreet and persistent. In bringing Chardonnay to Kimmeridgian clay the monks had brought forth one of the great wines of the world.

The town at Chablis flourished. Inhabitants still in legal serfdom became rich enough to buy their freedom. By 1403 there were more than 450 recorded private proprietors of vines who could afford, collectively, to finance a fortified wall for their protection and independence. The number had increased to seven hundred by the early sixteenth century. Their vines spread along the deposits of Kimmeridgian clay, avoiding, with rare exceptions, the Portland limestone that formed a plateau above the valley slopes and the cold, damp alluvial soil below. Carried by cart to Auxerre for shipment to Paris, to Rouen, and from there by sea to the ports and cities of the north, Chablis wine was first just a part of the trade in Auxerre wine, a name given indiscriminately to all wines that arrived by boat and barge from that city. But its own reputation was soon established. With the restoration of Charles II to the throne of England, for example, Chablis found its way to a luxury-loving court no less addicted to fine wine than was that of Louis XIV (records reveal generous stocks of Chablis in the Earl of Bedford's cellar at Woburn Abbey in the 1660s).

Consumption of cheap wine by the French urban poor grew steadily throughout the eighteenth century, encouraging the spread of varieties and practices that boosted production with little throught to quality. To serve whose economic advantage it is hard to say, but a struggle ensued in regions of easy access to big cities to protect the traditions of fine wine established there by the ecclesiastic and aristocratic estates of the Middle Ages. At first, when local ordinances, intended only to stop the loss of grain fields and pastures to an invasion of common, prolific vines, culminated in a royal decree of 1731 forbidding new vineyards, the problem seemed to have been contained. But the decree went further in requiring immediate uprooting of all vines recently planted on land not previously used for that purpose. In regions where landless peasants had staked everything on clearing and planting scrubby acres leased from landowners happy to put poor land to profitable use there was such a desperate outcry that social and political expediency forced a recersal. The 1731 decree was swept aside by another of 1759, and, if the first had gone further than wise government might have dictated, so did the second. With it all regulations on land use were abandoned and there was left no hindrance to an endless proliferation of common grapes of uncommon yield. Revolution thirty years later increased still further the demand for ordinary wine, and, because the great estates were broken up and sold as "public property," there was no compunction in smothering what had been fine vineyards with common, high-yielding varieties. Nor was there scruple or law to restrain extension of vineyards everywhere and anywhere with navigable access to big cities. Whatever else might have flowed as a result of the events of 1789, Louis Bosc, the encyclopedist, wrote in 1821 that the French Revolution produced a torrent of common wine.

Old Séchard, a character who appears in Balzac's novels *Les Illusions perdues* and *Splendeurs et Misères des Courtisanes*, spoke for a multitude who had inherited, divided, and extended the vineyards of the *ancien régime*: "Monsieur the marquis, monsieur the count, monsieur the this and that, they tell me my wine lacks quality. Of what use is their education if they are so befuddled? Listen: those fine gentlemen get seven, perhaps eight barrels to the acre and sell them for sixty francs apiece. At most and in a good year they clear four hundred francs an acre. Now I harvest twenty barrels and sell them for thirty francs—total, six hundred francs an acre. How is that wrong? Quality! What good is quality to me? Monsieur the marquis and monsieur the count can keep it. The only quality I'm interested in is cash profit."

The Auxerrois, easily connected by barge to the urban markets of the north, was one of the first areas to succumb to greed and speculation, the more tragically because it had been the first and most prestigious wine region of medieval France. Edme Restif, father of Restif de La Bretonne (the eighteenth-century French novelist who brought to perfection the art of titillation disguised as moralistic text), is said to have grown rich by leading the spread of the Sacy grape from his native plateau east of Chablis. It was a variety that gave an abundance of such poor wine that the president of the municipality of Vermenton, one of the towns along the Yonne that had long supplied quality wines of the Auxerrois, sought powers in 1782 to destroy the vines that were in effect destroying his community. Unfortunately spread of the grape could not be stopped, and degeneration of quality continued when railways brought even cheaper wine from the Midi. Despite a brief frenzy of renewed activity when the phylloxera louse temporarily devoured the vines of the south before, in turn, devouring those of the north, there was an end to Auxerre as a wine center.

Chablis was saved, said Professor Dion in his *Histoire de la Vigne et du Vin en France*, only because the cost of transportation twelve miles to the Yonne at Auxerre by cart was disproportionately high for cheap wine. He might have added that the narrow valley of the Serein, mild and charming to the eye, traps easily those masses of cold, spring air that freeze tender May vine shoots. The risk of losing three or more consecutive crops, not unknown in Chablis, was only worthwhile if successful crops were of a quality that could command high prices. Making a virtue of necessity, the growers of Chablis stayed faithful to the Chardonnay abandoned by others.

There were still several hundred growers of Chablis in the nineteenth century, their vines covering some two thousand acres that had spread into adjacent villages and hamlets but always within two or three miles of the town. Their holdings were small, many of them less than an acre, and few could support the cost of even rudimentary winemaking equipment for their grapes. In fact, the entire Chablis crop in the last century was brought to the huge wooden screw presses owned by a handful of families, the juice carried to the growers' homes in open tubs slung on poles. Regardless of what went on around them, the vineyards of Chablis remained intact, their wine holding, as Jules Guyot wrote in 1868, in a study of French vineyards sponsored by the government, "a prominent place among the best white wines of France. In spite of the fame they have long enjoyed," his report continued, "their true value . . . far exceeds their repute."

That repute, of course, led to the flattery of imitation in the new vineyards of California and Australia, where the name Chablis was applied to any white wine that satisfied the seller's subjective definition. (One need hardly say that such "generic" Chablis, pleasant though it might be, gives not even a hint of what true Chablis is all about.) In Chablis itself the confusion and commercial permissiveness that eventually followed in the wake of phylloxera blurred the lines traditionally limiting true Chablis from the ordinary white wines that surrounded it. A group of working vineyard owners drew together to protect the name and quality of their wine, and in 1923 and again in 1929 they were the first in France to succeed in obtaining legal definition of their product. That definition recognized the link between Chablis wine, Chardonnay grapes, and the layer of Kimmeridgian subsoil instinctively followed by the monks of Chablis and of Pontigny eight centuries before.

With the formation of the National Institute of Controlled Appellations in the 1930s, a consequence of the government's decision to reserve jurisdiction in such questions to technical experts in Paris rather than leave it to local judges and magistrates, that definition, covering Chablis and nineteen surrounding communities, was confirmed in 1938—with two differences. They seemed unimportant at the time, but they sowed controversy that now threatens Chablis as surely as did Edme Restif and his Sacy grape two hundred years ago.

First, if Kimmeridgian clay was of such importance, ruled the technical experts, then the area included within the limits of the *appellation* Chablis should be extended to *all* places within the twenty communities where Kimmeridgian clay emerges to the surface (or "flowers," as the Chablis people quaintly express it). That included woods and wheat fields, some of them locations never used for vines because, for any number of reasons, they were manifestly unsuitable. The defined area of 2,500 acres entitled to the *appellation* Chablis was, in theory anyway, increased by that ruling to 12,500 acres. Second, with an adroitness essential to the survival of detached government agencies, a sop was thrown to the few growers with Chardonnay vines outside the delimited areas but within the twenty communities. Without definition or limit they were to be allowed to call their wine Petit Chablis. It meant, in effect, that wine of the entire 50,000 acres of the twenty communities, other than what was already Chablis, could be called Petit Chablis. Inevitably, those whose vineyards had only a lack of Kimmeridgian, to impose a single but significant word, lost no time in pointing out some of the far more serious drawbacks of the woodlands and wheat fields that had been gratuitously elevated to full *appellation* status.

Since 1961 techniques of frost protection have reduced the risks of growing Chablis. The vineyards have spread, and land entitled to the *appellation* has increased in value. Those whose land was excluded from the *appellation* sought, and were successful in obtaining, a commission of inquiry, and battle polarized around two strong personalities of the region. Just as *Clochmerle*'s public convenience touched hilariously the deeper political passions of the time, so the principle of Kimmeridgian was allowed to take on the odor of doctrinaire inflexibility because it was defended by William Fèvre, head of the Syndicat de Défense de l'Appellation Chablis, a graduate of the key Ecole Nationale d'Administration, an administrator of France's *autoroutes*, and a man of declared leftwing sympathies. The attack was led by Jean Durup, head of the breakaway Fédération des Vignerons du Chablisien (the last word, meaning "Chablis area" rather than Chablis, gives a clear indication of what they might like the *appellation* Chablis to mean). Durup, a lawyer who formerly held a high position in the Ministry of Finance, was of declared freewheeling right-of-center sympathies, which would have appealed to the technocrats of the Giscard d'Estaing administration, eager to free France from what they perceived to be old-fashioned shackles.

Durup's Federation won the day, and in 1976 a decree, confirmed on appeal in 1980, further extended the Chablis *appellation* by converting more than two thousand acres of what had been Petit Chablis (of which barely two hundred were producing wine at the time). For the first time the *appellation* encompassed land with no link to Kimmeridgian clay, much of it still wooded and not even tested in the production of wine of any kind. More surprising, some of the acreage added to the *appellation* in 1938 in accordance with the experts' theory that all Kimmeridgian should be included, though still not planted in vines, has now been elevated to *premier cru*. There was a time when such distinction was accorded pragmatically and reflected a known, consistently high standard of wine. It is difficult to grasp how anyone can *know* in advance that land still covered in wood and scrub will produce, if planted with vines, not merely good wine but wine of *premier cru* quality.

Those who defend the changes claim, perhaps rightly, that exposure is as important as soil and that improvements in the art and science of winemaking over the centuries have established techniques that make a greater contribution to quality and style than does soil composition. But the basis of the controlled *appellation* system in France, right or wrong, is respect for the character of a defined terrain as expressed through the wine produced from it according to what is described in the statutes as "constant and loyal custom." If Jean Durup is right, then it is possible to make Chablis, the same extraordinary wine, divorced from Kimmeridgian clay. But that begs many questions: For example, how important are Miocene soils to the character of Châteauneuf-du-Pape or gravel to the Médoc or chalky hills to Champagne? Old Séchard would have had a very short answer. But do we?

Venerable Hermitage

THE CLOSET I use as a wine cellar has only the sketchiest semblance of order, a state of affairs I promise to correct whenever I search in exasperation for a bottle that I *know* to be there somewhere. Too much is crammed into too small a space, of course (a common complaint), and I make matters worse by lazily separating bottles from newly delivered cases to fill gaps here and there instead of taking the trouble to rearrange the bins. But in the resulting chaos I sometimes come across a wine that I thought finished long since and then feel the same joy as finding a favorite book, assumed lost, caught behind the stack or meeting in a faraway place a long-missed friend in circumstances that allow time for a drink and a gossip.

A few weeks ago, rummaging in the corner reserved for uncertain wines discreetly brought out for family drinking only, I came across a bottle of 1962 Hermitage that had been bottled in our company's former cellars in London. I didn't remember having brought any of it to San Francisco, and had I known it to be there I would have drunk it long ago. There was beef stew on the stove, the 1962 had been a good wine, and it seemed to be as appropriate a choice as any. I looked forward to seeing what had happened since I had last tasted it, at least five years before.

Expecting some deposit, I decanted the wine. There was very little sediment, but down one side of the bottle a light crust had formed. The color was deeper than I had expected, with hardly a hint of browning; the bouquet and taste showed vigor rather than complexity. Though considerably mellowed, the wine had taken seventeen years in its stride.

The crust recalled my earliest memory of drinking old Hermitage in London, during the late fifties. With some braised pigeons (an unfortunate choice for the evening, as I remember clearly; much of that morning had been spent coping with an obstinate pigeon stuck in our chimney), a friend had shared with me his last bottle of the great 1923. The wine had thrown a crust every bit as heavy and as firm as any Port would have done. To my bewilderment it had contradicted my bible of the time, P. Morton Shands' engagingly opinionated book on French wines. First qualifying his ever-dogmatic view with a mischievous "when not pasteurised," Shand says that Hermitage "throws a heavy deposit, like a violet mud, which is apt to precipitate itself to the bottom rather than adhere to the sides in the form of a hard crust . . ." But deposit or not, that wine, too, had amazed me by its unexpectedly vigorous color and lively quality after thirty years in bottle.

Perhaps it was an obvious promise of such long life that caused Hermitage, of all French wines, to be the first to be set aside for aging in bottle. Dr. Middleton, that eighteenth-century master of lucid English, theological controversy, and companionable drinking, gave Hermitage as one of the three wines that "did not compare," because of its capacity to "grow to an extreme old age." (The other two, oddly, were "port" and "hock," rather vague and all-embracing categories, one might have thought, to be put on such elevated pedestals.) Professor Saintsbury's much quoted description of Hermitage as the "manliest of wines" referred in fact to a specific 1846, drunk forty years after the vintage, and was probably an allusion to this same remarkable vigor-in-age. On the other hand, having once described an 1874 Hermitage in language so sensational that I hesitate to quote it directly, H. Warner Allen later regretted his early excess, saying that he had since drunk many bottles of Hermitage and of other wines and that "today I should be less extravagant in my eulogy." None of which is surprising, for though we look for subtleties and complex harmonies in most aged red wines as recompense for our patience in keeping them, my experience has been that the longevity of Hermitage is itself the chief attraction; the gradual but persistent ripening, on a sustained even note, is the aesthetic reward.

Like Falernian and Malmsey, Hermitage is a literary wine, one of legend and myth. With its southern exposure, rare in the Rhône Valley, the hill was first planted as a vineyard by the Greeks who traded along the valley from their settlement at Marseilles. By the time the Romans had made Vienne an important administrative post, the hill was already bearing the Syrah grapes still cultivated there, fanciful stories of this variety arriving from Persia in the knapsack of some errant medieval knight notwithstanding. The legend that the vines were planted (or replanted) by Saint Patrick himself is hardly credible; but Gaspard de Stérimberg's retirement there in 1224 to a hermitage that eventually gave the hill its name, is adequately documented, though the popular image of an ascetic soldier piously beating sword into plowshare to make wine flow from what was barren rock to the greater glory of God is at very least poetic exaggeration.

For a man seeking a life of self-denial and penitence, petitioning to possess the hill of Saint Christopher (as it was then called), which was already covered with vineyards that for over a thousand years had been reputed to produce the finest wines in France, was an unusual beginning. There must have been mutual, tacit under-standing that he was, in fact, asking his due for services rendered the French crown in the barbaric crusade against the Albigensians, a barely disguised military destruction of the Languedoc to geld the powerful counts of Toulouse.

We can imagine how impressive Hermitage, then known as *vin de Tournon*, must have seemed at the time. Even during those centuries when most other red wines, made to be drunk within months of the vintage, were closer to our idea of a rosé, it is im-possible that a wine made from Syrah grapes could have been any-thing other than solid and deep-colored. Louis XIV thought so highly of it that he included it in a gift to Charles II of England as evidence both of his affection and of the prestige of French wines; and other references show that, rare and expensive, it was re-garded as the optimal wine in seventeenth-century Paris.

But it was the opening of the Canal du Midi in 1681, linking the Mediterranean and Bordeaux, that finally brought Hermitage to the tables of northern Europe. Before the end of the century, at least one grower had started to ship his wines by that route; and, doubtless in the same way, Lord Townsend, British ambassador to The Hague, brought a quantity to the cellar of his embassy, the first recorded purchase of Hermitage by an Englishman. The Earl of Bristol, an ardent collector of French wines, followed Townsend's example in 1714 (but then he had long been an admirer of Rhône wines, having purchased "Avignon" wine—possibly what today we would call Châteauneuf-du-Pape—as early as 1704). A 1760 Hermitage stole the show at the Paris Exhibition of 1862, and at the Vienna Exhibition of 1875 Henry Vizetelly said that Châteauneuf-du-Pape was hardly to be noticed, such was the dominance of Hermitage as far as Rhône wines were concerned.

But these days Hermitage is a wine more often talked about than tasted. Production is small, and the speed with which modern wine merchants travel usually takes them straight from the *négociants* of Burgundy to the cooperatives of the lower Rhône, with hardly a pause at Tain-l'Hermitage. Though almost as far from Orange, the commercial wine center of the southern Rhône, as from Beaune, Hermitage, with its handful of associated *appellations* in the forty-mile stretch from Vienne to Valence, is too often seen as merely an adjunct to the lower Rhône. But apart from differences of scale (the eight *appellations* together rarely give more than 2 percent of the total output of wine of the Rhône Valley), the grapes used, method of cultivation, soil, and climate are quite different from those farther downstream. The wines have almost nothing in common.

Hermitage and Crozes-Hermitage adjacent to it seem to be exceptions to a rule that all the fine wines of what the French call the *Rhône septentrional* are produced on the granitic bluffs of the west bank. They start with the red wines of Côte Rôtie, opposite Vienne, continue through the white wines of Condrieu and Château Grillet, include red and white wines under the *appellation* St. Joseph, and end, opposite Valence, with the interlocking *appellations* of Cornas for red wines and Saint-Péray for white. Actually, Hermitage is less an exception to this rule than at first appears. A gigantic lump of granite, the hill of Hermitage must have been separated from its original formation through some primordial cataclysm. Geologically it, too, belongs to the west bank. Crozes, on the other hand, mostly clay, is exactly where it should be, possibly explaining why the red and white wines of Saint-Joseph more closely resemble in style and quality the red and white wines of Hermitage, though separated by the breadth of the river, than do those of the neighboring vineyards of Crozes-Hermitage.

Saint-Joseph is grown on terraced vineyards that meander through the little river port of Tournon, with its old *château fort* facing Tain-l'Hermitage, and neighboring *communes*. The wines were always sold as *vin de Mauves*, the name of one of the communes, in the nineteenth century and enjoyed a high reputation. But that name was rejected when the communes had to agree on a joint *appellation* in 1956. Perhaps Glun and Lemps, two of the villages with names obviously bereft of sales appeal, resented the idea of continuing to play second fiddle to their exotically named neighbor. Whatever the reason for the choice, the unfamiliarity of the name Saint-Joseph has since been a commercial obstacle. Crozes-Hermitage, with the advantage of the suffix and its proximity to Hermitage, commands as high a price as a good Saint-Joseph, though rarely is it as distinguished. Red Crozes doesn't age well and is inclined to be clumsy when young.

All three *appellations* are based on the Syrah grape for their red wines, though the statutes tolerate a slight admission of the permitted white grapes, Roussanne and Marsanne. The Syrah is a low-yielding, fragile vine that grows supported by stakes fixed in tripods, the better to resist the fierce winds that roar down the Rhône Valley. The wine it gives, deeply colored and vigorously tannic, has an unmistakable aroma of violets when made from fully ripened grapes; but this becomes less intense in time, and the style and bouquet of the wine then vary according to origin. French growers distinguish between *petite* Syrah and *grosse* Syrah, the latter having the advantage of yield rather than quality. Neither is related to what is called the Petite Sirah in California. That vine is thought to have been most likely developed from a variety propagated in France by a Dr. Duriff and named for him in the 1880s. Related or not, there are powerful examples of the California Petite Sirah that share certain sturdy characteristics of northern Rhône wines (the Robert Mondavi Petite Sirah 1973 is one), giving hope for better things to come. One or two California growers, however, notably Joseph Phelps on the Silverado Trail in Napa, have a few acres of true Syrah that are beginning to bear. It remains to be seen what this grape will give in California: early examples of the wine are still too raw to judge.

Saint-Joseph, without quite the intensity or weight of Hermitage, comes close and shares its capacity for aging. Shortly before I enjoyed my unexpected 1962 Hermitage I had shared a bottle of 1962 Saint-Joseph, which, had I been able to taste it alongside the Hermitage, would have lost little in the comparison. Both are very direct wines that need to be matched to substantial dishes, and other wines served with them at the same meal should be equally uncomplicated.

Hermitage, Saint-Joseph, and even Crozes-Hermitage are more robust than the red wines from the other two *appellations* of this mini-region: Côte Rôtie and Cornas. Côte Rôtie is still tempered by a proportion of white Viognier grapes (the variety used on its own to make Condrieu and Château Grillet), but the practice is diminishing. In those two wines, Viognier gives a distinctive smell of hawthorn blossom, and in Côte Rôtie—as I noticed again recently when by lucky chance I found a bottle of *cru* La Garde 1973 on a restaurant list in a suburb of San Francisco—Viognier brings an aromatic strain as well as softening the style of the Syrah. The wine made a perfect match for a *suprême* of pheasant, where an Hermitage or even a Saint-Joseph might have been overpowering.

Cornas, which I used to drink often at the Beau Rivage at Condrieu, is made from Syrah grapes alone, but much of the territory of the *appellation* extends over pebbly terrain that was once the bed of a torrent draining the Vivarais hills into the Rhône. Whether for this reason or for some other, Cornas wines have always seemed to me to have briskness in youth, rather than the sometimes brutal harshness of a young Hermitage, and in age less denseness, softening almost to a point of sweetness. The last time I was at the Beau Rivage I had just such a 1966 Cornas, elegant though still rather out of scale for the *volaille au poivre vert* that I had mistakenly elected to eat with it. But I had already chalked up a perfect match of *rouget en papillote*, the Mediterranean red mullet that was an obsession with wealthy Romans in the early years of the Empire (obviously for good reason), and a 1976 Condrieu.

Condrieu and its appendix, Château Grillet (the only single *domaine* in France, and a handkerchief-size one at that, to have an *appellation* of its own), are white wines that stand apart. I have already mentioned their distinctive aroma of hawthorn flower; with a year or two in bottle it seems to intensify as the wine fills out—not that I recommend long aging for these wines. In London we imported Château Grillet regularly, and it was quite disappointing after a few years in bottle.

Though often dismissed as unimportant, and admittedly unpredictable in quality, the white wines of Hermitage and Crozes-Hermitage have given me much pleasure. The first bottle of wine I paid for with my own earned money was a 1947 Hermitage Blanc. I bought it in 1950 from the wine shop that stood on the corner of Old Compton Street in London, an adjunct to Kettner's restaurant. Perhaps that has prejudiced me in its favor. Sadly, there has been a deterioration in recent years caused by the persistent replacement of Roussanne vines, their small yield giving grapes with zest and flavor, by more prolific but milder Marsanne. Both varieties are permitted, and ideally each would contribute to a perfect balance. But if your favorite Hermitage Blanc now has less assertive flavor than once it did, and ages more rapidly than it should, you can be sure that the vineyard has converted largely to Marsanne. A fine Hermitage Blanc, with a year or two in bottle, should develop a bouquet that I liken to macadamia nuts and honey.

White Crozes-Hermitage, grown on heavier soil, is not just a secondary Hermitage but a different style of wine. It needs, in particular, a chance to aerate. What might at first seem a dumb, tired wine often opens miraculously after a few minutes in the glass and a slight raising of the temperature (white Rhône wines are usually served too cold: they should be chilled, not iced). A Crozes-Hermitage Les Meysonniers 1976 that I had in a restaurant near Chicago last fall, for example, after a very disappointing start opened up with an astonishing bouquet redolent of almonds and glazed fruits.

At Saint-Péray the Roussanne and Marsanne grapes give wine of much less character, most of it made to sparkle by fermentation in the bottle, the *méthode champenoise*. Wagner was fond of it and was said to be drinking it copiously while composing *Parsifal*. It cannot be relied upon to have the same effect on others.

Southern Rhône, Wine Cellar of France

MANY WINE BOOKS and restaurant lists present the wines of
the Rhône Valley as a unity, and, if I once had difficulty
in understanding, let alone appreciating, Hermitage and
Châteauneuf-du-Pape, my problem stemmed, I am sure, from my
confused attempts to taste a connection between the two. Eventually I realized that the northern Rhône has as much to do with the
southern Rhône as either of them has with the unexceptional wines
of Bugey in the elbow of the Rhône above Lyon or with the wines
of the Valais—that stretch of the Rhône above Lake Geneva where
vineyards on an arid mountainside are watered by melting snows
through an intricate system of wooden conduits.

Some see the difference as just a matter of scale, because the
small production of Hermitage, Côte Rôtie, and the rest of the
northerly vineyards between Vienne and Valence bears no comparison with the massive output of the southern Rhône. Others
dismiss the whole thing as a mere divergence of style, like the
Côte de Beaune and Côte de Nuits in Burgundy or the Médoc and
Saint-Emilion in Bordeaux. The difference is in fact much more
stark.

Except for a traditional supplement of white Viognier grapes at
Côte Rôtie, all the northern Rhône red wines are made from the

Syrah alone, a black grape well adapted to unstable weather and difficult terrain. It has been the principal, if not the sole, red wine grape in the northern Rhône since the fourth century and probably was brought there even earlier by Greeks trading pots for metals. Vigorously harsh when young, superb when aged, its wines require a measured investment of patience, a final effort of concentration, to be fully enjoyed. In short, they are wines for laying down; and that implies time, money, and a certain way of thinking about wine.

In the south, the bulk of the production is ordinary red Côtes du Rhône, though that should not obscure the considerable quantity of distinguished red wines, especially those of Gigondas and Châteauneuf-du-Pape. They are all wines that can be appreciated sooner than those of the north and are more easily approached, even when more alcoholic, as they frequently are. Softer, rounder, fruitier, these southern wines are made, unlike those of the north, from a cornucopia of grape varieties that are shared, often under other names, with neighboring regions and neighboring countries. Indeed, they could be more accurately described as wines of Provence, of the Mediterranean. When Keats called for a "beaker full of the warm South . . . With beaded bubbles winking at the brim," he was probably hoping for a glass of young Côtes du Rhône, still purple, drawn from the wood.

A matter of words—but a matter of perception and use, too. In the south the enjoyment of wine is direct. There is no long view or distant expectation, no time lost analyzing or discussing a wine that has failed in its immediate essential—to satisfy. Despite highways, tractors, and power presses, the Rhône delta is an antique world where a bottle of wine is, after all, a bottle of wine. This unpretentiously serious local attitude led first to respect for a wine's natural origin, and from that the phenomenon of controlled geographic *appellations* developed in France. It was Baron Le Roy of Châteauneuf-du-Pape who initiated both the idea and the apparatus for putting it into effect. Ironically, the same down-to-earth view that wine is, well, wine, within two years extended the region's principal controlled *appellation*, Côtes du Rhône (which in 1935 defined the hill vineyards where wines had a distinction that was worth recognizing and preserving), to the plain between Orange and Avignon, land from which the wine is certainly drinkable but not the sort, if I might paraphrase Dr. Johnson, that one would *ask* a man to. It is this dilemma of reconciling the huge volume of sound, everyday wines—an achievement, I agree, that must contribute more to the total sum of human pleasure than does the sublime but minute quantity of, say, Richebourg—with the limited production of quality wines that causes problems for both growers and consumers. In fact, the lower Rhône, as the smug and simplistic phrase of our time would have it, has an identity problem.

The region I refer to starts in the *département* of the Drôme, extends south over most of the Vaucluse and then westward across the Rhône into the Gard. From above Bollène (though at that point there is hardly a vine to be seen from the *autoroute*) to below Avignon vineyards stretch east and west. To the east, they cover the alluvial plain, interspersed with orchards and market gardens, fill valleys, and spread over hills. They climb the slope of Mont Ventoux itself, a mountain dominating the area, as near perfect in its symmetry as Fuji. To the west of the Rhône, the vineyards reach the limits of the *garrigue*, the first tormented abutments of the Massif Central, where they merge with even vaster plantings of hybrids used for the nameless table wines of French grocery stores. In both directions the landscape has been molded by millennia of waters flowing from the pre-Alps on one side and the Cévennes on the other. Their deposits of pebble and rock, sand and clay have left a terrain so variable that uniformity of soil, even within one vineyard, is impossible to find.

In his classic ampelography, *Cépages et Vignobles de France*, Professor Galet of the University of Montpellier rationally breaks down the Vaucluse into seven principal areas and numerous subdivisions, let alone the extensions of the region into the Drôme and the Gard. For those whose interest is more general, the lower Rhône can be imagined as a lopsided, very irregular saucer with a slight rise in the center. To the northeast, vineyards cover the last spurs of the pre-Alps, descending to the river Aigues at Sérignan and Sainte Cécile-les-Vignes; to the east, beyond the Ouvèze river, a chalky bench extends from Mont Ventoux and the heights of Montmirail to support the sometimes gravelly, sometimes sandy, vineyards of Gigondas, Vacqueyras, Séguret, and Sablet.

Extending further east beyond Gigondas and Vacqueyras, the vineyards of Mont Ventoux could be said to start at Beaumes-de-Venise, a *commune* producing delicious Muscat dessert wine as well as robust reds. Soon after, they start to climb, hectare after hectare,

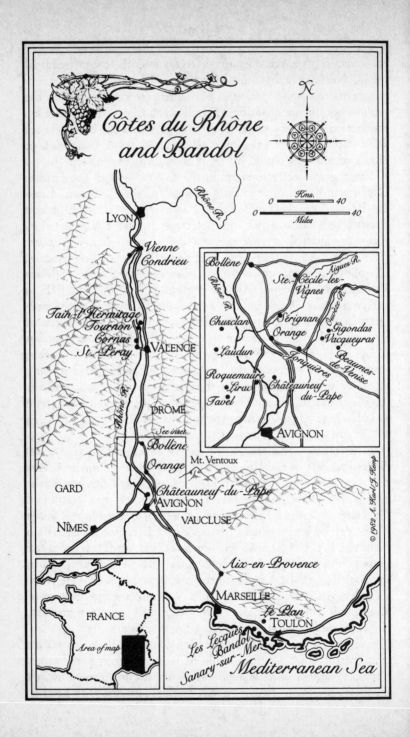

Côtes du Rhône
and Bandol

N

Rhône R.

Kms.
0   40
0   40
Miles

LYON

Vienne
Condrieu

Bollène

Ste.-Cécile-les-
Vignes

Aigues R.

Rhône R.

Chusclan

Sérignan

Orange

Ouvèze R.

Gigondas
Vacqueyras

Tain-l'Hermitage
Tournon
Cornas
St.-Péray

VALENCE

Laudun

Jonquières

Beaumes-
de-Venise

Rhône R.

Roquemaure
Lirac
Tavel

Châteauneuf-
du-Pape

DRÔME

See inset

Bollène

Orange

Mt. Ventoux

AVIGNON

© 1982 A. Karl/J. Kemp

Châteauneuf-du-Pape

GARD

AVIGNON

NÎMES

VAUCLUSE

Aix-en-Provence

MARSEILLE

FRANCE

Le Plan
TOULON

Area of map

Les Lecques
Bandol
Sanary-sur-Mer

Mediterranean Sea

to surround Puyméras, Mormoiron, and a score of other old villages, all of pale gray stones and faded stucco under worn, terracotta tiles. Their grapes are used to produce rosy-red wines, the mainstay of French cafés. Traditionally juice and skins are left to ferment together only overnight to make a soft, fruity, light red wine called, appropriately enough, *vin d'une nuit*. At Flassan, on the mountain, there is an inn where the wine can be drunk by the liter with locally cured ham and sausage. There might also be some *grisets de Ventoux* (wild mushrooms sautéed with garlic and oil), the thyme-scented thrush pâté of the region, and, if the proprietor has been lucky, a *civet de lièvre*.

To the southeast are the hills of Gardagne, producing red wines that were equated more than a century ago with the wines of Châteauneuf, and behind them the Lubéron, where some indifferent white wine is made; to the west across the Rhône, the cliff of Roquemaure at the end of the bridge appears to defend the vineyard slopes of Tavel and Lirac; and to the northwest are the series of slopes that make up the vineyards of Saint Gervais, Chusclan, and Laudun. In the middle is the plain of the Comtat Venaissin, papal land until the eighteenth century. It spreads from Orange and Avignon east to the plane tree–shaded villages of Travaillan, Violès, and Jonquières and reaches into the lower valleys of the Aigues and Ouvèze.

Châteauneuf-du-Pape is set on a rise in the center, and its vineyards are often referred to as covering a series of hills. In fact, the terrain is more like an undulating plateau, thickly covered with characteristic stones, round as pebbles and large and smooth as ostrich eggs.

The average vineyard holding in the lower Rhône is twenty-five acres, but thousands of growers, certainly the majority, have fewer than five. Because ordinary red Côtes du Rhône sells at prices that barely cover the rudimentary costs of cultivation, such small growers work at other crops and other jobs in addition to tending their vines. It would make little sense for them to be equipped for winemaking when their production is so small, and more than 70 percent of the grapes are taken to communal wineries.

The banding of small vineyard proprietors into cooperatives has been the strength and the bane of the region since it was resurrected after the phylloxera devastation of the late nineteenth century. Most have efficient, modern installations, professionally trained personnel, and the capacity to allow wine of consistent quality to be offered to large distributors. Some cooperatives, depending on the force of personality of the director as much as anything else, work with their members much as do California wineries with contracted growers, imposing vineyard and cropping standards, dictating the when and what of treatments, and deciding picking dates. They often use a system of bonus payments to encourage the planting of varieties that will improve the cooperative product.

Yet other cooperatives seem unable or unwilling to combat the apathy of their growers, who, removed from the personal ritual of making their own wine, find no satisfaction in the tens of thousands of hectoliters that issue from a winery to which each might have delivered his scant twenty tons of grapes. In such circumstances there can be no engagement of pride to inhibit pushing grape yields as far as the law will allow. This heavy cropping, especially when it occurs in the plain, almost inevitably lowers quality and swells supply. As a result, though sales of Rhône wines increase steadily, residual stocks have increased even faster. Despite inflation in France, winery bulk prices for Côtes du Rhône, the kind that is sold by the tankload to merchant-bottlers, slipped again in 1980 by as much as 10 percent compared with the previous year.

The tragedy (from the conscientious growers' point of view) is that all Côtes du Rhône prices are held down by the pressure of the quantity of ordinary wine. The market makes little price distinction between the unimpressive product of some cooperatives and the quality wines produced by others, not to mention the many private estates. That is why Côtes du Rhône wines tend to be underpriced and exceptional value can be found if discrimination is used.

The best are still those from areas that were first accorded the Côtes du Rhône *appellation* in 1935. In an attempt to restore something of the distinction recognized at that time, those wines are now entitled to use the superior *appellation* Côtes du Rhône Villages or to link their basic Côtes du Rhône *appellation* with village names such as Côtes du Rhône Vacqueyras or Côtes du Rhône Beaumes-de-Venise. (The village name Beaumes-de-Venise used alone, incidentally, is the *appellation* of the Muscat dessert wine produced there, not to be confused with its red table wine.) The *communes* concerned agree to stricter controls of vine varieties used, yields permitted, and minimum alcohol levels in the wines, a rough-and-ready indicator of grape maturity and quality at time of picking. Some *communes*, in addition to Châteauneuf-du-Pape, which had it from the beginning, have earned separate controlled *appellation* status: Gigondas, Lirac, and Tavel, the last for its rosés.

In this part of France, stricter control of vine varieties usually means eliminating or severely restricting the Carignan grape, a variety about which there is much ambivalence. Most basic Côtes du Rhône is made from a combination of Grenache and Carignan. To see these two vines together is to sense right away the contrasting wine that each will produce. The Grenache is luxuriant. Its smoothly shaped leaves, barely indented, protect large, floppy bunches of grapes. The rough, jagged leaves of the Carignan, on the other hand, are sharply indented, and its grapes are small and tightly compact. As one might expect, Grenache wine is structurally loose: high in alcohol, low in flavor, and dangerously quick to age. Carignan wine is hard, sometimes sharp, even bitter; it brings a tough, coarse element to blends even while adding stamina to an otherwise flabby Grenache. For this reason the Côtes du Rhône and the Côtes du Rhône Villages *appellation* statutes limit the quantities of Carignan that may legally be used. At Lirac and Tavel, it is allowed but discouraged; at Gigondas and Châteauneuf-du-Pape, it is not permitted at all.

That is all very well, but Grenache, if used alone, would be short of flavor and acidity as a young wine and lack backbone for aging. Apart from Carignan, however, there are eleven allowable varieties, some of which, in combination, can provide the necessary balance. Certain varieties are even compulsory now, though most are only acknowledged or merely tolerated. The two most widely encouraged, to give balance to local red wines, are Cinsault for its young, fresh bite and perfumed aroma, and Syrah, the grape of the northern Rhône, for its depth of flavor and its aging potential; most of the other grapes dutifully listed in all the texts—the Bourboulenc, Picpoul, Picardan, Vacarèse, and so on—have probably caused more ink to flow than wine. Their use is less than might be supposed, though every grower will claim that this or that nuance in his wine is due to a row or two of some obscure variety. Châteauneuf-du-Pape and Gigondas rely on ancillary varieties (especially Mourvèdre) more than do most other *communes*, and a firmer, richer, headier style is the result.

Growers at Châteauneuf-du-Pape experimented for a while in

the 1960s with fermentation techniques that made their wine more supple and faster maturing. But the characteristic force of a classic Châteauneuf-du-Pape was exactly what most enthusiasts wanted, and there has since been a complete return to the full-bodied style introduced by the Marquis de la Nerthe in the early 1800s, after centuries during which Châteauneuf-du-Pape had been neglected. De la Nerthe was notorious (and envied) for an erotic life that continued to an unprecedented and unseemly age. He claimed that the wine produced at his vineyard at Châteauneuf-du-Pape was "an elixir for prolonging youth and even life itself." His widespread reputation probably contributed in a small way to the revival of Châteauneuf-du-Pape's popularity during the last century, but his is not a claim that should be relied on in all circumstances.

Wherever red Côtes du Rhône is made, some rosé wine will be found, but the best is grown on the west bank. Using a high proportion of the elegant Cinsault with their heady Grenache, the growers of Tavel, for example, have succeeded in developing a rosé that has for long been a benchmark. It combines warmth and finesse to a rare degree and at its best has a sustained flavor that lifts it almost to the level of the great classics. Lirac, an *appellation* that covers four *communes*, produces a rosé that is almost indistinguishable from Tavel, but in the last ten years the growers have veered increasingly toward the production of red. Due to the emphasis on Cinsault in their grape proportions, however, even the red wines of Lirac are unusually aromatic when young and are elegantly structured. Chusclan, too, produces a good rosé, though heavier and less subtle than that of either Tavel or Lirac. Perhaps the grape mix is different. (The cooperative at Chusclan is one of the most efficient in the region.) At Laudun, one of the four *communes* first to be given the superior Côtes du Rhône Villages *appellation* in 1953, there is little rosé but some of the freshest and cleanest of the limited white wine production of the lower Rhône. Most other white wines of the region, I am sorry to say, are neutral at best and age too quickly to make them of interest for shipment overseas.

Though some years are especially memorable for their quality (in the last decade this is particularly true of 1971, despite a difficult flowering, and of 1978), the lower Rhône has less dramatic variation from year to year than does, say, Burgundy. In 1980, for example, a problematic year for much of France, the lower Rhône was conspicuously successful, and one of the finest bottles of

Châteauneuf-du-Pape that I have enjoyed recently was a 1977 (as difficult a year in the Rhône as it was in the rest of France) from the Clos de l'Oratoire des Papes. I drank it from a half bottle, in fact, when lunching alone at a restaurant in Châteauneuf-du-Pape itself. There was a bitterly cold mistral outside, and with my *boeuf carmarguais*, nothing could have been more restoring. The wine was richly colored and wonderfully full on nose and palate, smoothly balanced, imposing but neither heavy nor overbearing. Rhône wines, in fact, seem to me always to have just such a rich, autumnal quality appropriate to the "season of mists and mellow fruitfulness." So I wouldn't complain exactly if I were to find a forgotten case of that Clos de l'Oratoire in my cellar when the days start to shorten.

Graceful Wines
of Alsace

WITH A PILGRIMAGE to the Auberge de l'Ill at Illhaeusern almost mandatory these days, one might have thought that exposure to the refinement of the Haeberlin's kitchen and cellar would have converted more Americans to the wines of Alsace. If it has, the effect is hardly noticeable.

Although shipments of Alsace wines to the United States in 1977 and 1978 rose to almost 60,000 cases a year from a mere 40,000 cases in 1976, they have slumped back again in 1981—a consequence, I suppose, of the currently fashionable view that French wines are expensive. If it puzzles me that a frost or a storm in Bordeaux can lead some to assume the vintage ruined all over France, I am even more bewildered by those who allow the price of Pouilly-Fuissé to deprive them of moderately priced Rieslings and aromatic Gewürztraminers.

Those French wines that reach dizzy prices do so because they have a low production combined with an exaggeratedly high profile. In an abundant year, Pouilly-Fuissé produces 300,000 cases at best: not much to satisfy a thirsty world. But even in 1978, one of the smallest crops of the decade, Alsace produced 7 *million* cases of dry, fragrant, reasonably priced wine. It is difficult to understand why they don't do better here. To start with, the bulk of production—almost 100 percent of it—is white, at a time when there seems never to be enough white wine to go around; the labeling is probably the simplest to understand and remember among all French wines, based as it is on grape variety rather than on a complicated hierarchy of classified vineyards; the wines themselves—light, fruity, and dry—are very much to the taste of most Americans today; and the Comité Interprofessionnel du Vin d'Alsace (Committee of Growers and Shippers) has worked persistently over the years to show and explain its wines to the retailers of America.

The switchback history of Alsace during the past hundred years—from France to Germany to France to Germany and, finally, to France again—made it difficult for the region to enjoy the expanding reputation of other French wines during that period. The prestige it had in the sixteenth century, when its wines were the most prized in northern Europe (even Shakespeare had nice things to say about them), was lost in the appalling destruction of the Thirty Years' War, which culminated in Alsace being absorbed into the French kingdom of Louis XIV. Since 1918, and especially since 1945, the growers have followed a policy of improving and controlling quality that has been more rigorously self-enforced than that of any other wine region of France. Alsatians have had to work harder than those who could fall back on long familiar names of local classed growths or use the reflected glamour of a handful of aristocratic estates.

Although popularly associated with the Rhine (and for that reason often confused with the wine regions of Germany), the vineyards of Alsace are some twenty miles distant. Thirty thousand acres of them stretch for more than sixty miles from Marlenheim, near Strasbourg, in the north to Thann in the south, mostly on the lower slopes of the Vosges and more intimately connected with, and dependent on, the climate and terrain of the mountains than that of the riverbank. The Rhine, where it borders Alsace, is wide and shallow and was barely navigable until the Germans deepened and embanked it in the late nineteenth century. Frequent flooding had deterred settlement, and, except for the rare bridgehead (such as Strasbourg), towns and villages grew up at a safe distance from the water, usually on higher ground.

To the east beyond the Rhine, the massive Black Forest protects the towns and vineyards of Alsace from bleak east winds; and to the west the Vosges themselves, though seeming little more than a decorative crest when approached across the long, gentle tilt of the Lorraine plateau, provide a barrier to the Atlantic storms that sweep across northern France. Rainfall in Alsace is barely a quarter of what it is on the western side of the Vosges: Colmar is the driest town in France.

The long strip of vineyards mostly faces east, catching the morning sun, but growers take advantage of every thrusting knoll that might give a southeasterly or even a southern exposure to the vines. A complicated geological history has given them a variety of soils, unusual in such a compact zone. At Turckheim and Wintzenheim, for example, there are granitic terraces side by side with calcareous strips; sandstone and schist lie next to limestone and marl at Riquewihr; and throughout there are scattered layers of loess, the yellowish-gray loam for which the Rhine Valley is known. These chaotic soil patterns and the microclimates of the mountain folds have taught growers to match carefully each vine variety to a parcel of land best suited to it. In summer, when the vines are uniformly green, the subtle complications of this patchwork are difficult to discern, but in the fall, when each variety of vine changes color at its own pace and to its own autumnal shade, the slopes become a vast and brilliant tapestry.

An Alsace wine is identified by the grape variety from which it is made. Sylvaner is the grape most widely planted (more than a quarter of all bearing vineyards). Though not the most robust of vines, it produces regular and reasonably abundant crops that ripen late, an advantage in a region where dry and sunny autumns permit a late harvest. Sylvaner wines are mild, with freshness (and therefore youth) their chief quality; nevertheless, the grapes grown on the slope rather than on the plain can display a firm character more usually associated with Riesling wines.

The Riesling, most distinguished of the Alsace varieties, ripens latest of all. It continues to mature even in poor weather, which is why it lends itself to late harvest pickings wherever it is grown. With consistent yield, when grown on favored sites it will give wines of unmatched elegance and depth of flavor.

The variety most closely associated with Alsace, however, is the Gewürztraminer, an early-ripening grape descended from the old Traminer Rosé, first introduced about a century ago and now one of the most popular varieties. When picked at the precise moment of maturity, Gewürztraminer grapes give a wine of intense aroma and full flavor, more reminiscent of an old-fashioned damask rose than of spice. After these three classic varieties, the Pinot Blanc is presently spreading in Alsace because extensions to the vineyard are on the plain rather than the slope, and there Pinot Blanc is preferred. In cold soils it ripens more easily than either Riesling or Gewürztraminer and yet gives wines of more substance than Sylvaner.

The Chasselas of Alsace, once important for carafe wines, is disappearing. In the past ten years the acreage has dwindled to less than half. Pinot Gris, giving wine once more commonly (and confusingly) labeled Tokay d'Alsace, is grown only on a small scale in Alsace. The grapes ripen early and give wine that combines the characteristic intense fruitiness of Alsace with the body and softness of a Côte d'Or Burgundy. Though usually dry, in some years, contrary to normal practice in Alsace, it can retain a little residual sugar. I remember a Pinot Gris of the 1967 vintage (one of the great years of Alsace) with a slightly sweet finish that went perfectly with the roast veal and glazed carrots a grower served me for lunch a few years back. (On that same day, again contrary to what one is told about Alsace wines always being fermented dry, the grower served me a Special Reserve 1967 Gewürztraminer with 13.5 percent alcohol and 4.9 percent residual sugar. We drank it with an apple tart warm from the oven. I was in heaven.) A small amount of Pinot Noir is grown for the production of rosé.

Of all varieties, however, the most surprising to those unfamiliar with Alsace is Muscat d'Alsace. Whether made from the early-ripening Muscat d'Ottonel or the more intense Muscat à Petits Grains, a very late ripener, the wine is always dry and light, unexpected after such a beguiling aroma. Muscat d'Alsace makes an excellent apéritif.

Zwicker, or Edelzwicker, describes wine made from a blend of grape varieties. There was once a distinction between the two words based on the fact that Chasselas could be admitted into the blend of a Zwicker but not into an Edelzwicker. That distinction has now been dropped, and the shorter version will probably disappear.

Those who visit Alsace will find a carefully signposted Route du Vin passing through all the wine villages. It runs along the lower slope past the vineyards so that one can see close at hand the high training of the vines—to six feet or more—and the pitch of the vineyards, some so steep that cultivation must be done by hand or by winch rather than with tractor and plow. Though repeatedly battered by wars (there was not a doorpost standing in Bennwihr after a particularly fierce engagement between American and German troops in 1944), most towns and villages retain at least a few old houses, a church with stork nest on the steeple, or medieval fortifications. Dambach, with picturesque gateways and gabled houses; Barr, with its Renaissance mansions; and Riquewihr, with a mixture of Baroque and high Middle Ages, are enchanting places to visit. Less obvious, and maybe for that reason even more captivating, is the walled town of Turckheim, where one can walk round the old ramparts.

These towns and villages exude domestic order, well-being, and abundance. Gardens overflow with flowers, trees are heavy with fruit, and the dogs are sleepy. From kitchen windows the smell of cooking is rich and succulent: goose fat and cabbage, chicken poaching in Riesling, quetsch tarts. Alsatians like to eat well.

They like to drink well, too, their wines always cool but not too cool for fear of stunning the "fruit." They use the word in a special way. To others, "fruit" might mean the general redolence of fruit in the developed bouquet and flavor of a mature wine. But to Alsatians it means the aroma and flavor of a particular variety: they expect to find it again in the wine, transmuted and intensified, perhaps, but clearly identifiable. The better to enjoy it, they serve their wines in careful sequence, leading from light, discreet Sylvaners to assertive Rieslings before heady Gewürztraminers. The wines are versatile and adapt well, but each is matched to an appropriate dish. Sylvaner, young and fragrant, perfect with a savory quiche or an onion tart, mild ham or boiled sausage. Pinot Blanc, with more body, is good with *charcuterie*; but the richer texture of a pâté, especially foie gras, needs the full flavor of a Tokay d'Alsace or even a Gewürztraminer. Riesling is a natural partner for fish, especially from river or lake. Choose a *réserve* Riesling, or one from a big year like 1976, when the wine must balance a creamy sauce, yet notice how even a modest Riesling will bring out the hazelnut flavor of a freshly caught trout.

The style of Alsace wine is unlikely to change, but we might soon see unfamiliar words on the label. The spread of vineyards onto the plain has met resistance from those who feel that quality could be threatened, and there is talk of a compromise that will give a separate *appellation* to such lesser wines. At the other extreme, the words *grand cru*, used in the past to denote an exceptional wine, are now reserved for wines from specific, designated vineyard sites, rather like the *crus* of Burgundy. This new direction is not supported unanimously by the committee of growers and shippers. Some members argue that simplicity of *appellation* has been their strength. But others glance covetously at the complicated panoply of classifications in Bordeaux and Burgundy and reflect that, at least as far as the United States market is concerned, simplicity hasn't got them very far.

Bandol: A Personal Preference

THERE IS a point on Route Nationale 7 between Avignon and Aix-en-Provence where a slight rise leads through a cutting. Especially on a summer evening, it is here that a traveler on the road from Paris first breathes the air of the Mediterranean. I drive through that gap with a sense of release, of entering a world more languid yet more ardent, more elegant yet more sensuous, more intelligent yet more frivolous, with priorities ranged in good-humored perspective.

Along with the scent of thyme and pine, memories flow through the open car windows: familiar hilltop villages, buffeted by wind and bleached by sun, fade into visions of herb and lemon stalls in the Toulon street markets; images of fishermen at Sanary-sur-Mer, unloading their catch for early-morning sale under the manicured palms that surround, at a respectful distance, the very proper town bandstand, merge with remembrances of lazy afternoons on the beach at Les Lecques, shared, of course, with half the population of Marseilles, and memories of fresh-caught sardines grilled on the embers of vine cuttings at the kitchen door of the Peyrauds' house. Yes, above all, I think Mediterranean means to me the Peyrauds' house, the most loving and serene of ships, comfortably adrift in a sea of vines. Plain and gray, like many another Provençal *mas*, it speaks contentment, less in its signs of mellow calm—the patina of crumbled stucco and faded window shutters—than in the message of a child's worn swing that hangs from a lopsided cherry tree, in the umbrella pine that doubles as an outdoor family *salon*, protecting an old millstone table and a clutter of dusty wooden chairs from the late afternoon sun, in the ancient vine that curls over the west front of the house and covers an uneven brick terrace with a shady green canopy, and in the wide front door with its fist-size key.

One evening in early summer, a few years back, I took the familiar turn off the highway at Le Canet, through the hills of Le Beausset, and then followed the narrow, high-banked road that leads to Le Plan-du-Castellet, to the Peyrauds'. The drive from Paris is long, and it was almost nine o'clock when the noise of the engine and the barking of the dogs brought the family out to greet me. There were Lucie and Lucien Peyraud (it is strange that two such names should come together, like the shepherd and shepherdess in an early Mozart opera); their sons, François and Jean-Marie; their sons' wives, Catherine and Paule; Veronique, the last daughter to remain at home; and in the background, shyly, some sleepy grandchildren. With a glass of Champagne we crossed the year that had elapsed since we had last seen each other, and by the time we went into the dining room it was as if I had left them only yesterday.

Lucie Tempier Peyraud is known to everyone as Lulu. Descended from a line of Marseilles merchants, she inherited this country *mas*, the Domaine Tempier, originally built for her great-great-grandmother. The vineyards around it, mostly spilling down narrow, terraced ledges that the labor of centuries created, were destroyed by phylloxera about a hundred years ago, and their replanting and regeneration has been an act of faith and courage. Lucien Peyraud's devotion to the Tempier vineyards is almost mystical, as if in marrying Lulu he had also married these few scattered acres that remain attached to their steep hillsides only through the will of God and backbreaking work on the supporting terrace walls. Some of the ledges, rarely more than thirty or forty yards long, are so narrow that they can hold only a row or two of vines each, and most of the cultivation must be done by hand. His face and hands roughened by sun and wind, Lucien Peyraud is a down-to-earth man if ever there was one, yet he is as proud and tender in his regard for his vines as any father for his child. No other vine-yard I know is nourished by passion to equal his.

The wine region of Bandol is one of the oldest is France. We can be certain that the Greeks, whose settlements led to the founding of the cities of Marseilles and Nice, brought vines and planted them where they seemed most likely to flourish. They undoubtedly saw, as we still can see today, that the hills above the bay of Bandol, quite close to Marseilles, form an arena protected by the mountains behind them. Here, vine-covered slopes face south and benefit from the clear sunlight reflected off the sea, as well as from the tempering effect of the water.

There is evidence of trading in Bandol wines as far back as Roman times. Wine jars, or fragments of them, continually turn up in the nets of local fishermen, and in a geography of Provence, published in 1787, the region was lauded for its red wines "of first quality . . . mostly highly prized. They sum up quite simply the real virtues of the Provençal soil and its products: honesty, finesse and ardour." By the mid-nineteenth century wines from all the villages that surround the port were being shipped to markets as far away as Brazil and India. Just as Bordeaux—on a much grander scale, of course—gave its name to the whole region that shipped from its quays, so Bandol gave its name to the wines of La Cadière-d'Azur, Le Plan-du-Castellet, Le Castellet, Le Beausset, Saint-Cyr-sur-Mer, Sanary-sur-Mer, Ollioules, Le Brulat and Sainte-Anne-d'Evenos. It is impossible to say whether the million gallons of wine exported each year by the close of the Second Empire were all Bandol in the sense that the *appellation* is defined today, but the region, if fully planted, is capable of producing that much wine. In 1941, when a decree officially granted Bandol growers their own *appellation contrôlée*, annual production of wine from the entire area had dropped to barely 30,000 cases. Production in 1981 was about 300,000 cases of red, rosé, and white wines, from the vine-yards of some two hundred small growers—a fragmented, but very personal, wine region.

There was, and is, very little white wine. In that climate it is difficult to produce the crispness that one would most want. Clairette and Ugni Blanc grapes are used, primarily for wines to be consumed by the grower's family. Oddly enough, the fishing vil-lage of Cassis, only a few miles away, manages to produce a quite passable white wine from the same grapes; but then the deep *calanques* that bring cool sea air well into the hillsides there probably help. The best white wine of Bandol that I remember was from Château Milhière, near Sanary, a vineyard now threatened with extinction by the spread of grotesque little villas. Monsieur Roethlisberger, a Swiss winegrower, had brought a light touch with white wines from his native Alpine vineyards and until his death produced wines of delicacy and flavor.

The rosés, found in every good restaurant from Marseilles to Nice, have more character than most others and are superior to the general run of Provence rosés. Over the years that I shipped them regularly to London—where they met with some success— I found that, though delicious when young, they aged well, developing an aroma of ripe pears. Ranging from the heavy, tannic wines of Château Pradeaux at Saint-Cyr to the racy, elegant wines of Lucien Peyraud at the Domaine Tempier, the reds are obviously in a class with wines from far more distinguished regions. They repay keeping.

Grenache vines are common throughout the south, and are as important in Bandol as they are at nearby Châteauneuf-du-Pape and Gigondas. Important, too, is the Cinsault vine, thought, because of its country name of *le romain*, to have been brought to the region by some wandering centurion. These two varieties are the basis of the rosé wines of Bandol, but small patches of the uncommon Tibouren or the local Pécoui-Touar are to be found here and there, adding a more subtle strain of flavor.

The special quality of the reds is due entirely to the Mourvèdre and its adaptation to the particular conditions of Bandol. It is a variety of vine that spread through southern France from the Mediterranean coast of Spain during the Middle Ages. In most areas its popularity was short-lived. Though vigorous in growth, it is low in yield; and the wine, deep-colored and tannic, has an intense personality that needs careful aging to give of its best. There are Mourvèdre vines at Châteauneuf-du-Pape and even as far away as Cognac in the Charentes (where it has the inexplicable name of Balzac Noir), but it seems to have found its natural home in the band of chalk and silica that runs through the Bandol hills. In most cases I have found that the quality of any red wine of Bandol can be directly related to the proportion of Mourvèdre in the vineyard. The *appellation* law has established that, of the vine varieties permitted, a minimum of 10 percent must be Mourvèdre;

and although a wine made entirely from Mourvèdre grapes might
be overwhelming in scale even when mature, I am certain that the
basis of Lucien Peyraud's quality is the sacrifice he makes to maintain such a high proportion of these vines, difficult and ungenerous
though he knows them to be.

Altitude also affects the quality of the wine, but whether this is
a result of the greater exposure to sunlight, the cooling effect of
the breezes, or the more arid spare soils one finds on the hilltops,
I wouldn't like to say. Perhaps it is a combination of all three.
Lucien ferments separately the grapes from each small lot of vines,
eventually blending them to produce a uniform wine for each
vintage. Checking the young wines with him, noting the differences
of character and style that mark each one, is an exciting experience. At a tasting the morning after my arrival, a colleague traveling with me, a man whose training and experience had been in the
wider acres of California, was astounded at the family's care to
preserve every nuance of their wines and at their familiarity with
the shading of taste that each small terrace brings.

Before dinner that night we drank a neighbor's white wine
because Lucien doesn't produce one. With it we ate the typical
hors d'oeuvre of Provence: cold spinach omelet, purée of egg-
plant, *tapenade* of olive and anchovy. They were followed by a
superb *mérou*, a Mediterranean fish related to the grouper, gently
poached and served simply with lemon and a fruity olive oil as
sauce. Lucien produced a rosé in an unfamiliar bottle. It was from
Bellet, a village above Nice possessing one of the few other *appellations contrôlées* in the south of France. It was at least fifteen
years since I had last tasted one, on a visit to that very village, to
the personal vineyard of a prosperous Nice wine merchant. Standing at the roadside near his house, I had seen how the suburbs of
Nice were poised to engulf his vines. The wine, as I remember it,
artfully packaged in a dumpy bottle with gold thread around it,
was among the less distinguished wines that I have tasted; and,
though it might seem uncharitable, I was able to contemplate its
possible end without feeling much distress.

But here was a wine from Bellet from a grower I hadn't known
of, a wine that showed why this tiny enclave of vines had been
recognized with an *appellation* of its own in the first place. It was
delicately fruity, crisply dry, and with a fresh, lingering aftertaste.
It was lighter than most of the Bandol rosés, which, though not

particularly alcoholic, seem to have a richness of glycerin that gives them a muscular, full-bodied style.

Lucien followed the rosé with both the 1969 and 1970 reds of the Domaine Tempier, while Lulu produced a leg of lamb, fragrant with garlic and pungent herbs of the *garrigue*, to accompany them. The 1969, with which I was already familiar thanks to a small stock at home in San Francisco, was one of Lucien's most elegant wines—dark, with a bouquet that I found, perhaps fancifully, to have an echo of the thyme and pine perfume of those hills. Well balanced, it was soft enough to enjoy and zesty enough to promise pleasure for quite some time. The 1970, which I had previously tasted only in wood, was a bigger wine, heavier than the 1969, less revealing in bouquet and flavor, its youthful tannin still quite bold. We preferred first the pleasure of one, then the promise of the other, and then weren't sure, and went on tasting and talking and nibbling at fresh little Banon cheeses that had appeared on the table. Nobody noticed how late it was getting to be.

Wine of Holy Satyrs:
Sancerre

I<small>N THE EARLY</small> 1950s in London, no serious merchant would have considered buying a wine until it had completed its first year in wood and could be evaluated calmly. Bordeaux might have to make up its mind sooner, but London rarely made a commitment to a vintage until the following autumn.

The frosts of 1956 changed all that. Shortages became so acute (or we thought they were so acute) that London importers were persuaded to buy their wines on the vine, contracting for quantities mostly, but not only, of the classed growths before the grapes were visible, let alone transformed into wine.

Though it reduced a skilled trade to the level of dealing in pork-belly futures, the growers, impoverished by the war years and the low prices paid in the period after them, were compelled to do business as best they could while they financed the replanting of their devastated vineyards. Smaller crops and reduced income deprived them of the means to carry a crop on the field, let alone two vintages in wood in the *chais*. Needless to say, with pounds sterling maturing on Cabernet vines in the Médoc, the weather in southwestern France became a subject of passionate interest in London; even members of the British wine trade on Scottish moors in September were less perturbed by the thought of a storm interfering with a day's shooting than they were by news of a light shower a thousand miles away in Bordeaux.

Once the growers had overcome their need for an accelerated cash flow, the practice of such early buying largely disappeared. But there was never a return to the slower, more patient ways in which the trade had taken a year to reach its conclusion about a vintage. In those earlier days, I should add, wines that *had* to be judged sooner—especially some of the lighter whites that often needed drinking within the year, let alone assessing—were largely ignored as unimportant, or dismissed with that catchall phrase, "Won't travel, old boy."

Now, whether the wine is for early shipping or for long keeping, international merchants make their buying decisions at the first round of tastings, once the initial rackings from the murk of heavy lees just make possible a notion of quality and future style. In January and February—and sometimes even before Christmas— the side roads of France are filled with merchants, scurrying under leafless trees to be the first at the best barrel. Young red wines, rude with tannin, and whites that have lost their grapiness and have not yet recomposed themselves are hardly prescribed drinking on a frosty morning: there is much of absorbing interest but little of sybaritic delight in these wintry jaunts.

What a relief it is, then, to arrive at Sancerre, where, no matter how young, the wines seem always to be tender and delightful. Even a cold cellar on a raw February day cannot spoil the pleasure of these young Sauvignon Blanc wines. They shimmer with aroma and flavor, recalling first a ripe white peach, then perhaps a whiff of caraway or a smoky hint of gunpowder. Sancerre is so close to Paris—hardly more than a hundred miles—that I usually make it the last stop on a long trip round the wine regions, a reward for all that has gone before.

Isolated on a low hill that nevertheless dominates the Loire at this point, the town is some distance from the folds of hills surrounding it. Those hills were covered with vines before the Romans arrived in the wake of Julius Caesar, and over the centuries references to Sancerre wines have been frequent enough to show that their delicacy is no new phenomenon.

The Sauvignon Blanc grape is thought to have originated there in the Middle Ages and later to have spread to Bordeaux rather than the other way around. Monks of the neighboring Abbey of

Saint-Satur, active in viticultural experiments almost a thousand
years ago, probably made the selection of cuttings that led to the
varietal grape as we know it today. (The name Saint-Satur, incidentally, is linked to the Roman name for Sancerre itself, *castrum
sancti satyri*, "fort of the holy satyrs," an appropriately Dionysiac
reference in a region noted for its vines and its goats, but one that
it might be tactless to examine too closely.)

For those who like comfort and rather grand food, the elegant
Auberge des Templiers at Les Bézards, about thirty miles north of
Sancerre, will offer every luxury, including the opportunity to
taste Sancerre wines from some of the best producers. But I prefer
a modest inn in Saint-Thibault, the village by the Loire at the foot
of the Sancerre hill, where the rooms are small if pleasant, and
where there is a particular pleasure in coming downstairs to homemade jams and fresh croissants in the cozy bar *cum* parlor.

As is so often the case in France, the *appellation* Sancerre doesn't
belong just to the town of that name. Wines grown in some parts
of at least a dozen adjoining *communes* are entitled to it, too, but
vineyards are important in only seven of them. Overall, there are
about 3,000 acres planted with vines and entitled to the *appellation*,
compared with barely 1,000 twenty-five years ago. And where
there was, perhaps, an annual production of 100,000 cases in the
1950s, Sancerre now produces 400,000 to 500,000 cases of wine
every year. It seems a lot, but such is the demand in Paris alone
that there is never enough, and scarcity is aggravated by the scale
of the growers' holdings—an average of two acres of vines each,
and that usually split into at least ten tiny parcels scattered over
a hillside and, on occasion, over two or three neighboring hamlets.
It is instructive as well as delightful to stand at the top of one of
the hills and look down at the patchwork of vineyards surrounding the villages. In recent years there has been some attempt to
rationalize by exchanging land, but growers here are traditional
and tenacious. Does one need to explain that a small patch of land
is infinitely more precious than a huge estate? Besides, with good
reason, many growers believe that their scattered holdings are an
insurance against frost or hail damage; and then, depending on
where his parcels of land are, each man's wine is often improved
by its diverse origin.

Essentially chalky, the hills of Sancerre range from the compact
chalk of the low hills and of the bases of the higher ones—known

as *caillotes*—to marl on the upper parts of the higher slopes. The plateaus above the slopes are clay and are not used for vineyards. *Caillotes* give wines of great finesse with exuberant aroma, wines that are best bottled young and consumed as soon after the vintage as possible. These are the wines, especially, that brighten those chilly morning tastings. The Clos du Chêne Marchand at Bué is entirely on *caillotes*; so are Les Cous de Brault at Chavignol, Le Paradis at Sancerre, and L'Epée at Amigny.

Marl vineyards, on the other hand, known as *terres blanches*, give wines that are bigger, less aromatic, with more definite character and yet more suppleness. And although Sancerre should never be thought of as a wine for long keeping, wines from the *terres blanches* do keep and develop better than those from the *caillotes*. A combination of the two, however, gives wine that is better than either, so that a grower whose parcels include some of each is unwilling to give up one or the other. The best vineyards, in fact, for reasons that are easily understood, are halfway down slopes where the terrain is something of a mixture of the two soil types. To make the connection between soil and style clear, Sancerre growers are never content to explain their wines on the sole basis of what they themselves produce. One is led to taste in a neighbor's cellar, the better to understand some fine point of *caillote* or exposure, and each is as proud of his neighbor's wine as he is of his own.

In addition to Sauvignon Blanc, there have always been some patches of Pinot Noir, much of it in Sury-en-Vaux, north of Sancerre, but more has been planted in recent years. Until 1959 the red wine made from it was sold as nameless *vin rouge*, but in that year the Sancerre *appellation* was extended to cover red wine as well as white. There is an annual production of red Sancerre close to 100,000 cases, as much as there was of the white twenty-five years ago, though in poor years a large portion of it is vinified as rosé. Despite this considerable quantity, it is hard to find, even in France, and I am not sure where it all goes. In style not unlike a light red Burgundy, it has sometimes a more intense Pinot Noir character than do wines of the Côte d'Or but rarely as much weight or depth of flavor.

I remember well how much I enjoyed my first taste of the 1959, the first vintage of Pinot Noir that could be called Sancerre. I drank it with a local grower who invited me to share his lunch of a hare that had foolishly strayed across his path. Roasted and served with baked celeriac (a vegetable that until then, I must confess, I thought was compulsorily served in strips drenched in *sauce rémoulade*—what a revelation), the hare was as perfect as the wine. Inevitably, we followed it with mature *crottins* of Chavignol, the tiny goat cheeses of Sancerre, just at that point when the outer surface is mottled delicately blue-gray and the cheese crumbles without being dry. My memory fails me, but I shouldn't be surprised if we didn't drink a second bottle with them.

Fresh *crottins*, chalk-white and creamy textured, are served with bread still warm from the oven for cellar tastings, and although the admonition of those who taught me always rings in my head ("Buy on bread, sell on cheese"), a day that starts with fresh *crottins*, a warm crust, and a cold glass of Sancerre is moving in the right direction. *Crottins* were once made mostly by the growers' wives. Ten years ago every household still had half a dozen goats. Haltered with triangles of sticks round their necks to deter them from penetrating too far into the vines, they were allowed to eat what they could find. An assortment of grasses and herbs enriched the milk and improved its flavor, and if one of the goats chose to rummage in a neighbor's flower patch or nibble some tender vine shoots from his vineyard, one could always pretend not to see.

Money from the cheeses kept the family going from one vintage to the next and provided a means to survive if there was a total loss of the crop. The growers still live modestly, but, because there is less economic need for the goats, few families have more than one or two to provide for their own consumption of cheese. *Crottins* on sale in the stores are now produced from commercial flocks, and the Sancerrois are convinced that they don't have quite the same flavor.

Some of the best *crottins* of the growers' kitchens find their way to the Espérance restaurant across the river at Pouilly-sur-Loire; but there, of course, one will accompany them with a Pouilly-Fumé rather than a Sancerre. There is no hostility, nor even rivalry, between the two banks, but it just wouldn't occur to anyone to drink wine from the other side. Though the past twenty-five years have seen changes at Pouilly, too, there has not been an expansion of the vineyards as there has at Sancerre. Vineyards in Pouilly itself and in the neighboring *communes* of Saint-Andelain and

Tracy, close to the river, have been extended, and vineyards have been switched from the humble Chasselas to Sauvignon Blanc. But in other *communes* with the right to the Pouilly *appellation* vineyards have been abandoned, especially those that slope to the east and the southeast, where repeated spring frosts have demoralized the growers. In 1977, for example, when the growers of Sancerre scraped by with partial loss from the frosts in April, many growers at Pouilly lost all but a quarter of their crop—and on such tiny holdings that means penury.

The Chasselas is not used to produce Pouilly-Fumé, but only the rather undistinguished wine known simply as Pouilly-sur-Loire. Sauvignon Blanc is the only grape allowed for Pouilly-Fumé (or Blanc Fumé de Pouilly, as the wine is also called, Blanc Fumé being a local name for the grape). Even in a normal year there is only half as much Pouilly-Fumé as there is Sancerre. What distinguishes one from the other is the absence of *caillotes* on the Pouilly side of the river. The slopes of Pouilly, though less high than those of Sancerre and less sharply inclined, are mostly marl mixed with chalk and quartz. Thus the wines have less of the bright, early aroma of certain Sancerre wines and more of the slow-developing qualities that one finds, for example, in Sancerre of Les Monts Damnés and other *terres blanches* vineyards. For this reason, Pouilly-Fumé, unlike Sancerre, is almost always at its best a year from the vintage; and, although it would be foolish to suggest that it ages well, Pouilly-Fumé from a big year—like 1976—can be astonishing with a year or two in bottle.

Sauvignon Blanc vines are also grown at Quincy, some thirty-five miles southwest of Sancerre, on a plateau that slopes gently to the banks of the river Cher. The river once flowed over the land, leaving a thick bed of gravel and quartz that assures the wine an unusual combination of body and delicacy; it is more muscular than Sancerre, and with that wine's intensely fruity aroma much subdued. In France it is considered the perfect wine for oysters, and I have always found it the ideal white to precede red wines that are classically made but suffer from what we would call, these days, nonassertiveness.

A few miles farther southwest is another small *appellation* based on Sauvignon Blanc, but the white wines of Reuilly are rare to the point of having almost disappeared except in the village where they grow. With apologies for my own insensitivity in the matter, I must say that the few examples I have met do not inspire me with much concern for a revival. On the other hand, recent plantings there of Pinot Gris, vinified as a golden-pink rosé, have been successful and are now recognized with an *appellation contrôlée* of their own.

Sauvignon Blanc vines have long been planted in California, but until recently the wines made from them were usually sold as "sauterne," without a final *s* and, unlike French Sauternes, usually dry. They were dull, heavy wines; and, whatever success they might have had in the past, they were not the most sought-after in recent years.

Then Robert Mondavi, a few years ago, brought out a Sauvignon Blanc wine that he labeled Fumé Blanc, using an inversion of the alternative French name for the grape. He did it to get away from the name "sauterne" (he has always followed a laudable policy of avoiding French geographic names) and also to draw attention to the way in which his wine differed from what was usually expected of Sauvignon Blanc in California. Our soils are nothing like those of Pouilly and Sancerre, but with low-temperature fermentation (something the Sancerrois had always had naturally, thanks to the chill of their underground cellars) he was able to produce a wine with more grace and more aroma than before. It was bigger and rounder than the Sauvignon Blancs of the Loire, but the experiment has been a success, and others have followed suit. It is significant that whereas there were only some 600 acres of Sauvignon Blanc vineyards in California in 1970, the popularity of Fumé Blanc has caused expansion to more than 7,000 acres within a decade. There are now at least half a dozen California wineries producing varied Fumé Blancs; in addition to the wine of Robert Mondavi, now settled down to its rather plump style, the crisply perfumed Fumé Blanc of Château St. Jean in Sonoma County is a favorite of mine. None duplicates a Pouilly-Fumé or a Sancerre, but there is no reason to expect that. The diversity of wine adds to our pleasure.

Bordeaux First Growths: A Diversion

T HERE IS something tongue-in-cheek about San Francisco's First Growth Club, an echo, perhaps, of those improbably named dining clubs spawned in the coffeehouses of eighteenth-century London. The Sublime Society of Beefsteaks, the Sçavoir Vivre, the Lying Club (the chairman of which was always to be the member uttering the most "stupendous improbability"), and the Dilettanti Society gave rise to some of London's most distinguished men's clubs. Others—the names of which are all too descriptive—provided unusually diverting entertainment for their members after dinner. But the essence of them all was the pleasure that like-minded men found in each other's company over a few shared bottles of wine.

Such is true of the First Growth Club, a group of men who had long known each other and who found that since they were sharing the contents of each other's cellars anyway, they might as well share in the choice of what should be in them. Whenever the reputation of the year seems to warrant it, they subscribe together to buy a case or two of each of the eight First Growths of Bordeaux; and every few weeks, at a moveable feast that settles on each member's house in turn, they dine together to fulfill the self-imposed obligation of keeping check on the development of their wines. On each occasion they draw from the communal stock a bottle of each of the eight growths of the year chosen for review.

Eight? Yes, eight. In a stylish gesture, and long before the French government followed their lead, they elevated Château Mouton-Rothschild from its erstwhile secondary status to join the four Firsts of the 1855 Classification (Lafite, Latour, Margaux, and Haut-Brion). Then they included two Firsts of the 1955 Classification of Saint-Emilion (Ausone and Cheval-Blanc), and, with unself-conscious grandeur, they also confirmed Pétrus as First of the Pomerols, a status that had been merely honorary before.

A member unable to attend has the option of sending a guest in his place, and that is why I found myself strolling down Russian Hill on a Thursday in 1977 in pleasant anticipation of a fine evening. Dinner was to be provided by a member who is both a neighbor and an old friend, a bachelor of some gastronomic distinction in San Francisco. His apartment is typical of a certain period in the city: stairways and loggias give the feeling of entering the Casbah at very least; round oriel windows spring airily (and against all engineering logic) from the corners of rooms to provide unexpected, even mysterious, glimpses of town and bay; and the high-ceilinged kitchen and dining room are given significantly more space and prominence than his sitting room. He is a man who delights in the detail of his life; on every side there are empty bottles to recall past pleasures, letters stacked to be relished again, books and papers to be enjoyed in lazy hours ahead (if he has any). And in the midst of this magnificent eighteenth-century disorder his table is always set with the finest linen, brilliant glass, mellow silver, and the rich magnificence of old Crown Derby.

Awaiting the eight of us, and already decanted, were eight bottles of the 1966 vintage. But first, with a tray of dry sausage from the Italian grocers of North Beach, we drank a magnum of Krug 1962, a Champagne of which I am particularly fond. The house style of Krug combines steely dryness with considerable body, not always a happy association; but 1962 was a year of great finesse in Champagne, and in this vintage the styles of year and house combine to give a wine of rare elegance. In magnum it had held its freshness very well.

As we turned our attention to the red wines, conversation

dropped. They were poured blind so that we could taste and discuss them without the influence of preconceived notions and prejudices.

At its first assessment by the trade, in the spring of 1967, the 1966 vintage was pronounced, cautiously, "satisfactory." It was a large crop in Bordeaux (though not as big as the record-breaking one of 1962) that had somehow overcome unhelpful weather. July and part of August were too cool, and wet besides. September was fine and warm, but at that point, when the vines at last *needed* water to complete the ripening process, there was none, and sugar levels were sometimes disappointing as a result. Too late to be of help, rain came at the end of September, when picking had already started. The effect was not as serious as heavy rain had been during the 1964 harvest, but it tended to weaken some wines without strengthening others. In Pomerol and Saint-Emilion the rain had no effect because picking is always earlier there and most growers had finished. And our group choice eleven years later, perhaps not coincidentally, placed Pétrus of Pomerol and Cheval-Blanc of Saint-Emilion ahead of all the Médoc wines.

I first tasted the 1966 wines of the Médoc early in 1967. My notes refer to "high tannin without much acidity." In my notebook I wondered about their probable outcome, because I thought they would need years to lose their asperity, and at the time I wondered whether there was sufficient acidity for development of bouquet and flavor while this was going on.

In any event, the Médoc wines we tasted that evening were distinctive, in the sense that each had individuality, and they were, for the most part, both graceful and subdued. Some did indeed show austerity, and I attributed that to a lack of those flavors and aromas which give charm and at least an illusion of roundness to a wine.

But by tasting them alongside Pétrus and Cheval-Blanc, I am not sure that we were allowing those Médoc wines to show at their best. The current passion for comparative tastings is taken to extremes, it seems to me, and too often a wine is judged not for what it is, but, in comparison with an unrelated wine, for what it isn't. There are times when that can be instructive but not always is it the way to enjoy the best of a glass of wine. By chance, and very soon after this particular evening, I sampled several of these 1966 wines again in the course of lunches and dinners during a visit to Bordeaux. Tasted in the normal context of preceding wines planned to bring out the quality of each, they seemed silkier and more elegant. In particular, the austerity that had been so marked against the voluptuous styles of Pétrus and Cheval-Blanc was hardly apparent.

My own favorite Médoc of the evening was Lafite, though my opinion was not shared. The others much preferred Latour, which certainly had better weight but which was the sole wine I found to be brutally out of balance. The Lafite had a dry finish, as did they all, but it also had an attractively clear Pauillac-Cabernet nose, so pronounced that when tasting blind I had assumed the wine to be Mouton, usually identifiable from this very characteristic.

With serious consideration of the wines over, we proceeded to empty our eight glasses with broiled lamb chops, followed by a superb Brie, and the club members resumed the conversation they had started in 1962 and that has been running, with interruptions, ever since.

The First Growths of Bordeaux were not selected competitively in the course of a gigantic taste-off. They selected themselves, in a way, by doing the right things at the right time. Until the seventeenth century Bordeaux wines were not sold by name. Wine was a simple agricultural commodity like any other, and quality was rarely attributed to a particular source. In any case, the making and handling of wines was often so primitive that the consumer felt himself blessed if the wine was palatable, let alone distinguished. A wine fleet sailed from Bordeaux each November, with wine barely finished fermenting in the casks, in order to have the current vintage in London taverns for Christmas. The previous year's wine, kept in ullaged casks, open to air and spoilage of every kind in the pre-Pasteur era, was by then distinctly disagreeable. Unlike modern wine, it took a steep drop in price as it got older, especially once the new year's wine was available.

In the 1660s Arnaud de Pontac, a rich and influential wine-grower from Bordeaux, used his position and intelligence to change the marketing pattern of Bordeaux wines and, as a result, the pattern of winegrowing as well. First president of the local Parlement de Guienne in the mid-seventeenth century and later ambassador to London, he decided to use his connections and the prestige of his name to promote the wine from his estate at Haut-

Brion, near Bordeaux. Soon, in 1663, Samuel Pepys was writing in his diary that at the Royall Oake Taverne he drank "a sort of French wine called Ho Bryan, that hath a good and most perticular taste that I never met with." It was the first *named* Bordeau château wine offered for sale anywhere. Later the Pontac family opened a fashionable eating house in London at which, need we say, Haut-Brion was the wine offered.

Pontac's wine sold at prices up to two and three times more than other Bordeaux wine in London. Bordeaux wine, previously considered tavern tipple, became smart and fit for respectable tables. Others followed Pontac's success, and, by the first years of the eighteenth century, the *London Gazette* carried advertisements for three Bordeaux wines in addition to Haut-Brion. When we read their names, we note that these are the very ones that emerged, one hundred and fifty years later, as the four Firsts of the 1855 Classification.

Of course, the connection could be that only the best-managed wine estates on the best sites making the finest wines could afford this early self-distinction and promotion. But if it is true that fine wine commands a high price, it is equally true that a high price can often guarantee fine wine because it allows the rigorous selection of vines, the sharp control of yield, and the strict rejection of below-standard batches that are essential for high quality.

The emergence of named châteaux in the Médoc (in itself a novelty: much of the region was newly planted at that time); the development of the cylindrical bottle with cork closure, without which few Médoc wines could have aged to the point of revealing their charm; new money (brought to Bordeaux by the flourishing trade with the Caribbean) invested in developing the new vine-yards and financing the aging of the bottled wines; the new desire in France for delicacy at the table (François Marin's *Délices de la Table*, the first work of its kind, was published only in 1739); and the eighteenth-century passion for classifying everything from wild flowers to vineyards led to many attempts to rationalize the maze of new names in the Médoc. The wine brokers of Bordeaux classified them according to vineyard and year, the latter playing a much stronger role in deciding the price category for a wine than the vineyard of origin. In the early nineteenth century, for example, Lafite, Latour, and Margaux could command 3,000 francs a *tonneau* (equivalent to about a hundred cases) in a good year but only 400 francs in a bad one, less than what the wine of even the meanest vineyard of the Médoc fetched in a good year.

More significant, however, is the modest margin by which the First Growths in those days topped the prices of the wines below them. When the First sold for 3,000 francs, Léoville, Lascombe, Rausan, and others sold for 2,700 and yet others for 2,400. Today, the First Growths tower in price above the other classified Growths, such is their prestige, and the prices they command can be almost as high in a middling to poor year as in a fine one.

But until the 1855 Classification—in fact, nothing more than a public dissemination of the status quo in that particular year as part of the exhibit of French arts and industry at the International Exhibition in Paris—there was still considerable flexibility. In 1851 Cyrus Redding wrote (in his *History and Description of Modern Wines*):

The growers use all their efforts to place their wines in a higher class, and thus emulation is kindled, and they are justified in their efforts by the profits. The prices of their wines . . . is less governed by particular merit, than by the number which they occupy in the scale of classification. It often costs them sacrifices to reach that object. They will keep their wine many years to give it a superior title, instead of selling it the first year according to custom. By this means an individual will get his wine changed from the fourth to the third class, which he had perhaps occupied before for many successive years.

The emergence of the leading châteaux in Saint-Emilion and Pomerol has been more erratic and much more recent. Cheval-Blanc won recognition with its 1921 vintage, one of *the* great wines of Bordeaux, a success later confirmed by its outstanding 1947 wine, still, in 1982, magnificently lively, almost black-red in color and as fruitily rich as Port wine. In the 1850s, Cocks and Féret, the Debrett of Bordeaux, had ranked Cheval-Blanc only among the second-grade Saint-Emilions. What changes, I wonder, might have occurred in the Médoc classification during the course of the last century, had it remained as flexible as that of Saint-Emilion?

Pomerol did not exist as an *appellation* separate from Saint-Emilion until 1923, and although Pétrus first won attention (and a gold medal) at the 1878 Paris Exhibition, it is only in the last twenty years or so that it has been able to command the prices of

Lafite and Mouton. It was without doubt the best of the 1966s we tasted on that occasion.

The evening mellowed, and so did we. Bowls of ripe California strawberries appeared, along with plums and sections of papaya with lime—the last an exquisite accompaniment to a 1959 Eitelsbacher Karthäuserhofberg Beerenauslese, a richly shimmering treat.

And, as befits a gentlemen's dining club, we talked into the new day with Port and nuts—in this case a Sandeman's 1945, rather light for a vintage Port, but ideal for a fogbound summer night by the Pacific.

Bordeaux Classed Growths

N INETEEN EIGHTY-THREE Bordeaux classed growths raised
little enthusiasm when first offered on a pre-arrival basis.
Every superlative (and most resources) had been lavished
on 1982, and little could be done, or even said, about its sequel
that had not already been done and said to excess. The pity is that
among the 1938s are many wines that could possibly outclass the
1982s—to the astonishment of some and to the embarrassment of
others.

To understand why, we need a brief botanical review (those
allergic can skip to the last paragraph), and a comparison of the
Bordeaux weather in 1983 and 1982. A look at 1981 and 1984, too,
will put all these recent vintages into context and perspective.

Sun, wind, and rain affect a vine during its growing season
through the leaf-pores, or, more accurately, the *stomata*, that open
and close in response to the rate at which the vine loses water to
the air relative to its ability to find and to draw up more from the
soil. By way of these same *stomata*, plant oxygen is exchanged for
atmospheric carbon-dioxide, transformed, with solar energy, into
the vine's life staple. Even bright sun is of little use if a drying wind,
excessive heat, or lack of ground moisture to replace leaf water-
loss causes the *stomata* to close defensively, inhibiting an exchange

of the gases. On the other hand, a free movement of gases doesn't achieve much if the sun's rays are muffled in a blanket of cloud, or if the vine is too cold or too hot. Vines function best within the same extremes—from roughly 55° to 95°—that we ourselves, unless exceptionally fragile, find tolerable for work. Timing is of the essence, too. Crucial periods of the growing, flowering, fruiting, and maturing cycle need more consistent energy and more building material than others. Healthy shoot growth in May doesn't guarantee a faultless flowering in June, and a perfect fruit-set in June still needs balanced weather from July to September for balanced ripening, preferably with good sun in the final stages of sugar-accumulation just before picking. A replenishing rain in August will have a different effect from one in late September or in June, especially if, in June, it coincides with the vine's flowering.

In 1981, flowering occurred in dry weather in the first half of June, the usual time for Bordeaux. July was wet and lacked the sun and warmth to get the grapes off to a good start, but at least it ensured adequate ground moisture to keep things moving should conditions change. August, with less sunshine than ideal, was warm, and, fortunately, September was both warmer and sunnier than average, despite a downpour late in the month with recurring showers during picking. The crop was healthy even though the vines had twice missed hours of sunshine at crucial times: first in July, when the berries were just formed and starting to grow, and again in the final, sugar-accumulating days before and during harvest. This weather pattern is not unusual for Bordeaux, and is the basis for wines that we normally think of as typical of the region—well proportioned and well put together. But a slow start in July, and, more significantly, an imperfect finish, will hardly ever bring, in addition, that full, rich style associated with Bordeaux's most successful years.

When first tasted from barrel early the following year, the 1981 classed growths did, in fact, show impressive balance and structure. Though no more full-bodied than average, they were firm, well defined, and had good flavor. They were, in other words, of classic Bordeaux style. A year later, continuing to develop well, they had acquired greater distinction, even if assuming, against the newly presented and richly concentrated 1982s, a more austere, a more angular, a more subdued aspect than when tasted alone. Finally, in the spring of 1984, when they had been bottled and shipped to the United States, and were at the awkward stage when a young red Bordeaux wine, having mostly shed its enticing early aroma, has yet hardly begun to develop bouquet, they showed clearly the compact, graceful structure that had been their characteristic from the beginning, and that continues to be so now. They will eventually give pleasure all the more satisfying for its subtlety.

Quotations for the 1981s opened moderately in Bordeaux and soon languished when the world got caught up in 1982 fever, so that bargains abounded when the wines first arrived here. Their market prices began to increase in Bordeaux in 1985, however, following the trend in demand for all classed growths generated by the 1982s. Fortunately, some stocks remain, here and in Bordeaux, in reserve for United States importers paid for when the dollar carried a higher premium than it does now. Dazzled by the 1982s, many of us overlooked the 1981s: there is still a chance to make good the omission.

Flowering at the end of May and early June, the 1982 vintage showed itself from the start to be both precocious and prolific. The advantage of such an early bloom, provided the rest of the summer works out well, is that the grapes, instead of reaching the sugar-accumulating stage in September, when days are shorter, will do so in August. In fact, after a bright, warm July which advanced the grapes further, August 1982 was generously sunny, followed by a pleasantly warm September also blessed with abundant sunshine. Some rain in August had kept the moisture balance right, despite the grumbles of growers who complained that without it, 1982 would have been a perfect year. (By and large, they were the same growers who had complained that 1970 would have been a perfect year if only there had been a little rain in August . . .) Easy and early flowering, a good fruit set, a replenishment of water when it was needed to keep the *stomata* working, and more than normal sun in July, August, and September make a good prescription for a successful wine.

The 1982 Bordeaux wines are as superb as anyone would guess just from reading the weather data. And at first (and in retrospect), prices were not excessive for what was offered, thanks to a strong dollar. But with many more wine merchants offering 1982 "futures" than had been the case when the 1970 vintage had swept in with similar commotion, sales pressure was intense and relentless. The 1982s warranted an enthusiastic reception, yet anyone can empathize with those who reacted by playing down the vintage if only to mark their disapproval of a fuss that bordered on hype. Most 1982 classed growths are now sold, and only the certainty of beatific visions could justify the prices of those that remain. But, who knows? Even in this worldly age, somewhere a wine merchant of old-fashioned simplicity might be harboring in his store an odd bargain or two . . .

By the time first reports of the 1983s began to circulate we were all vintaged out: the last thing we were ready to cope with was more good news. In fact, even when the supply of 1982s has almost run dry, we might still reasonably ask if it is possible to think about the wines of 1983 objectively, away from glare and tambourines. More than money was invested by those who bought 1982s heavily, buying at the same time the idea that to do so was the imperative of a decade and perhaps of a generation ("One of the Great Vintages of Our Lifetime," proclaimed one critic, who stopped short of describing it as The Vintage of the Century, he explained, only because that was, in his view, an "overused expression"). Those who didn't, nevertheless, resent those who did, and they have an equally strong need to prove the virtue of their restraint and the wisdom of their judgment.

But if the Bordeaux summer of 1982 shaped so clearly the style and quality of the wine, didn't that of 1983 do the same? A wet spring provided a good moisture reserve, before fine weather during the first ten days of June guaranteed normal flowering. The hottest July ever recorded in Bordeaux gave the season a surging start, followed by a hot and, on occasion, stormy August. September, too, was warmer than average, and, of greater significance, the grapes, not picked until the end of the month, two weeks later than in 1982, had the advantage of 221 hours of sunshine compared with a Bordeaux September average of only 176. In fact, talking numbers, Bordeaux had a total of 434 hours of sunshine in the crucial maturing months of August and September 1983, compared with 424 in the same two months in 1982. Despite those sporadic August rainstorms in the Médoc, especially from the northerly tip down to Saint-Estephe and Pauillac, it is reasonable to expect well of a season with the warmest average temperature in 60 years, adequate replenishment of water during the growing season to keep the *stomata* functioning, and an exceptional amount of sunshine. Of course the wines vary to the same extent as do the sources from which the weather averages are drawn (an average vineyard can be found about as frequently as an average 2.75-member American household), but the indicators alone for 1983, at least as favorable as those of 1982, give good reason to pay close attention to this vintage.

If storms left patchy results in the lower Médoc (and some Saint-Estephes, in particular, do not measure up to others), 1983 red wines of the Graves and of Margaux, especially, and most Saint-Juliens and Pauillacs, are striking for their depth and persistence of flavor. In fact, when compared with the emphatic and shapely refinement of many 1983s, 1982s often seem merely exuberant. A few 1983 Saint-Emilions and Pomerols show signs of over-ripe grapes, but on that side of Bordeaux, too, success is general for this vintage. The Château Cheval Blanc 1983 tasted from barrel just before lunch at the property in June 1984 was so good that it overshadowed all the wines we had later at table.

And 1984? Winston Smith's boss in the Ministry of Truth would have had a tough job revising the weather reports for May. The whole of western Europe was cold and sopping. Flowering, toward the end of June, was very late—a sign that the crucial final ripening would be pushed back to shorter days with an increased risk of sunshine curtailed when most needed. Equally ominous, rain returned during the flowering. Merlot vines, which make up a substantial proportion of many Médoc vineyards, and dominate those of Pomerol and Saint-Emilion, drop their blossom easily in such adverse conditions. Wines known for a high proportion of Merlot will be seen in their 1984 vintage in a different key. At Château Cos d'Estournel in Saint-Estephe, for example, Merlot grown on a lower chalky section of the vineyard where Cabernet Sauvignon would not ripen well (and would have too aggressive a flavor if it did), usually accounts for roughly 35 percent of the finished wine; but in 1984, the proportion fell to 15 percent. At Château Petit-Village in Pomerol, owned by the same Prats family interests, Merlot is the mainstay, representing 80 percent of production. In 1984, the proportion fell to 50 percent—still substantial, but reduced by an extent that is bound to affect the style significantly. There are those who have taken the deficiency of Merlot as a signal to avoid properties where it represents an important factor, especially those of Saint-Emilion and Pomerol. Yet some of the best years there (1961 and 1971 will serve as examples),

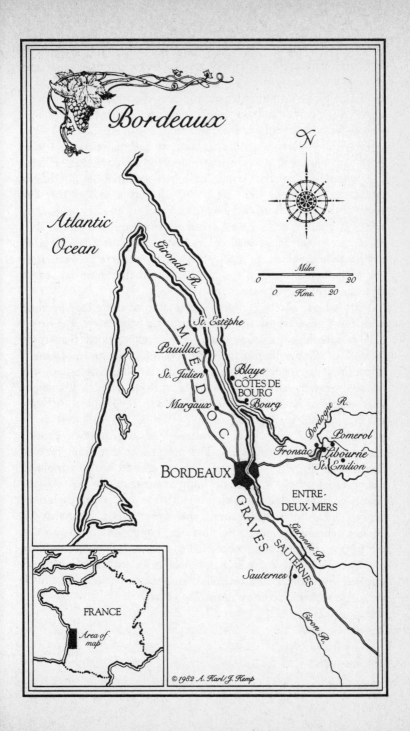

Bordeaux

Atlantic
Ocean

N

Gironde R.

Miles
0   20
0   Kms.   20

St. Estèphe

Pauillac

St. Julien

M
É
D
O
C

Blaye
CÔTES DE
BOURG

Margaux

Bourg

Dordogne R.

Pomerol

Fronsac

Libourne

St. Emilion

BORDEAUX

ENTRE-
DEUX-MERS

G
R
A
V
E
S

SAUTERNES

Garonne R.

Sauternes

Ciron R.

FRANCE

Area of
map

© 1982 A. Karl/J. Kemp

and certainly some of the best years of Château Pétrus, the leading growth of Pomerol made almost entirely from Merlot, have been those in which a crop thinned, as it were, by nature came to perfect maturity in conditions that might sometimes have been less auspicious had the vines been fully burdened.

July and August 1984 were, in fact, dry and reasonably warm in Bordeaux, with well above average hours of sunshine. Alas, September, when good weather would have been essential because of the lateness of the crop, went from bad to worse: cool at first and rainy at the close. Bordeaux lost the chance to fill out those many wines that had started with a measure of handicap. The 1984s tasted so far are nevertheless well-colored, straightforward, and better, in fact, than expected. In quality they lie somewhere between 1981 and 1980, by no means a condemnation; but they have an abrupt style and are generally short in flavor.

With a logic barely comprehensible even to those long familiar with the folk ways of the classed growth proprietors, the 1984s have nonetheless opened at prices considerably higher than those quoted for the opening of the 1982 and 1983 vintages. *Sud Ouest*, Bordeaux's daily paper, wrote ironically of "the anguish of the [classed growth] proprietor" who must keep up with his neighbors' prices or lose rank. "If I sell for less," the owner of a fashionable growth was quoted to say, "it is as if I admitted to be slipping. There are [price] clusters, and one mustn't change cluster without good reason." The problem is that from time to time certain growths—Château Pichon Lalande is an example in recent years—show a dramatic improvement, or for less obvious reason acquire sudden notoriety. With the release of each successive vintage of such a growth the owner tries to capitalize on greater demand by increasing his price, hoping eventually to slip out of one cluster into another. When the rest of the cluster tries to move with him, there is a round of price increases sometimes justified, but in any case tolerable, in successful years, but which gives rise to "proprietor's anguish" in others.

Trocken-Trocken

THE MATUSCHKA-GREIFFENCLAU family began the massive pile that is now Schloss Vollrads in the fourteenth century, and in all senses of the word the structure stands at the heart of their vineyard estate. Clang and clatter in the courtyard recently reminded us that ever since its beginnings there have been additions, changes, and restorations. Over a period of two years, Erwein, the newest Graf, restored the medieval roof. Starting with the steep-pitched beam structure and replacing dozens of tiny attic gables, he rehung thousands of the scalloped blue-black slates that cling like scales to a monstrous fish. The new roof of Vollrads is a signal that Graf Erwein is prepared to tackle problems fundamentally at considerable effort (and cost) for what he thinks worth preserving. Less apparent but with wider effect, he has adopted an equally energetic and fundamental attitude in a polemic that presently engulfs the entire *hoch Feinschmeckerei*.

The ferment in France to scrutinize all that had been previously taken for granted in wine and food found an echo in Germany. Already *nouvelle cuisine* seems a wistfully dated expression—whether it really represented anything particularly new is a debate we can leave to others—but there is no doubt it revitalized interest in our own taste buds, reminded us that fresh ingredients tasting of themselves are the basis of all good cooking (*nouvelle, ancienne,* and just plain Grandma's), and reemphasized that lightness and fragrance, in wine as well as food, are desirable qualities.

In Germany, wines were already lighter and more fragrant than the lightest of French wines—that is their essence—so controversy there focused on the question of sweetness. By way of background we should recall that in the late fifties German wine producers financed a study that seemed to indicate that more Germans would drink more wine if it were slightly sweeter than was then the case. At that time the sweetness of a wine (I generalize, of course) depended on its quality. Spätlese and Auslese wines, known for their naturally sweet style, were made from late-picked grapes and inevitably carried both higher production costs and higher prices on the shelf. For a number of reasons cheap sweet wines were rarely as satisfactory. But a technique was then perfected to overcome this. By retaining a proportion of the unfermented grape juice and reintroducing it judiciously into the finished wine, the level of sweetness could be adjusted even in a wine made from grapes with only delicate sugar content. The presence of even a little unfermented grape juice will intensify the grapy quality of a wine's aroma (an obvious advantage in many cases) and the practice enhanced even the most ordinary wine, increasing its charm manyfold.

In the decade from 1963 to 1973, annual consumption of wine per head rose in Germany by roughly 70 percent—and this at a time when consumption in France, the most traditional of all wine-drinking countries, fell by 20 percent. Because of this success, sweetness became the dominating characteristic of German wines. But it was one thing to make everyday wines more palatable, quite another heedlessly to mask the quality and personality of finer products, and reaction was inevitable. A one-way pendulum has yet to be discovered, however, and, to the dismay of Graf Erwein and of those who share his view, the gastronomic new wave is replacing one exaggeration with another. A passion for bone-dry wines has seized the fashionable wine and food establishment in Germany. Increasingly, on labels and on wine lists, one sees the word *trocken* (boldly underlined), not as reference to the dry state of raisinlike grapes, picked late and overripe for luscious dessert wines (as in Trockenbeerenauslese), but to "dry" according to the English usage, describing absence of any perceptible sweetness in a wine.

"Dry" and "sweet" are relative, even subjective, terms. A light, crisply acid Mosel wine with twenty-five grams of residual grape sugar in the bottle, for example, will taste less sweet than a rounder, more alcoholically powerful Rheinhessen wine with only fifteen grams. Finding the right sweet-dry balance for any German wine is difficult (as in so much else, it is a question of deciding how far art might discreetly support nature).

But a German wine of quality depends on a sweet-sharp sensation so finely in balance that neither part dominates. Such a wine provokes and soothes the palate simultaneously, suggesting a universe of tastes and smells but presenting only one. Intense, complex, integrated, it should have what the Germans call "harmony." The higher alcohol levels of most French and Italian wines contribute warmth and fullness sufficient to balance their lower acidities. German wines, the most northerly of Europe, owe their exquisite flavor to the relatively high acidity in the grapes from which they are made, and high alcohol alone could not provide a necessary balance. Even if means were found to "improve" the alcohol to the required level, it would have to be so high that the wine would finish hard and disagreeable, its delicacy of aroma and flavor wrecked. That is why the elegance and style of fine German wines can be preserved only through a carefully judged relationship between acid and grape sugar.

The role of residual sugar in this balance was illuminated recently in a brief comment in the *New York Times*. Frank Prial, then the paper's wine columnist, had tasted a number of new-style *trocken* wines from Germany and found that they reminded him of Alsatian wines (produced from similar grapes in a more southerly and sheltered part of the Rhine and almost always made without residual sugar), except, he complained, for their lack of body. Of course, Alsatian wines have more alcohol, and the high acidity natural to German wines needs either that or sugar if the wine is not to taste thin, or downright scrawny.

To accept the sweet-sharp theory of harmony in German wines is one thing, to make it work in relation to food is another; many are daunted at the prospect of matching German wines to classic dishes. There is a tendency to shrug the question aside, suggesting on the one hand that German wines are best drunk without food (which is true for some but not for all) or that, willy-nilly, they "go with everything" (which is true if one is not overly concerned with subtle combinations of wine and food or if one's preference for German wines is so overwhelming that the more logical choice for certain circumstances would be less pleasurable personally).

To demonstrate the compatibility of German wines with the classic dishes of France and Germany, Matuschka-Greiffenclau invites German restaurateurs and other professionals to Schloss Vollrads for dinners where the finely graded range of his wines is matched to appropriate foods. Schloss Vollrads uses a color code to indicate the quality of the wines, as defined by German law, and supplements the code with a silver or a gold band to indicate the degree of dryness.

For some years Germany has divided wines into three quality categories, based on the degree of ripeness of the grapes at the time of picking. Wines made from grapes with less than a certain level of natural sugar, and which therefore need enriching at the time of the crush prior to fermentation, are described as *Tafelwein* ("table wine"). Few wines of this quality are exported; mostly they are used for everyday drinking in Germany. Wines made from grapes with more sugar than this minimum, but that still need some enriching to be of satisfactory strength, are described as *Qualitätswein* ("quality wine"). Wines made from grapes that need no enrichment at all are described as *Qualitätswein mit Prädikat* ("quality wine with description"). These last always have a descriptive word that can range from Kabinett (a flag word to distinguish "quality wine with description" from an ordinary "quality wine") through Spätlese (made from late-picked grapes, and, though not stated, conforming to more stringent standards than plain Kabinett), Auslese (made from grapes picked bunch by bunch as each becomes ripe), and Beerenauslese (made from grapes picked one at a time to ensure perfect ripeness) to Trockebeeren-auslese (made from grapes picked one at a time, each when over-ripe to a point of dried, raisinlike consistency).

By linking the quality grading to a standard of the grapes at the time of picking and not just to a geographic location (as is the case with *appellations contrôlées* in France), a wine is systematically downgraded in category, no matter where it was grown, if conditions at the time of picking were not propitious for making fine wine. With equal logic, a wine of humble geographic origin is entitled to the appropriate descriptive phrase when unusual vintage conditions create a product of high quality. None of this is automatic. A German wine of "quality" status or above must be submitted to a government tasting panel before it can be sold under the category claimed. The color code used by Schloss Vollrads is green for ordinary "quality wines," blue for Kabinett, pink for Spätlese, white for Auslese, and gold for Beerenauslese. The vineyard adds a distinctive band when the sugar levels are more (or less) than one might reasonably suppose from the quality designation. A silver band denotes a wine drier than one might expect; a gold band, sweeter. But the degree of sweetness (or lack of it) is decided only in accordance with what an individual wine needs to be in harmony because, Graf Erwein will tell you, wines in balance are neither sweet nor dry.

The residual sugar in most balanced German wines is compatible with sauces, whether they are made from reductions or thickened with cream. But German wines do not need the buffer of sauces to marry well with dishes of all kinds. A full-bodied Rhine wine will stand up to most meats and game, though Graf Erwein acknowledges that a red is best with plain roast beef. In Germany the food I eat is usually of the simplest kind, and the wines always seem to be perfect matches. I have enjoyed full-blown Deidesheim wines with roast partridge and cabbage; *Saumagen* (pig's stomach stuffed with chopped pork, carrots, potatoes, and herbs, boiled and roasted, and served sliced thick like a huge sausage) is a superb foil for any Rheinhessen wine; and I remember particularly a Niersteiner, sharp-sweet as any I have had, deliciously in key with pheasant livers and wild mushrooms, served on a bed of creamy mashed potatoes.

One of the finest partnerships of German wines with food that I have ever enjoyed was a pair of 1969 Auslesen from Schloss Rheinhart, one an Ockfener Herrenberg, the other an Ockfener Bockstein, served together at a San Francisco dinner with a plain sauté of cod accompanied by new potatoes rolled in butter and lightly sprinkled with sea salt. The buttery quality of fish and potatoes made an exquisite marriage with the wines, something impossible had they been bone dry. And in a local restaurant just a few months ago, I was served a 1976 Steinberger Kabinett, hardly a dry wine, with a terrine of leeks. A *coulis* of tomato brought out the sweetness of the wine and linked it to the terrine perfectly.

A fine Beerenauslese can be as magnificent on its own as with dessert. The choice of dessert for such a wine, however, must be made with great care; an excessively sweet dish can overpower its delicate sweetness and make the wine seem both dry and characterless. The best accompaniment is a ripe peach; the worst, apart from anything with chocolate, is a creamy, sweet pastry. Matuschka-Greiffenclau claims that upside-down apple cake is best to show off a rich German wine, but the ripe papaya and lime once served to me with a 1959 Eitelsbacher Karthäuserhofberg Beerenauslese was a revelation, and the memory of a 1959 Hallgartner Deutelsberg Beerenauslese served to me with a fresh pear sorbet only last night has been an aid and stimulus as I have been writing.

The most successful conclusion to the *trocken* controversy will be recognition of what German wines are and can be rather than imposition of a style that is fashionable but irrelevant (another wistfully dated word) to German vineyards. Whatever the outcome, however, the battle itself has stimulated fresh and intelligent concern for wine within Germany, and growers always do better for that.

Baden-Württemberg

With sales of basic Rhine and Moselle wines increasing dramatically despite higher prices, it is surprising to discover that roughly one bottle of German wine in four is now made from grapes grown in Baden-Württemberg, a region we hardly ever hear of. In 1981, more than 200 million bottles of wine were produced there, at least twice as much as in the Moselle. But local consumption (Badeners cheerfully drink twice as much wine per capita as other Germans do) and growing demand elsewhere, particularly from northern Germany, is such that there is never enough, despite extensions to the vineyards in recent years. Considering this, I suppose the absence of Baden wines from this side of the Atlantic should not be unexpected.

Tucked into the southwestern corner of Germany, Baden-Württemberg (the two regions are usually thought of together) is a viticultural backwater to most. I have yet to stumble into a discussion of its wines conducted with the fervor usually reserved for the growths of the middle Moselle or the more pronounceable parts of the Rheingau. To be fair, I am not sure that even the best of Baden can equal the best of what we think of as the traditional stretches of the Rhine; but taken as a whole, and particularly in the price range of wines that we meet in the ordinary course of

events, I find Baden wines incomparably more charming than
other German wines. They are lighter than Alsace wines from
across the river (Baden lies between the Rhine and the Black
Forest), drier than Rhine wines as they are made today, and,
though often as fragrant as most Moselles, they are much softer.

Baden, a long, narrow wine region that stretches from Heidelberg to the Swiss frontier, is divided into a number of areas, each
with slightly different characteristics. Württemberg is just to the
north and east—in and adjacent to the valley of the Neckar—and
extends from Stuttgart to Heilbronn. The vineyards of both regions are among the most romantic in the world: they tumble
down precipitous slopes from impenetrable castles in the Ortenau,
spread in terraces through Hansel-and-Gretel villages of the once-
volcanic Kaiserstuhl, carpet with lush green the sides of the
Staufenberg above Heilbronn, and run like leafy ribbons through
the pink baroque palaces of Meersburg to the shore of Lake Constance. The Black Forest protects them from the cold east winds,
and the Vosges Mountains keep back the Atlantic rains. Baden
is Germany's driest and sunniest region. It is also, perhaps, its
most beautiful. As if the setting between mountain and river were
not already enough, the villages, nestled in vineyard and orchard,
are smothered in flowers from spring to fall, with geraniums
massed on balconies and windowsills.

Every restaurant and *Weinstube* offers Baden wines in open
carafe, and, even when sold without particulars of vineyard or
grape, the wines always have a distinctive light, flowery style. The
names on the bottles of labeled wines will at first strike a familiar
chord. Sylvaner and Riesling, after all, are to be found up and
down the Rhine. In Baden-Württemberg they are used together,
separately, or in one of the several hybrids that have been cross-
bred from them. Müller-Thurgau, for example, which takes up
fully a third of the vineyard acreage in Baden, brings the zest of
Riesling to the good yields and mild flavor of Sylvaner. It shows
a sturdier resistance to adverse weather than does the Riesling and
a better balance in the finished wine than a Sylvaner.

A closer look at a Baden wine list, however, reveals names of
vines quite unfamiliar, or, at least, quite unexpected in Germany.
Pinot Gris, for example, known here as Ruländer, is planted
extensively in Baden and yields white wine with a style somewhere
between that of a plump white Burgundy and a fruity Moselle.

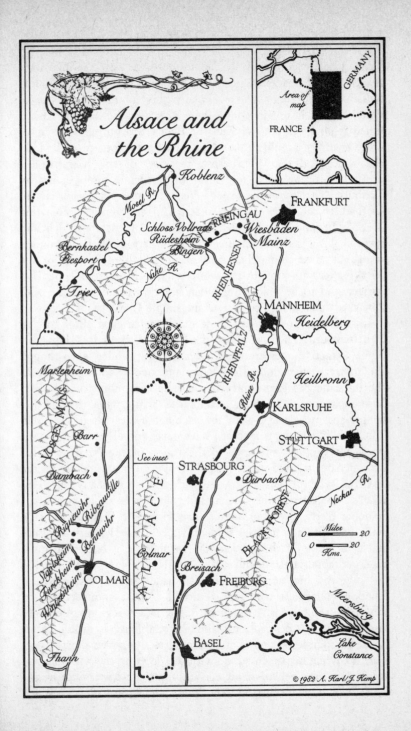

Alsace and
the Rhine

FRANCE

Area of
map

GERMANY

Koblenz

FRANKFURT

Mosel R.

Schloss Vollrads   RHEINGAU
Rüdesheim   Wiesbaden
Bingen   Mainz

Bernkastel
Piesport

Nahe R.

Trier

RHEINHESSEN

N

MANNHEIM

Heidelberg

RHEINPFALZ

Heilbronn

Rhine R.

KARLSRUHE

Marlenheim

STUTTGART

VOSGES MTNS.

See inset

STRASBOURG

Durbach

Neckar R.

Barr

A L S A C E

BLACK FOREST

Dambach

Miles   20

Riquewihr   Ribeauville
             Bernwihr

Colmar

Kms.   20

Sigolsheim
Kientzheim
Winzenheim   COLMAR

Breisach

FREIBURG

Meersburg

Thann

BASEL

Lake
Constance

© 1982 A. Karl / J. Kemp

Traminer, labeled locally as Clevner until the new German wine
law of 1971 forbade the practice ("What is not approved is for-
bidden"—bureaucrats will eventually tidy all the magic out of
wine), is less heady in Baden than is usually the case in Alsace,
but it is no less aromatic. And the Blauer Spätburgunder is none
other than the familiar Pinot Noir, used here both for soft, light
red wines and for Weissherbst, the rosé of the Kaiserstuhl—
created, it is said, solely to assuage the academic rigors of nearby
Freiburg. (Freiburg must be a very rigorous place: it is also
soothed by the wine of the Glottertal, made from a combination
of Spätburgunder and Ruländer and one of the most delicious
rosés in the world.) Pinot Blanc, known here as Weissburgunder,
is grown in small patches; and in the south of Baden, in the
Markgräflerland, most of the white wine is made from Gutedel, a
variety said to be unique to Baden but that produces wine with
a marked resemblance to that of the simple Chasselas of Alsace.

In different proportions, most of these varieties also grow in
Württemberg. There, emphasis is on red and rosé wines, however.
Some attractive ones are made from Spätburgunder, even though
the growers have adopted the Rhine practice of adding a little of
the unfermented grape juice to their Spätburgunder wines. Perhaps enhancing to a thin or characterless white wine, the addition
brings an unnecessary—and unwelcome—sweet finish to a red.
The Trollinger, a variety that I have never found elsewhere, is the
grape more commonly used in the valley of the Neckar. It has
little personality and seems most agreeable to me when fermented
as a rosé, when it is usually mixed with white grapes anyway. This
rosé is a specialty of the Neckar and is known as Schillerwein, not
in honor of the poet, but because it is iridescent. It is also the café
wine of Stuttgart and the student wine of Heidelberg. Another
red wine grape of the Neckar, the Lemberger, is becoming quite
rare, perhaps understandably.

I owe my first acquaintance with Baden wines to one of my
London colleagues who had returned from a summer visit to
cousins in the Ortenau (the heart of the Baden region) glowingly
enthusiastic. His description of bucolic simplicity in an old farm-
house surrounded by vines and plum trees was given sharper perspective when he presented me with the notes on the wines he had
tasted from the cellars of his cousins and their aristocratic neighbors. "Lords are lordliest in their wine," said Milton, and it seemed

as if my friend had indeed caught a glimpse of paradise regained. At that point there was little doubt that I would allow time to see Baden for myself on my next trip to Germany.

That first visit was enchanting. By good fortune I arrived in the Ortenau in early spring, when the orchards were in bloom and young shoots were just appearing in the vineyards. The new wines —the delicious 1964s—were just ready to be sampled, and they were as tender and fresh as everything I saw around me.

I started my tasting tour at the vineyards of Freiherr von Neveu above the pretty village of Durbach. They cover barely thirty acres, most of them surrounding his house and a few at Ortenberg, five miles or so to the south. The vineyards are so steep that they can be plowed only with the aid of a winch. A man sits on the plow and guides it as it is hauled up by motor-driven wire. And after every storm the topsoil must be laboriously carried back up the slopes in baskets.

My host first offered me his Ortenberger Freudental, made from a Riesling-Sylvaner cross, and I could not have had a more delightful introduction to his wines. It was light, fresh, and clear. We tasted from almost every batch in his cellar, including some wines from older vintages. His 1962 Durbacher Grillenhalde (a vineyard name that has been swallowed in the reorganization of German vineyards) made from late-picked Traminer grapes, was one that I bought for our London cellars. The wine was pale gold in color, and the original aroma of the Traminer grape had delicately fused into the more complex bouquet developed in the bottle. Though velvety full, it was not heavy, and the sweetness, perfectly in balance, seemed only to complete—logically, to "close"—the wine.

The vineyard at Schloss Staufenberg, a knightly manor belonging to the Markgraf Max von Baden, sits on the other side of the valley from von Neveu's house. The manor was built in the eleventh century, and the view it commands across the Rhine to the Vosges beyond suggests that the choice of site was not dictated by viticultural needs alone. When I arrived, a checkered cloth had already been spread on a table in the shade of an old linden tree in the courtyard so that we could taste and enjoy the panorama at the same time.

Herr Duhr, the vineyard administrator, began our tasting with a wine from one of the smaller, outlying von Baden vineyards north of Durbach: Schloss Ebersteiner Grafensprung. He intended it as a curtain raiser, nothing more. But delighting in its fragrance and delicacy, I began to realize that the Baden growers take these characteristics so for granted that they no longer perceive them as qualities. They offer graceful wines as a foil for their more complex wines, those with which they wish to please and impress. But the simple wines of Baden are as impressive in their way as the most extraordinary, and therein lies the charm of the region.

We went on to taste each of the other wines produced by Herr Duhr, including the clean, fresh Spätburgunder from Schloss Eberstein; but the wine that pleased me most was again a Traminer, from the Staufenberger Schlossberg. It was a heavy wine, detectably Traminer on the palate, but with a bouquet reminiscent of roses.

I continued my tasting at the third of the great Durbach estates, that of Graf Metternich. I was no longer surprised at my pleasure in the least significant of the wines—this time a Durbacher Hatsbach made from Müller-Thurgau grapes, crisp, clean, and with a bouquet that was almost spicy. Herr Schilli, the manager of the Metternich'sches Weingut, is widely respected in Baden for the skill with which he preserves in each wine the sharp characteristic of its grape variety and the personality of each particular vineyard site. Trained in France and Italy as well as in Germany, Schilli brings an unusual breadth of view to his winemaking. He produced for us a Durbacher Annaberg Spätlese Eiswein, an exceptional wine with a sustained bouquet and the flavor of pears; a Durbacher Herrenberg Sauvignon Blanc, from what are thought to be the only Sauvignon Blanc vines in Germany; an Auslese of incredible richness and fruitier than any Sauternes I have tasted; and what was again my favorite, a Traminer from the Durbacher Schlossberg that was full-flavored, firm, and muscular.

It can hardly be accidental that the three leading wine estates of Baden are all to be found at Durbach, but in terms of commercial activity the center of the Baden wine region is Breisach, an old town on the Rhine close to Freiburg and the Kaiserstuhl. It is the home of the Baden central wine cooperative, the largest and probably the most up-to-date in Europe. At the end of World War II the vineyards of Baden were disorganized, the wines poorly distributed and in chronic surplus. The central cooperative was founded in 1952 as a marketing channel rather than as a means to rationalize production. But gradually the two concepts have become one, and, as I have learned from successive visits, Baden is now by far the best organized viticultural region in the world.

What is especially striking is the care taken in handling even the smallest batches of grapes, despite the scale of the cellar operations. Unlike most other cooperatives that feel compelled to combine all grades of grapes from their members, at Breisach every batch is sorted according to varietal, vineyard origin, time of picking, and quality. Gleaming like a space-age fantasy, Breisach was among the first to practice low-temperature fermentation (one of the reasons why Baden wines are so fragrant) and has been a source of technical know-how to wineries everywhere, including California. The quantities of wine that leave Breisach every day are indeed huge, but the numbers are impressive only because every single bottle is a delight and does credit to the growers.

To make a visit to Breisach even more agreeable, the cooperative has funded a small, elegant hotel in the old part of town, with spectacular Rhine views from the dining room and a kitchen to show off the region's best dishes. Or one can drive into the Black Forest and spend a weekend in Hinterzarten, a chocolate-box village where the Park Hotel Adler gives the visitor the illusion of having stepped back in time—but with the latest, and most delicious, Baden wines to accompany him.

Piedmont: A Changing World

A VISIT TO PIEDMONT a number of years ago rid me of at least one illusion. We had spent a week skiing in Val-d'Isère, and because the Col de l'Iseran was closed for the winter we had to take the long route, backtracking almost as far as Chambéry to reach Modane, the French terminus of the Mont Cenis Tunnel. After the stinging chill of the high Solaise, there was a mild smell of spring in the valley, a foretaste, I thought, of what awaited us once through the mountains. Dazed by bright sunshine, we would emerge into Italy symbolically reborn, to green fields, even wild flowers, perhaps, in the soft drift of Mediterranean air.

Alas, my fantasy was shattered at Bardonecchia, as we swept out and into a blizzard worse than anything we had experienced all winter north of the Alps, and our descent into Turin presented a challenge to downhill courage greater than any slope we had tackled the previous week. Twice we landed in a ditch, and the car, in a final sulk, packed up its windshield wipers so that the last exhausting hour was spent with both side windows down and driver and passenger doing their best with numbed hands to maintain some visibility and avoid total disaster. Dazed, indeed.

Relaxed and restored by a warm bath and a hot rum toddy, we set off for dinner, walking to the Ristorante del Cambio on the

Piazza Carignano. I love the formal arcades of central Turin, and the illuminated snow and recessed shadows gave sharp patterns to the façades of the streets. Our appetites had become pretty sharp, too, in the cold air, and we were glad to arrive in the welcoming atmosphere of the Cambio.

Every time I have been to Turin I have visited this restaurant, but as it is now some years since I was there I can only hope that the changes that have engulfed the city have left undisturbed at least this one distillation of sedate Piedmontese charm. The old-fashioned dining room took its age gracefully, linen stiffly starched and waiters gently courteous. One ignored occasional signs of wear in the red plush, of course, or a random weak spring in the banquettes, with the same respect with which one does not notice the wavering voice of an elderly orator or see the unsteady foot of an older, beautiful woman.

The wine list included the most extensive collection of Piedmont wines I had ever seen, and the selections, I was later to realize, were chosen from among the best growers in the area. Repairs to the car kept me in Turin (not the most miserable of fates), and I was able to sample further the contents of the cellars of the Cambio, as instructive an introduction to the wines of Piedmont as one could have.

The northern romantic sees the vineyards of Piedmont as an extension of the prolific arbors and trellises of the south. But the region is on roughly the same latitude as Bordeaux and the French Massif Central and shares the brusque shifts of weather typical of a sub-Alpine climate. The Piedmont vineyards, small and orderly, are often on steep terraces and produce wines of wide variety. Some of the wines are as big as the imagination allows, though rarely with the intemperate swagger so falsely associated with Italian wines; in Piedmont, alcoholic strength and full body are usually balanced by good acidity and delicacy of flavor. Others, Grignolino, for example, and Freisa—the latter on occasion so perfumed that one might be forgiven for suspecting a fruit essence in the wine—are light, mild, and often slightly sweet.

With wines so varied, the layman (and often the professional) has a hard time making sense of the taste of Piedmont, let alone the names and categories of the wines, despite the introduction of Denominazione di Origine Controllata (the Italian version of *appellation contrôlée*) in the 1960s.

It is confusing that some wines are identified and labeled geographically—Barolo and Barbaresco are both named for the legally
defined zones where they are grown—whereas others, such as
Dolcetto and Brachetto, are named for the grapes from which
they are made, and yet others are named both geographically and
varietally: Barbera d'Asti, for example, or Barbera del Monferrato
(a wine in which, to complete the confusion, Italian law allows a
proportion of grapes other than Barbera).

There are those who will disagree with me, but I find I make
sense of Piedmont only if I distinguish between wines made from
Nebbiolo and Barbera grapes, wines that I regard as serious, and
those made from other grapes, which, charming though they can
be, are country wines in the best sense—right for drinking on the
spot, and not too critically. Brachetto, Dolcetto, and Freisa grapes
make simple wines, often with a light sparkle artfully introduced
and sometimes with unfermented grape sugar deliberately retained
to give an *amabile* style that may be pleasing but is rarely flattering
in the course of a serious dinner.

The best of this "other" group is Grignolino. Drunk young,
when its bright ruby color has an unusual orange cast, it is delight-
fully undemanding. There are good examples in every *trattoria* in
Turin, where new Grignolino is held in much the same affectionate
regard as young Beaujolais is in Lyon, and for the same reasons. It
tastes attractively of the grape and is mild in both alcohol and
acidity. Unfortunately, the Grignolino vine is disappearing in Piedmont, unable to resist a virulent vine mold. Even in California,
where there was once extensive acreage, there now stand barely a
hundred acres of Grignolino (and some maintain darkly that those
survive only because they actually contain a hybrid of Grignolino
and Brachetto rather than Grignolino itself).

Nebbiolo wines, however, are not to be trifled with. Dark and
rich, they are full of tannin when young and sometimes retain a
faintly bitter zest even at their peak. Each vineyard gives its own
distinct style, and so does the choice of subvarietal (there are
several subvarietals of Nebbiolo, of which two are widely used).
Barbera wine, without the complexity of flavor and bouquet of
Nebbiolo, lacks none of its strength or color. As a varietal it is
stable—in the sense that subvarieties are few—and the Barbera
vine is recognizably the same wherever it grows, whether in
Piedmont or California.

The province of Cuneo, between Turin and Genoa, is the center for Nebbiolo. Production encircles the town of Alba, also distinguished as the commercial source of Piedmont white truffles. To the southwest, Barolo spreads its vines across two valleys of the Langhe hills. To the northeast lies Barbaresco, seemingly larger in area than Barolo but made up of many scattered pockets of vines, which together give an annual yield barely a quarter of that of Barolo. Lastly, to the northwest is the zone where wines called Nebbiolo d'Alba are grown. Barolo has a production of almost half a million cases of wine a year, and roughly the equivalent of 300,000 cases are produced each year with the right to the denomination Nebbiolo d'Alba.

Barbaresco sounds like the name of a character in a minor Mozart opera; Barolo has a full-bellied ring. The wines share something of this simplistic contrast, with Barbaresco less assertive and less robust than its neighbor. Barolo is referred to as the "king of wines and wine of kings," no doubt an allusion and compliment to the House of Savoy, which rose from its Piedmont origins to rule unified Italy until deposed after World War II. All Italians (even those who have never tasted it) will tell you of the excellence of Barolo, as if belief in its superiority were a matter of national pride. Yet despite the hyperbole, enough to drive the most charitable to skepticism, Barolo does indeed stand above all other Italian wines for the consistency with which examples will touch our highest expectations of red wines.

Vineyard holdings in Barolo are small, with few exceptions. Many growers sell their grapes because their acreage hardly justifies the expense of equipping a winery. La Morra, a commune with more than a third of the vineyards entitled to the Barolo denomination, might be a patchwork of tiny farms, but it is more important as a winegrowing center than Barolo itself. Its vineyards face southwest and bear grapes that ripen easily in afternoon sun to yield soft, fat wines. Southeastward, across the valley to the commune of Barolo and then across the watershed to Serralunga d'Alba, the wines get progressively firmer, harder. The subvariety of Nebbiolo most widely used for Barolo is Lampia, a vine of prolific and untidy growth. Michet, less common (and hardly found at all in Barbaresco), is a tight, neat vine giving tight, neat wines. Rosé, a Nebbiolo variety that, as its name suggests, produces light-colored wines, is rarely found now, though it was once

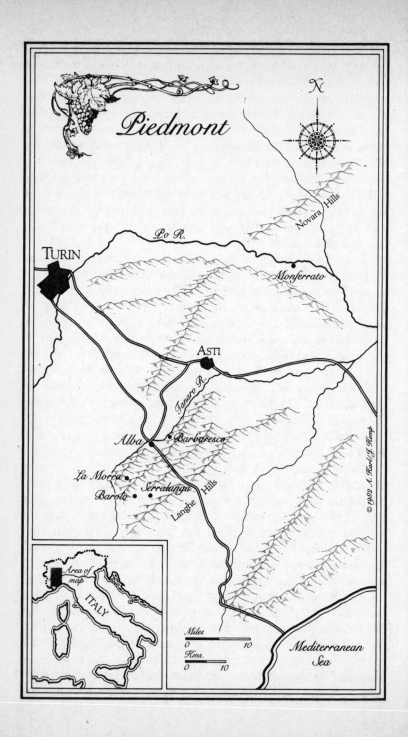

popular. In the chalky soils of the Barolo hills, Lampia and Michet give intensely flavored wines with good color and a capacity for long aging. Barbaresco wines, more perfumed when young, are less forceful and age less well. Nebbiolo d'Alba, grown on the sandier soils across the Tanaro, has the characteristics of wines grown on sand everywhere—fragrance, quick development, and lack of depth.

Other Nebbiolo wines of Piedmont include Spanna, a synonym for Nebbiolo, grown without geographic delimitation; Gattinara from the province of Vercelli; and Ghemme and Sizzano from the hills of Novara. (I once found an amazing wine at Sizzano, made not from Nebbiolo but from Fogarino vines brought back from Sicily by Giuseppe Bianchi. Neighbors mocked, were even scandalized, and his father forbade him to sell the wine he made from these alien grapes. When his father died, Bianchi submitted a sample to the annual wine fair of Piedmont, *the* classic wine event of the year in Italy, just as a lark. He won the top award with his Fogarino wine, to his own and everyone else's astonishment. I tasted his 1958 vintage in his kitchen while we enjoyed a country soup that Signora Bianchi had enriched with a cloud of beaten egg, bread crumbs, and grated Parmesan cheese. I acknowledge that it might have added to both my pleasure and satisfaction in the wine.)

But Gattinara, Ghemme, and Sizzano are made on a small scale and are not found easily outside Italy. Consumed mostly by those who make them, they have changed little over the years.

Barolo, Barbaresco, even the Barberas of Piedmont, on the other hand, have changed quite a lot. When I first went exploring in the region twenty-five years ago, I was more than surprised at some of the things I saw. Young wines were commonly left on the gross lees of their casks long after they had fallen bright, a practice that sometimes gave Piedmont wines a lees-y taste. Even when racked promptly, wines were kept in wood interminably, adding to the harsh, dry qualities of Nebbiolo instead of mellowing them. And wines bottled at the appropriate time, when mature, were often decanted into fresh bottles for shipment to eliminate any deposit that might have formed.

Once, touring the cellars of a distinguished wine company in Piedmont, I entered a room filled with an exquisite aroma. Girls sitting at long tables were decanting hundreds of bottles of old

Barolo so that the wine could be shipped bright to New York. Along with the deposit, the bouquet that had taken twenty years to form was also left behind. (I wonder if those who fuss about the natural deposit that forms in mature wines know what they surrender in order to avoid it?)

Nothing was as strange to me, however, as the technique of a winemaker in Alba. From oval casks I tasted his young red wines: without exception they were extraordinary. But when I tasted his bottled wines, even those newly under cork, I found them miserable—flat, maderized, and uninteresting. I soon learned why. He took me onto the roof and proudly showed me row upon row of five-gallon glass demijohns filled with wine "taking the sun." He gave this treatment to all his red wines for several months between barrel and bottle, a sure method, he explained to me, of guaranteeing stability. Pasteurization by solar energy is the way modern ecologists might describe it.

In order to persuade the grower to sell me in barrel some of the sound, young wines that I coveted, I vowed that once arrived in London, and before bottling, the wine would be transvased into demijohns and given the benefit of a Thames-side sunning above our Tower Hill cellars. The satisfaction of knowing the pleasure I gave our customers by making these wines available in an unadulterated state still barely stifles my twinges of guilt at so deliberately misleading him.

In recent years, there has been a revolution in the making of Piedmont wines. One generation has succeeded another, and new ideas prevail. Prompt racking, early bottling, careful aging are now the general rule, and it is rare that any wine made within the last decade will show the characteristics of old-style Barolo. The grower now aims to produce softer, fresher, fruitier wines. To my taste, these changes, in keeping with current practice everywhere, are improvements.

The difference between old and new was presented to me with unintentional but dramatic clarity at a recent dinner in Berkeley. A sequence of wines was served made by two generations of the Mascarello family of Piedmont, first some wines made by the son, Mauro, winemaker since 1967, and then older wines made by his father, Giuseppe. We started with a 1974 Nebbiolo d'Alba made by Mauro, a suave and elegant wine, followed by a 1971 Barbera d'Alba, which was generous, fruity and easy to enjoy.

The first of the Barolos, a 1970 from the family's Monprivato vineyard, was surprisingly delicate in style, as was the 1968, in which I caught a hint of mirabelle. Then we passed to a 1964 Barolo made by Giuseppe, and the old style was immediately apparent. The wine was woodier, and its complexity was matched by harsher qualities than the younger wines had shown. In a final 1961 we had a perfect example of old-style Barolo, with its strange suggestions of vanilla and old Oloroso.

The dishes that accompanied these wines were both unconventional and splendid. I was the guest of a music historian of some distinction who teaches at Berkeley and moonlights as a wine importer. With the chef of Il Pavone, he had planned a dinner of red snapper, poached in Nebbiolo and served with gnocchi no larger than peas; sorbet of Barbera wine and Barbera grapes; broth enriched with Barolo; and veal with herbs and truffles. My host told me how he had been drawn to Italian wine and food in the 1960s, while living in Bologna and working on his doctoral thesis. It seems he must have spent as much time ferreting out fine wines as he spent researching old manuscripts. When he returned to teach at Harvard, he put Boston wine merchants in touch with his favorite growers so he could continue to enjoy their wines. Soon he was departing for Italy each summer with commissions to find more wine that the world had overlooked, gradually slipping into the role of broker.

A few days later, watching him at work on a risotto milanese in his kitchen, I returned to our earlier talk of Piedmont wines. He produced for me a bottle of the 1970 Barbera d'Alba to compare with the 1971 we had drunk together at Il Pavone. It was lighter, with more bouquet and even a suggestion of bead on the tongue, a far cry from the stolid Barberas of the 1960s. Barbera d'Alba is not the most abundant of the three Barbera denominations (Barbera d'Asti is produced from double the acreage), but it is considered the best and the most fit for aging; Barbera d'Asti is finer and lighter; Barbera del Monferrato, perhaps because of the admixture of other grapes, is more perfumed but has a less robust flavor.

Sadly, many small growers of fine wines in Piedmont are inhibited from exporting their wines by the very procedures set up to help them. The bureaucratic controls imposed on all who wish to export wines from Italy, whether large shipper or small grower,

were established to protect the reputation of Italian wines overseas
—but they are time-consuming and costly. Growers who have
little difficulty in selling their small and highly sought-after crops
locally won't bother with the complications inherent in selling to
an overseas market, a story that is not restricted to Piedmont, unfortunately. My friend is convinced, nevertheless, that we shall see
more good wine arriving from Piedmont in the years ahead. Given
the quality and the reasonable prices, I hope he is right.

Chianti:
An Old Wine,
A New Shape

M Y FAVORITE small restaurant in Florence is hardly a guitar strum from the Ponte Vecchio, but, fortunately, its unprepossessing entrance is enough to deter those who would misunderstand its simplicity. It's just a crowded cellar, down six precipitous steps from an already obscure arched alley. But there one eats real Tuscan food—fresh and abundant. With it, naturally, the proprietor serves pitchers of young Chianti—zesty, sprightly, fruity, exuberant, and eminently quaffable Chianti.

When I think of Chianti, I tend to wax nostalgic about my little Florentine *taverna* rather than the fine estates I have visited because, like everyone else, I suppose, I have enjoyed Chianti most often in just such a carefree setting, without ceremony. This popular image of Chianti has caused problems for the growers, however, even while winning them friends; because there is more to Chianti than checkered tablecloths. Young Chianti in its romantic straw-covered flask might have been the greatest impediment to our discovering the fine, mature wines of the region, and the winegrowers of Tuscany have been engaged in a long, and sometimes painful, reassessment of what they want Chianti to mean.

The seven zones that produce Chianti are not extensive, yet they are diverse. Each one, tucked in a valley or fold of the Tuscan hills, claims a style of its own quite apart from the distinction, jealously maintained, between the *classico* zone and the rest. But one division cuts through all of them. On the one hand are Chianti wines made deliberately to be drunk young and traditionally bottled in the straw-covered flask, the very symbol of Chianti. On the other are wines so different in style, let alone quality, that the distance between them and the flask Chiantis is the distance between a *cru* like Moulin-à-Vent and simple Beaujolais, or between a first-rate Hermitage and a no-nonsense Côtes du Rhône. Matured in Yugoslav oak casks, such Chiantis are aged further in bottle— not in flasks, which cannot be binned, but in the shouldered bottle usually associated with Bordeaux wines and used, in fact, wherever red wines are expected to throw a deposit when aged. (The shoulder helps catch the deposit when decanting.) Chianti made for early drinking can be released for sale in March after the vintage, but quality Chianti (known in Italy as *vecchio*) cannot be released, by law, for two years. Wines labeled *riserva* must be held for an additional third year before release. In addition, of course, there are higher minimum quality standards imposed for both *vecchio* and *riserva* wines.

Though some parts of the Chianti region are better endowed than others to produce such wines appropriate for aging, most growers make both kinds in proportions that vary from year to year, depending on the conditions of the vintage. There is a practical reason, too, why growers prefer to make some wine for early consumption as well as some for aging. If the produce of an entire vintage were to be reserved in the cellars, first in wood and then in bottle, with others following in succession, there could easily be a stock of three or four years' production of wine held at any one time. Few growers could find the money to finance such a quantity; and, at the present time, when the finest aged Chianti will fetch a price not much more than the most youthful, there is little incentive for the grower to incur the expense even if he could. With at least part of his crop made into wine that can be released, sold, and enjoyed at once, a grower can pay his bills, and the cost of carrying the balance for aging is easier to bear.

Why would a grower want to age wine at all if it doesn't pay him to do so? Pride, the respect of his peers, personal satisfaction—

all contribute more to winemaking decisions everywhere than do plain economics.

Wine for aging is made from more rigorously selected grapes, perhaps from older vines on sections of a vineyard known to produce consistently high quality. But the conditions of each batch at the time of actual picking dictate what the grower will do with it. By varying the proportions of the different varietals used to make Chianti and by adapting his method of fermentation, a grower can either hasten a wine to early drinkability or reinforce the qualities necessary for long development in bottle. For example, all Chianti, no matter from which zone it comes, *classico* or not, must now have at least 75 percent of its volume from the Sangiovese grape, to bring body and aroma to the wine. According to new regulations that came into effect in 1984, there must also be at least 5 and no more than 10 percent Canaiolo, a black grape that softens the effect of the Sangiovese. If a grower uses even more Sangiovese, his wine will be darker, stouter, more tannic for aging; if he should take Canaiolo to the maximum permitted, his wine will be softer. He can now also introduce into his blend up to 10 percent of other black grapes, thus allowing increased experimental use of small lots of Cabernet Sauvignon, for example. But where there was formerly an obligation to include at least 10 percent of white grapes— Malvasia, Trebbiano, or a mixture of both—to lighten the wine and to give additional flavor, the law now imposes a minimum of only 5 percent (2 percent for Chianti Classico) with a maximum of 10 percent (5 percent for Chianti Classico), a dramatic change that represents a victory for those who prefer Chianti to be thought of as a wine for keeping, and not as one for mere quaffing.

Before the new regulations, each grower could make up his own mind about the *governo*, a practice traditional to Tuscany whereby the scarcely finished young wine, weeks after the vintage, is provoked into a second fermentation by introducing the juice of grapes held back from the original crush and dried in order to concentrate their sugar. The warmth and activity generated by the renewed fermentation encourage what we call malolactic fermentation as well. Naturally and effectively, malic acid (the acid, present in young wines in large doses, that makes green apples taste green) is transformed into lactic acid (associated with milk). After the *governo* a young wine tastes less harsh, and because the fermentation leaves a slight "bead" in the wine, preserved when bottling as far as possible, it adds that sprightliness, felt on the tongue rather than seen, that is so characteristic of young Chianti, and is why the *governo* is now obligatory for wines to be sold in their first year.

The differences among the seven zones of Chianti production are easier to recognize, obviously, in wines of the quality that requires aging. Since these are generally the best of the crop of each grower, they are therefore more likely to show individual character and style; furthermore, the aging helps develop these distinctive characteristics.

Foremost among the seven zones, inevitably, is the region officially described as Chianti Classico. It lies between Florence and Siena, on a gravelly, sandy ridge, the ancient heart of Chianti. *Noblesse oblige*: Chianti Classico (and to some extent, Rufina and Colli Fiorentini) must conform to minimum standards slightly more stringent than those applied to other Chianti districts. An association of growers had already agreed on regulations to control standards of Chianti Classico long before the Denominazione di Origine Controllata laws were instituted in 1967, using the symbol of a black cockerel to identify the products of their members.

Following Chianti Classico, the zones of most importance are those of the Sienese hills (to the south) and the Florentine hills (to the north), Chianti Colli Senesi and Chianti Colli Fiorentini as they are known in Italian. But neither these names nor the names Chianti Colline Pisane (near Pisa), Chianti Colli Aretini (around Arezzo), or Chianti Montalbano (near Pistoia) are generally found on wine labels. They are generally sold just as "Chianti," even when they are estate-bottled. Chianti Rufina, the seventh zone, with a special reputation for its full-bodied wines, should not be confused with Ruffino, the brand.

There was yet another association of growers, who became known as the Consorzio del Chianti Putto after the *putto*, or cherub, that they used as their distinguishing symbol. Founded by growers of the Colli Fiorentini, they too established quality standards for their members before the *denominazione* regulations were written, but they extended membership to *all* Chianti growers of *all* zones who were prepared to accept the criteria of quality that they applied. Today neither *putto* nor black cockerel has the significance it once did as a guarantee of quality because laws now impose on all those who use the name Chianti standards that were once accepted voluntarily by only a few.

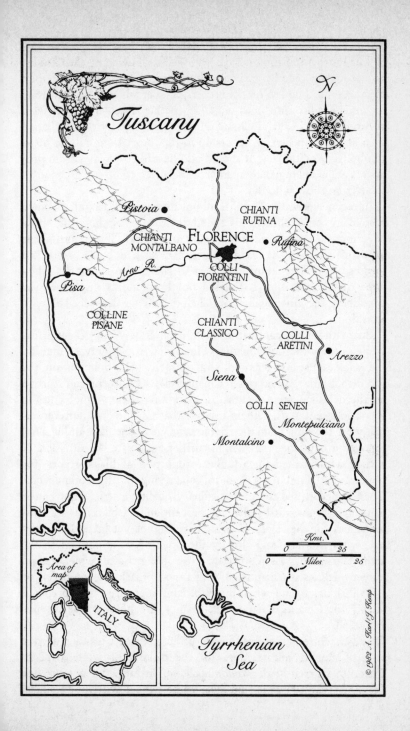

The Putto association has ceased to exist as such, and the Classico group remain together principally to promote the wines of their membership. The use or nonuse of the symbols can be confusing to buyers, who sometimes wonder whether absence of the black cockerel from a Chianti Classico means that the wine is less *classico* than another. In fact, membership in the association and use of its symbol is discretionary. It should also be said that wines from producers who belonged to neither association could be as good as wine from those who did.

In recent years, the flask has all but disappeared. Countrywomen who were once content to spend their days binding the straw coverings can now find more profitable work. Chianti producers have turned to an alternative, elegantly shaped bottle, restricted to Tuscany. They know that part of the charm is lost, but they hope that if attention is focused on the contents instead of the container, the finer wines of Chianti will at last receive more attention.

But without the captivating flask, exports of young Chianti fell, while sales of the finer, mature wines grew too slowly to take up the slack. Tuscany pulsated with fiercely held opinions on the problem. Some wanted to see Chianti follow California and certain northern Italian wine regions by marketing their young wines in liter-and-a-half jugs. Others insisted that Chianti had suffered already for too long from the frivolous image of the flask and wanted to avoid a container that would further aggravate the situation. It is they who pressed for a higher proportion of black grapes, for tighter yield limitations, and for qualifying tasting commissions. They hoped to see the more ordinary quality lose its right to the name as a step toward a changed perception of Chianti. With consequences for the region of which we cannot yet be certain, they have won the day, and already the price of wine entitled to the name Chianti has risen smartly. How the mass of wine that no longer qualifies as Chianti will find a world market when bereft of a familiar name, and what, in truth, consumers are really prepared to pay for Chianti, whatever its quality, are questions as yet unanswered.

Fewer white grapes used in the production of Chianti red wine will, of course, release more for the making of white wine in Tuscany. Currently the *denominazione* Chianti does not provide for other than red wine, and most white wine is without an official appellation. One of the finest white wines of Tuscany, for example, produced on the Pomino estate of the Frescobaldi family, is entitled to no *denominazione* at all, save that of plain "Tuscan white wine." Surprisingly, the first recorded use of the name Chianti was for *white* wine made from Trebbiano and Malvasia grapes; red wine grown in the area was referred to simply as *vermiglio*. Such was the case at least until the fourteenth century. How the red grapes infiltrated the white and took over the name is not certain. Today so little white wine is produced in Tuscany, compared with the large output of red, and so small is the proportion of it entitled to a *denominazione*, that statistics are scant and reveal little. Bianco Vergine della Valdichiana is the white *denominazione* most frequently seen. Roughly 7 or 8 million bottles of it are produced each year from vineyards around Arezzo. With a pale straw color and crisp, not-too-assertive taste, it is especially good with Tuscan ham and the local herbed sausage. Vernaccia di San Gimignano, better known, though of more limited production, is also dry, but more ample. Sometimes it has the pungent aroma and flavor of certain Sauvignon Blanc wines, and its fullness makes it an admirable accompaniment to pasta. In the summer of 1977 in Castellina in Chianti, I drank a 1976 Vernaccia from La Quercia with gnocchi in a sauce of Gorgonzola and Parmesan cheese and cream. Both wine and dish seemed to be perfect, but then each brought out something more in the other.

In an effort to promote white wine, growers of the Chianti Classico zone have now formed a consortium to establish Bianco della Lega as the eventual white *denominazione* for the region. A separate group of growers have formed a consortium to promote Galestro as the future *denominazione*. For the moment neither name has the force of law, but both wines are based on the traditional white grapes of Tuscany, Trebbiano, and Malvasia, with small proportions of Pinot Bianco, Sauvignon Blanc, and even Chardonnay. The Galestro regulations, self-imposed by the consortium who produce it, include a requirement of fermentation at low temperature and, most unusually, impose a *maximum* alcoholic strength of 10.5 percent, to ensure that Galestro is always light and fruity.

Supporters of the view that Chianti needs fewer white grapes in the blend are paying an unspoken compliment to the Brunello wines of Montalcino, within the Chianti region, south of Siena, but

defiantly sold with a *denominazione* of their own. At about the
time, a hundred years ago, that Baron Ricasoli was carrying out his
varietal experiments at Brolio, which led to the classic grape combination of Sangiovese-Canaiolo-Malvasia-Trebbiano for Chianti,
Ferruccio Biondi-Santi of Montalcino was experimenting with
wine made solely from a clone of Sangiovese, known locally in
Montalcino as Brunello. As one might expect, given the characteristics of the Sangiovese, it is heavier and longer-lived than traditional
Chianti made from its combination of grapes. Today there are
more than seventy growers producing Brunello di Montalcino,
including Biondi-Santi's grandson. Their wines have become something of a cult, older vintages fetching prices within Italy that exceed anything paid for comparable vintages of the classed growths
of Bordeaux; for as they age, Brunello wines seem to fill out and
develop in an extraordinary way. Recently I had the good fortune
to taste a series of vintages ranging from 1973 to 1945, all in the
course of a leisurely luncheon in the Biondi-Santi's kitchen at
Montalcino. We tasted examples of each of the successful vintages
during that span of almost thirty years, and it must have been more
than the chance style of each year that made them show better as
each wine succeeded a younger one. The 1945, with its deep, lively
color, was richly full-bodied, its bouquet and flavor giving delicate hints of cherries and vanilla.

The success of the growers of Montalcino has disconcerted the
growers of Chianti, for the former have followed not only their
own winemaking ideas but their own name, eschewing the *denominazione* Chianti to which they would have been entitled. Nor is
Brunello di Montalcino the only wine within Chianti to follow its
own course. Vino Nobile di Montepulciano has a history longer
than that of Brunello—in fact, it is as old as Chianti itself—yet its
reputation has remained largely local. A mixture of red and white
grapes is used, as in traditional Chianti, to produce a wine of elegance and velvety softness. I have not tasted Montepulciano wines
with more than ten years of aging, so I do not know if they continue to develop beyond that, but I remember a 1969 that accompanied a roast pigeon in a *taverna* of the town a year or two ago
that was as near perfect a wine as any I have had. Here, too, the
growers emphasize aged rather than young wines.

While the growers of Chianti debated their future, they continued to produce wines of uncommon grace. The *riservas* of the

1975 and 1977 vintages lent weight to arguments in support of more wine of this style and quality. Despite inflation, unpredictable currency exchange rates, and the host of other woes that combine to deprive us of so many classic wines, they were priced modestly and were among the most undervalued fine wines in the world. That is all changing now, and the prices of older vintages are rising to match the new. If we do not take advantage of our good fortune while we can, how shall we answer our grandchildren when they ask: "Where were you when the best Chiantis were practically given away?"

Chardonnay and Oak

TRISTRAM SHANDY'S mother, you will remember, received his father's affections on the first Sunday of the month because that was the day he would wind the large house-clock on the stairs, and with one economical jog to his memory he could then be free from all "other little family concernments . . . at one time, and be no more plagued and pestered with them the rest of the month." It is no wonder that the poor woman developed confused ideas and associations that had no connection in nature.

We can all learn from her difficulty: to confuse ideas that are only circumstantially connected is all too human.

As far as Chardonnay and oak are concerned, in California the two were brought together by the late James D. Zellerbach, one-time Chairman of the Crown Zellerbach Corporation and a United States Ambassador to Italy. For his eventual retirement pleasure he created, in the early 1950s, an exquisite rendering of a small, fine Burgundy *clos*, said to be modeled on the Clos Vougeot. He took his fancy as a simple *vigneron* far more seriously than Marie-Antoinette took her afternoons as a shepherdess, playing with washed and beribboned lambs.

Perched on a hillside in southern Sonoma County, Hanzell Vineyards (a contraction of his wife's first and last names) is just large enough to handle the grapes of the attached twenty acres of terraced vines. Zellerbach sought perfection in Pinot Noir and Chardonnay, the great varietals of Burgundy that he cared so much about, and he had the resources to leave little to chance in his efforts to achieve it.

His winemaking neighbors were amused when he insisted on using small barrels of Limousin oak—imported from the master coopers of Burgundy—for aging his wines. After all, perfectly good barrels of American oak were available. The French barrels, with the rustic splitwood hoops that distinguish fat Burgundian *pièces* from slightly elongated Bordeaux *barriques*, gave an air of sturdy tradition to the aging room of the new winery. The first Chardonnay, produced from the 1956 vintage, was matured in them, and eventually Zellerbach had a few cases shipped to him at the embassy in Rome. To everyone's amazement, including his own, the wine had the elusive but unmistakable quality and flavor that had always been associated exclusively with the fine Chardonnay wines of the Côte d'Or—or, more particularly, the wines of the Côte de Beaune within the Côte d'Or.

Much of the quality, of course, was a direct result of the care with which all vineyard and winery operations had been carried out. Pruning was severe, to limit yield per acre; picking—ripe bunch by ripe bunch only—was selective; fermentation was at controlled low temperatures—Hanzell was one of the first California wineries to adopt this technique, which preserves delicate flavors in white wines; and nitrogen was used to protect the young wines from contact with air during the complex procedures of racking, storage, and bottling.

But it was clear that the key to the characteristic that had eluded California winemakers until then lay in the Limousin oak used to mature Chardonnay wines in parts of Burgundy. The two main oak species grown in Europe for wine casks differ from those found in the United States. Whether it is that difference or the way in which the wood is subsequently dried, treated, and prepared for cooperage that subsequently affects the taste of the wine is still moot; but no one denies that the flavor extracted by Chardonnay wines from European oak, and Limousin oak in particular, is distinct and easily recognized.

At first gradually, and then more rapidly, other wineries in California followed the Hanzell lead. It was a relatively simple change for the smaller wineries for whom the investment required to put modest stocks of wine into French oak was of manageable proportions. The larger wineries, faced with the logistics of acquiring and housing several thousand barrels, in addition to the cost and the magnitude of possible error (who was to say that the different taste introduced by oak would be acceptable to a wide American public, let alone pronounce on whether *different* was also better?), approached the new dogma with caution. For this reason oak-aged Chardonnays first appeared from the small wineries and, in the minds of many, have become associated with the concept of small-scale winemaking.

Unfortunately, the converted in all matters are notorious for their excess, and in twenty-five years it has become common for California Chardonnays to be judged simply by the degree of oak in the wine. The taste of oak itself, often oppressively exaggerated, has become so confused with what should be the varietal taste of Chardonnay that many assume the taste of oak to be the taste of Chardonnay, and they can sometimes be heard lamenting the lack of varietal character in a wine, when what they really miss is the flavor of oak.

The circumstantial nature of the Chardonnay and oak partnership, not to mention sundry other digressive matters, was brought to mind when I dined with one of the partners of the tiny Chalone Vineyard, far off the beaten track on a limestone bench in the Gavilans in the general area of the Pinnacles. To accompany a delicious salmon—cooked in a clay pot and served with a sauce that was adroitly created from some homemade mayonnaise, the pot juices, and tarragon while we sat chatting in the kitchen—he served the vineyard's 1973 Chardonnay together with a 1970 Corton-Charlemagne of Louis Latour. Both wines were superb: the Chalone was huge, robust, heavy; the Corton-Charlemagne, soft, light, and unassertive as many 1970 Burgundies, both white and red, are inclined to be.

At first, I was so overwhelmed by the Chalone with its slap-on-the-palate, well-met, open style that the Corton-Charlemagne seemed prissily withdrawn and its flavor excessively low-key. But as I retasted and reflected I wasn't sure that I didn't prefer the Corton-

Charlemagne. The intrinsic balance of the wine had been scrupulously respected. No one had overlaid its delicate silkiness with a jot more oak than needed. It gave me aesthetic satisfaction and a jolt, too, by making me realize how easily we all fall into the trap of overresponding to heavily oaked wines merely because they shout louder. And, of course, it is the vociferous praise of oak for its own sake, rather than for what it can contribute to a wine, that encourages its insensitive and excessive use, so that it overwhelms any other characteristic and even, on occasion, produces a disagreeable, barely drinkable result.

The drawbacks to avoiding oak or to handling it with timidity, however, were well illustrated at lunch another day. Served to accompany sole stuffed with a purée of sorrel were two Napa Valley Chardonnays of the 1972 vintage: a Beaulieu Vineyard and a Chateau Montelena. 1972 was not the most successful year of the decade in Napa, but it was clear that the Montelena had good flavor and a moderately generous style that it probably owed entirely to the judicious support of oak aging. In comparison, the Beaulieu wine seemed light, and, unlike the Montelena and that earlier Corton-Charlemagne, each with its careful measure of oak, it showed little sign of oak at all, not even the touch that would have done so much to add interest now that its early fruit had faded. But the benefits of at least restrained use of oak have become obvious to California winemakers, and Chardonnays that do not rely on oak—and some of them are delicious when young—are becoming the exceptions rather than the rule.

A perfect example of the elegant balance between fruit and wood that demonstrates a winemaker's real understanding of the role of oak was the 1973 Chardonnay of Spring Mountain, which I had the good fortune to be offered twice when the wine was at its prime. It reminded me of the same perfect balance that I discovered in the 1971 Mayacamas Chardonnay—today, alas, hardly to be found.

In Burgundy, it is rare to find a wine out of balance in this respect; unlike so many factors of winemaking, it is completely within the control of the winemaker. Chablis, in northern Burgundy, follows a different practice from the Côte de Beaune. (The amount of white wine produced on the Côte de Nuits is insignificant and can be ignored.) In the latter region, oak aging is *de rigueur*: I do not know of a grower there who does not give his wine a period in oak, varying the length of time with the "weight" and style of the particular year and *cuvée*. In Chablis, on the other hand, small oak casks are the exception. There wines are both fermented and allowed to fall bright in huge vats, usually of glass-lined concrete. Large wooden *foudres*, holding anywhere from five hundred to a thousand gallons, are sometimes used for short-term storage; but the small cask, the *feuillette* of Chablis, was abandoned long ago and when found serves only to transport wine from cellar to cellar.

At least as much as the Kimmeridgian clay, for which the *grands crus* slope of Chablis above the little Serein river is known, this absence of oak aging establishes the style of Chablis—light and silky, soft yet dry. By their fresh, young flavor, Chablis wines are distinguished from those of the Côte de Beaune. It could be that since Chablis wines are universally crisper and more delicate than the plumper white wines of Meursault and Montrachet, trial and error through the centuries has shown that oak overwhelms these wines and should be avoided.

In the Mâconnais, it is possible to find both practices. Sometimes in the same cellar Pouilly-Fuissé receiving small barrel oak aging will be held apart from another lot stored in an enameled *cuve* until bottling. Generally speaking, it is the better wines, especially those destined for bottling by the grower, that will be matured in oak and the wines intended for sale to the local *négociants* that are kept in bulk. Since all growers believe that certain nuances of flavor are passed on from year to year through contact of their wines with their casks (though no one can be sure if the aromas originate in the wood itself or if it is the organisms harbored in the wood that provoke subtle changes in the composition of the wine as it ages), they become fiercely attached to the wood in their cellars.

Some years ago I found a batch of six hogsheads of Pouilly-Fuissé in the cellar of a grower at Solutré. At that time, following the disastrous 1963 vintage, Pouilly-Fuissé wines were in short supply, and all six casks were exceptionally good. The old man and I went through the ritual of tasting together, and we patiently arrived at a price that was acceptable to both of us. He had never before sold directly to a foreigner, and I sensed, mingled with a certain satisfaction that a wine merchant from London had sought out *his* wine in *his* cellar, the natural suspicion of an old country-man for one whose ways were unfamiliar.

It was the practice at Asher Storey to bottle almost all of our French wines ourselves in the firm's cellars under Tower Hill, and I told him that I would arrange for a local carrier to collect the six hogsheads the following week. When he realized that his casks would not be traveling the expected few miles to the cellars of a *négociant* in Mâcon for local bottling but to London and back, he became worried. I assured him that the casks would be well cared for, which was true; and, in what I hoped would be a clinching argument, I pointed out that if I sent other casks for the wine to travel in, as he wished me to do, the change of wood would probably change the style and balance of the wine. And that, I told him with more passion than was really necessary, would be a tragedy.

He was adamant. (For centuries the people of the Mâconnais lived a border life between the kingdom of France and the Holy Roman Empire, and few are as stubborn as they.) I told him I would go in search of the best casks in Mâcon and make arrangements for them to be sent up. The wine could be racked into them without delay for transport to England. To find what I wanted in the coopers' sheds took the better part of the next day. It was already four o'clock, and the February day was drawing to a raw close when I drove back to the house where the old man lived alone. He was not there, and his cellar door was shut and bolted. I drove in the direction of his vineyard, and from the road I caught sight of him, high up on the slope, guiding the plow behind his horse. I stopped the car and hailed him from the grass shoulder, but he didn't seem to hear me.

The freshly turned, muddy earth clung to my shoes as I started up the slope toward him. He *must* have been anxious to finish his plowing before nightfall, because even when I knew he must be able to hear me, he didn't stop. I drew alongside him and talked as we plodded across the field.

"I've found six good casks," I said. "They'll be here on Friday for the wine."

"*Je n'en veux pas*," he said gruffly, not even looking in my direction.

"But why not?" I asked. "Have you changed your mind about letting your own casks come to London?"

"*Non*," he said curtly. In two sentences he told me that it was out of the question for his casks to go so far, out of the hands of fellow Burgundians.

But my well-articulated arguments of the risks inherent in transferring the wine to unknown casks, of the importance of balance in wood flavors, had been only too persuasive. No less than James D. Zellerbach, the old man, too, hankered after perfection, and he preferred to lose a sale rather than risk destroying the well-judged balance of his wine.

California Cabernet Sauvignon

CABERNET SAUVIGNON was introduced to California in or before the 1880s with other varieties from Southwestern France, including those traditionally associated with Cabernet Sauvignon in the vineyards of Bordeaux and some, such as Tannat, used for less opulent wines grown in the Béarnais region closer to the Pyrenees. As in France, these varieties were seen as means to an end—the production of claretlike red wine—not as ends in themselves. No more than in France did California growers at that time seem to be seeking to make a "Cabernet Sauvignon," and, with rare exceptions, it was only after Prohibition, when attempts were made to break with European place names applied generically to California wines, that Cabernet Sauvignon became the name of a *wine* as well as of a grape variety, thereby confounding end and means in a way that is still not resolved. Most of us can only guess at the style and quality of those pre-Prohibition wines made from Cabernet Sauvignon grown in California, though a half bottle of the 1936 vintage from E. H. Rixford's legendary La Questa vineyard at Woodside, tasted recently, gave me some idea of how they might have been. La Questa's reputation ("the most expensive Cabernet listed . . . on most . . . California wine lists of the early 1900s," according to Frank Schoonmaker in

American Wines), was based on "red Bordeaux varieties planted," says Charles L. Sullivan in *Like Modern Edens*, "in the precise proportion as they were then grown at Château Margaux."

A half bottle almost fifty years old cannot be relied on, and when I broke the blob of wax that sealed the cork and poured wine directly, without decanting, I was expecting little more than a ghostly curiosity. To my surprise, the wine was deep red, almost opaque, merely tinged with terra cotta at the glass edge; there was that immediate and extraordinary bouquet with hints of chocolate, charcoal, and cassis we associate with distinguished classed growths of the Médoc; on the palate the wine was lively, intense, impeccably balanced. It was, in fact, among the best wines of Cabernet Sauvignon genre that I have tasted.

A more recent, and therefore more practically influential, legacy of California Cabernet Sauvignon has been handed down by Louis M. Martini, Charles Krug, Inglenook, and Beaulieu Vineyard, Napa wineries that alone from the end of Prohibition until the renaissance of the 1960s and 1970s ensured a continuum of fine winemaking in the state. During that time, they invested their skill and greatest effort in Cabernet Sauvignon wines. Remarkably, we can still see, within the scope of the disparate styles they chose, the seeds of all options available to winemakers today. They composed a theme that has since been taken up in ever widening fugue and variation. At Charles Krug, for example, Cabernet Sauvignon was unblended, and aged in well-seasoned vats and barrels; at Inglenook proportions of Cabernet Franc and, in later years, Merlot were introduced in quantities carefully judged to give subtlety without changing the essential character of Cabernet Sauvignon—a character further protected by aging in neutral German oak ovals; considerable varietal and geographic blending at Louis M. Martini, on the other hand, produced agreeable wines ready to be drunk early and with less regard for varietal purity; and at Beaulieu, of course, young American oak was used to dramatic effect on intense, unblended Cabernet Sauvignon to create the Private Reserve of Georges de Latour.

The contrasts in these familiar styles were etched in my memory at a dinner in the fall of 1979 when the 1951 Cabernet Sauvignons of Beaulieu Vineyard and Louis M. Martini were served with a 1956 Charles Krug and a 1941 Inglenook. The wines were presented to us in receding order of vintage—first the Charles Krug, with fruit so persistent and finish so soft that the wine left a sweet impression against which the Louis Martini seemed at first to be austere. It was certainly less direct than the others, but eventually revealed a youthful, berrylike bouquet that softened the wine and flattered the palate. The Beaulieu Vineyard Private Reserve that followed, richly preserving all those characteristics associated with Rutherford, with Cabernet Sauvignon, and with American oak that André Tchelistcheff combined into one of the most particular and consistent wines made anywhere, brought us more bluntly to the essence of Cabernet Sauvignon; and that was carried on by the Inglenook 1941, an immense, muscular wine, dark almost to the point of blackness, yet with bouquet unexpectedly fresh and elegant. Despite its size, there was no burn of excessive alcohol, no distortion of flavor or character: it had the perfect balance then characteristic of this estate.

These extraordinary wines of the 1940s and 1950s with an occasional glimpse or guess at pre-Prohibition production, remind us that Cabernet Sauvignon has a history in the state, and is certainly not a product of the recent wine revival. They provide a perspective in which we can better judge the potential and what seems to be the natural style of Cabernet Sauvignon in California. True, peroccupation with the grape is fostered by its associations with the great classed growths of Bordeaux (though none uses it to the exclusion of all others), a challenge as compelling to any winemaker as the Matterhorn is to a mountain climber, but that would soon be over if the wines to which Cabernet Sauvignon contributes did not so frequently touch our highest expectations of red wine.

In his *Bordeaux Antique*, R. Etienne suggests that evidence enough exists to show that today's Cabernet Sauvignon grape descends from Biturica, which in turn descended from Balisca, brought to Bordeaux in antiquity from the eastern shore of the Adriatic, where modern Albania now is. Pliny the Elder was familiar with Biturica in the first century and wrote (I quote and translate loosely) that "it flowers well, is resistant to wind and rain, and does rather better in cool than in warm regions," all of which makes sense to us today. Columella (according to René Pijassou of the University of Bordeaux: I have searched for the exact quote without success) confirmed Pliny's observation that

Biturica stood up well to rain, and added another attribute familiar to us—it gave wine that kept well and improved with age.

Cabernet Sauvignon vines grow not exuberantly, but vigorously, and, when properly cultivated, yield sparingly. Their buds open late, an advantage in areas prone to spring frost, as are both the Médoc and the floor of Napa Valley. The dark green leaves are indented deeply in a way that causes the lobes to overlap slightly, a varietal characteristic. Its fruit is most appreciated by winemakers for reliable acidity and for the intensity of color and flavor inherent in the tough, resistant skin. Bunches are small and irregularly shaped, but the berries are perfectly spherical, black, and tightly packed together. They have a high proportion of seed and little juice.

Cabernet Sauvignon grapes give a wine that is distinctive, and most who have tasted it would recognize it again even when blended with other grape varieties. The characteristic smell and flavor bring forth references to violets, black currants, eucalyptus, tar, and, in older wines, chocolate and charcoal. In California, vocabulary has recently been extended to include vegetables of various kinds, perhaps through a misconception of the French tasting word *végétal*, which means "vegetable" only in the sense that we distinguish plant life from animal and mineral. It should not be surprising to find echoes of fruits and flowers in Cabernet Sauvignon, however: all wines share at least traces of most of the acids, alcohols, and esters occurring in everything from pineapple to roses. It is Cabernet Sauvignon's richness in this respect that makes the variety such an important component of a great wine.

But Bordeaux has always been more concerned with terrain, with the "best sections" of a vineyard and what to plant there than with grape varieties as such and where to plant them. The great growths of Bordeaux, and therefore Bordeaux wine as we know it today, evolved from the discovery that a knoll of sand and gravel at Haut-Brion, though barely different from land that surrounded it, nevertheless produced wine of greater distinction. John Locke, the philosopher, went there in 1677 to see for himself, and described in his journal "a little rise of ground, lieing open most to the west. It is noe thing but pure white sand, mixd with a little gravel," he continued. "One would imagin it scarce fit to beare any thing. . . . This, however, they say, & that men of skill and credit, that the wine in the very next vineyard, though in all things seeming equall to me, is not soe good." Arnaud de Pontac, the owner of Haut-Brion at that time, was a man of influence and wealth, able to ensure exposure of his wine to those best able to appreciate and recommend it. The style of winemaking in Bordeaux changed to accommodate this newly understood potential as much as to adjust to new market needs, and claret was transformed from the uneven beverage it had been since the Middle Ages to what the London Gazette, in the early eighteenth century, referred to repeatedly, and with determined fascination, as New French Claret. But "if the *régisseurs* gave great importance to the role of the soil," says René Pijassou, in his 1980 treatise *Le Médoc*, "they gave no recognition to the virtues of grape variety as a factor of quality." In the carefully detailed working instructions left by Berlon, Château Margaux's great *régisseur* at the time of transformation, there was no indication at all of which grape varieties were to be used. At that time, white grapes were freely mixed with black in the château's vineyard (the white vines of Château Latour were grafted to black only in 1813), and Merlot was still unknown in the vineyards of the Médoc.

The emergence of Cabernet Sauvignon as the preferred grape of Bordeaux, after 1815, was probably due more to the properties of the vine than to the quality and style of the wine produced from it. Writing in 1850, Edouard Lawton, the well-known Bordeaux broker of the period, said that Cabernet Sauvignon (then referred to as Carmenet Sauvignon) had been planted in the vineyards extensively during the preceding twenty-five years because the variety budded late, a protection from spring frosts, and was resistant to flower-drop in wet and cold seasons. As late as the 1830s, Château Latour continued to experiment with all manner of grapes, including Syrah from the Rhone, and only in 1849 was there a policy established that, since terrain was of prime importance, selection of grape varieties was to be made in accordance with soil compatibility. Most Bordeaux châteaux today still use grape varieties in proportions dictated by the soil composition of their vineyards. Rarely do they plant varieties specifically with a predetermined style in mind, disregarding soil. It is in this sense, above all, that the soils of a Bordeaux château dictate the recognizable style of its wine. Bordeaux still thinks vineyard first and vine variety second. Though by 1970 Cabernet Sauvignon dominated the Médoc through the style it imposes, it represented only 48.6 percent of the vines planted there, and an even smaller proportion of the vines of Saint-Emilion and Pomerol.

In California, on the other hand, emphasis on winemaking rather than on grape growing has allowed, indeed encouraged, more play to a winemaker's expression of the character inherent in specific grape varieties, than to the style and quality dictated by a particular vineyard site. It is a difference of attitude accentuated by giving grape and wine the same name in California, creating an assumption, at least, that one should faithfully reflect the other. For some varieties, particularly most whites, depending on fruit aromas and flavor for their character and style, that might be justified. But Cabernet Sauvignon develops through the transformations of age, acquiring grace and subtlety, flavor and bouquet not present in its early youth. We value mature Cabernet Sauvignon wines because they *are* so much more than the fermented juice of a particular grape.

Yet even in those instances where much is made of origin— Martha's Vineyard in the Napa Valley, for example—its importance seems to lie in the extent to which it brings out the character of Cabernet Sauvignon planted there. Few California winemakers would be comfortable expressing the style of a particular vineyard, using without concern whatever grape variety or varieties seemed most apt to the location. Most, consciously or not, seek out growers whose vineyards give the greatest opportunity to express best the variety of special interest to them. This is notably true of Cabernet Sauvignon. Joe Heitz, a distinguished proponent of vineyard identification, says, nevertheless, that he "tries to make a first-rate California Cabernet Sauvignon, one that reflects the character of the vineyard." He does not say that he "tries to make a first-rate Martha's Vineyard, one that reflects the character of Cabernet Sauvignon." He thinks Cabernet Sauvignon, makes his wine from Cabernet Sauvignon alone, and is impatient with those who prefer to blend. "They look to France," he says, "when our soils and our climate are different." In one respect, at least, Michael Rowan of Jordan Vineyard in Alexander Valley agrees. "Vineyards in Bordeaux are traditionally on meager soils. Producing fine wine from richer California vineyards is a new art. We cannot rely on the experience of Bordeaux. The expression of Cabernet Sauvignon is changed here, and we learn as we go." Ric Forman, previously with Sterling Vineyards, also accepts that California's climate, in particular, brings out greater richness, but complains that it has been too often presented in a heavy-handed way, just for effect. "It is an added quality that we should use," he says, "but not to the extent of wrecking the inherent finesse of Cabernet Sauvignon. Bigger is not better."

The "heavy hand" originated in a system by which growers were paid for grape sugar rather than grapes. In 1975, for example, when a cool, slow ripening season delayed sugar formation, there were stories of growers who cut the canes to allow dehydration to concentrate low sugar in the grapes. Today, wineries often agree in advance to pay the price for 24° Brix grapes, marginally high for elegance, if they can retain the right, should they prefer, to have the grapes picked at a lower sugar concentration for the same price. In the early seventies, a "heavy hand" also reflected the eagerness of a new generation of winemakers to explore the extent to which they could push the varietal's intensity. A key sentence in the edition of Amerine and Joslyn's *Table Wines* then in use as a standard text at the University of California may have spurred them on. "The most common defect of California wines," ran its message, "is their lack of distinctive aroma or bouquet rather than the presence of any specific disease or defect." Whether or not that was true of wines of the Central Valley, the mass-production area closest to the Davis campus, it probably was never intended to refer to the limited production of coastal Cabernet Sauvignon wines.

"It was a time," says Warren Winiarski of Stag's Leap Wine Cellars, referring to the early 1970s, "when California winemakers were asking what Cabernet Sauvignon grapes *could* give, as opposed to what they *should* give." Massive, often charmless wines found ready acceptance among those who, often new to wine, allowed themselves to be impressed by scale before they had learned to recognise standards of balance, subtlety, and just plain drinkability. Dense, oversized wines matched the abundant enthusiasm typical of the newly converted. But such wines crushed any balanced, restrained wine tasted alongside them, so that the rosettes, medals, and endless accolades bestowed on them by county fairs, newsletters, and tasting groups further encouraged excess. The public, lacking guidance, accepted the rosettes and medals as recommendations, and were disappointed to find so many of them attached to wines that were unacceptably harsh and coarsely flavored. It was no consolation to be told that the wines would "live" forever.

Fortunately, the tradition preserved by Martini, Krug, Inglenook, and Beaulieu Vineyard, now strengthened and extended by others, continued, without fanfare, to provide balanced wines that perseptibly evolved from, and maintained, earlier styles. The point at which balance was again recognized as the key quality of a California Cabernet Sauvignon, as it is of any wine, was marked by the 1976 tasting in Paris at which Winiarski's Stag's Leap Wine Cellars' 1973 Cabernet Sauvignon was acknowledged the peer of any in the world. Stag's Leap had had some recognition in California, too, but the benchmark there at the time was still set by intense, exceedingly tannic wines that overwhelmed Stag's Leap in any direct comparison. European tasters had few preconceived ideas of how California wines were supposed to taste, and even fewer of the criteria by which they were being judged so articulately in California. Winiarski claims that he did not aim at any particular style for his 1973, but admits, at least, on reflection, to having sought moderation in all decisions along the way. Balance and moderation are now his consciously defined goals, increasingly shared by most other winemakers in California, however diverse the paths they use to arrive at them.

Balance in wine starts in balanced grapes, and Louis P. Martini says "perfect grapes grown in a perfect spot, would need little help. But not much in this world," he is quick to add, "is perfect." Martini blends to achieve the particular balance he prefers in his wines, bringing Cabernet Sauvignon grapes from his old vines in the Mayacamas mountains between Napa and Sonoma to add strength and a certain soft richness to the flowery, more pointedly acid, fruit of equally mature Cabernet Sauvignon vines grown in the cool Carneros region close to the Bay. He uses Merlot, too, to round out his blends, but only enough to arrive at the balance he seeks. Though it is an article of faith with him that no wine need be undrinkable when young in order to age, a Cabernet Sauvignon, he believes, is better for having all the Cabernet Sauvignon that balance and harmony will allow.

To Joe Heitz, "all the Cabernet Sauvignon" means *only* Cabernet Sauvignon. He feels that in the otherwise imperfect world lamented by Louis Martini, his own perfect grapes are indeed grown in perfect spots. "Blending," he says, "is all right for those who have to buy up lots here and there of what they can find. But the best wines are vineyard wines made from grapes where everything necessary is there within the fruit." André Tchelistcheff would once have agreed with him. Unblended and clearly defined Cabernet Sauvignon from designated vineyards was, and is, what Beaulieu Vineyards' Georges de Latour Private Reserve is all about. But though Tchelistcheff feels that a classic like the Georges de Latour Private Reserve must meticulously maintain its consistency of style, he now believes that softer, less assertive, more complex and more pleasing wines can be made from California Cabernet Sauvignon by blending, especially with 10 to 15 percent Merlot.

It is a philosophy widely shared in California; indeed, those using 100 percent Cabernet Sauvignon for production of fine wines seem to be in the minority. But with less than 2,600 acres of Merlot vines bearing in 1980, compared with over 22,000 acres of Cabernet Sauvignon, it is clear that California is far from the proportions of Merlot and Cabernet Sauvignon often common in Bordeaux. Freemark Abbey adds 12–15 percent Merlot to the Cabernet Sauvignon of its Bosché Vineyard wines. Charles Carpy, claiming that it enriches and rounds out the Cabernet Sauvignon, says "it also adds a hair of color," acknowledging that in California, at least, Merlot is often more deeply colored, stronger in alcohol, and richer in texture than is Cabernet Sauvignon. That is exactly what Michael Rowan likes about Merlot: "its concentrated, almost candy-like, fruit." "It is a flavor," he says, "that gets under the Cabernet Sauvignon and seems to push it forward, making it both more vibrant and more accessible." He uses roughly 10 percent Merlot in all his blends.

The strength and richness of California Merlot is a problem to Cathy Corison of Chappellet. She seeks a lean style for her Cabernet Sauvignon, picking carefully to keep grape sugar under control so that no Chappellet Cabernet Sauvignon need ever exceed 12.5 percent alcohol. "Merlot," she explains, "is sometimes bigger than Cabernet, and I trial-blend to check proportions to suit each vintage." But despite the problems, she would not want to work without the extra dimension of flavor and texture that Merlot brings.

In Monterey County, Bill Jekel, of Jekey Vineyard, uses no Merlot at all. He would, he says, if he felt his wines needed some softening influence, but learning to adapt to conditions in Monterey County—"so different from Napa and Sonoma"—he has also learned how to draw the best from the grapes of his Cabernet Sauvignon vines. A number of new factors came together in Monterey: ungrafted new clones of heat-treated Cabernet Sauvignon were set in a cool climate with low rainfall on soils that varied from sand and gravel to hard adobe clay. Greater control of water through irrigation was both a blessing and a disaster until the growers had learned how to handle it. On their own roots, Cabernet Sauvignon vines in Monterey were vigorous, but those who tended them, often new to viticulture, did not understand that the vines needed to be stressed at certain critical periods. Some say that improvement in Monterey Cabernet Sauvignon is due to maturing of the vines over the past decade, but Jekey disagrees. "We have learned how to handle the vines," he explains, "how to adapt our winemaking to the grapes produced here." He refers to better water control, fermentation techinques that drive off excessive aromatics, and aging procedures that bring out a distinctive style for Monterey Cabernet Sauvignon. "I don't see why Monterey Cabernet Sauvignon must taste like a Napa wine. All that is important is that it should be enjoyable. Local identity is part of the pleasure of wine."

Accepting such differences has not been easy in California. At recent public hearings that preceded labeling regulation changes for California (and all other U.S.) wines, one wine enthusiast, a lawyer, argued that he liked best Beaulieu Vineyard Private Reserve and fell into the common error of assuming that what he preferred must be, in some way, intrinsically superior. When he found that the wine was made from 100 percent Cabernet Sauvignon, he decided to campaign in favor of 100 percent Cabernet Sauvignon for *all* California Cabernet Sauvignon wines so that they could *all* taste like the Private Reserve. He was insensitive to the many variants possible and permissible in California Cabernet Sauvignon, and expected them all to conform to some predetermined type. As Peter Quimme (John Frederick Walker and Elin McCoy) said in *American Wines*, no one should "hold a wine's own unique character against it as if it were a defect."

The unique character of a California Cabernet Sauvignon, whatever it owes to the region where the grapes were grown and the proportion of other varieties introduced, is also based on the wood in which it is barrel-aged. The neutral German oak ovals brought to Inglenook by its founder, Finnish sea captain Gustave Ferdinand Niebaum, continued in use throughout the years from 1939 to 1964 when his widow's grandnephew, John Daniel, was in charge. Bordeaux wines, too, had been aged in Baltic oak until the early nineteenth century. Perhaps it was the British naval blockade of the Napoleonic era that first forced Bordeaux growers to use wood from nearby Limousin forests. Whatever the cause, the effect was to add a further strand to the flavor of a fine Bordeaux wine. In California, French oak was first used consistently, as everyone knows, at Hanzell Vineyard in the 1950s. Until then, redwood vats and American oak barrels had been the standard aging vessels. Both Louis Martini and Charles Krug had used well-seasoned barrels to avoid oak flavor, whereas Beaulieu Vineyard had deliberately included a proportion of new oak for the Private Reserve. "I liked the vanilla aroma of American oak," says André Tchelistcheff. "It brought a richer and distinctive style to the Georges de Latour." Beaulieu Vineyard Private Reserve still spends two years in American oak before bottling. Paul Draper of Ridge also uses American oak to enrich his Monte Bello Cabernet Sauvignons, and at Jordan Vineyard, too, American oak plays an important stylistic role. After normal fermentation in stainless steel, the Cabernet Sauvignon is racked into large American oak vats for malolactic fermentation before transfer to small French oak barrels and American oak barrels for aging. Michael Rowan finds the character that each wood gives complements the other, and each brings out a different strain of fruit and flavor in Cabernet Sauvignon. Ric Forman and Robert Mondavi use French oak alone, and both study carefully the type and condition of the wood they use. Mondavi tries to ensure that his top reserve wines go into new wood, as do the Bordeaux first growths. "I find it gives backbone and vitality to the wine," he claims, and uses it for the same reason that he prefers Cabernet Franc to Merlot in his blends (though he uses both). "Working with the French," he says, "has taught me that elegance and vigor can go together. I have learned what can be done to sculpt a wine and give it structure."

The different uses of woods, the what, how much, and if-at-all of blending, the choice of yeast and control of fermentation itself, the varied microclimates and terrains of California—all play their part in determining the style of an individual wine. It is easy to generalize and claim that California Cabernet Sauvignon is richer than its Bordeaux counterpart, and then be silenced by a comparison of Clos du Val's classically reserved style with the exuberance of La Mission Haut-Brion. It is easy to suggest that California Cabernet Sauvignon is "forward" and less durable than Bordeaux and then remember the Rixford La Questa 1936. It is easy to imagine that California Cabernet Sauvignon (as if there were only one) cannot match the variety of Bordeaux. Easy, that is, until we try to imagine what that one wine would be.

1980 and 1981 Vintages in California

W HEN WERE two consecutive years in California more wildly opposed than 1980 and 1981? The early spring of 1980 was followed by the kind of bizarre summer, with endless foggy mornings and bracing afternoons, that brings out songsters, humorists, and closet Californiaphobes. Unusually late, the wine harvest was declared to be "saved" by a welcome, if violent, burst of heat at the end of September that didn't so much ripen the grapes as it did dehydrate them on the vine.

A miserable start to 1981, on the other hand, was quickly forgotten in the balm of June days that encouraged vines to shoot with the fury of Jack's beanstalk. Cloudless days of a perfect summer brought an early harvest to a faultless conclusion. By mid-September picking was all but finished at a time when, the previous year, growers had still been searching for grapes—any grapes—halfway ripe enough to pick.

And yet, despite these extreme differences, as far as Cabernet Sauvignon was concerned, the two crops brought to the crushers at first showed surprising similarities. For a start, both crops had scant juice in the grapes in proportion to seed and skin; but, whereas the evenly ripened bunches of 1981 had remained small, with tight, undersized berries all through that consistently warm summer, those of 1980 had shriveled up just before picking. Both Cabernet crops had good grape sugars, too—one of the key indicators of quality in a year. But the swift dehydration that had concentrated the 1980 grapes to degrees of sugar even higher than those attained by the normal ripening of 1981 had concentrated acids and green tannins as well, and to levels rare in California. There is a Russian proverb that he who asks a boon of God should remember that sometimes He is listening; in that last fierce burst of summer in 1980, California winemakers got more than they might have prayed for.

"There was too much of everything," admitted Forrest Tancer of Iron Horse Vineyards. "All the components you could want for a classic, oversize California monster," added Rex Geitner, new winemaker of Robert Keenan Winery. By 1980 California wine-makers no longer wanted the massive style of prize-catching Caber-net Sauvignons that had seemed important to them in the 1970s and to find themselves confronted with the densely concentrated grapes of the 1980 vintage at such a time was ironic.

William Hill of Napa Valley said recently, with significance that still eludes me, "1980 was a year when California winemakers came of age." It was a year, and perhaps this is what he meant, when they had to do more than pay lip service to the newly fashionable wine vocabulary. Words like "powerful," "big," and "concentrated" were already out; newly acceptable words (we'll ignore the em-barrassingly inane "food wine") were "elegant," "focused" (also pronounced "directed"), and "well-knit." To most winemakers "elegant" meant lean, even light: "focused" meant wine with a simple, one-dimensional varietal identity; and, if "well-knit" meant anything, it meant a firm, clean-cut wine with its ends tucked in, so to speak.

When such words are used loosely without agreed definitions can there be agreement on how to attain the qualities they fail to define? Of two broad "elegance-in-red-wine" schools, the broadest was in favor of cutting back on everything that went into red wine from the start. Picking early, winemakers believed, would restrain sugar (and therefore alcohol); removing the juice from the skins and pressing as soon as vat fermentation was complete—and some-time before that—could reduce the asperity and bulk of tannin; and using wooden barrels with discretion would control enrichment and diffusion of flavor. The opposition preferred, in Rex Geitner's urgent phrase, to "shove it all in" and then, as he explained, to "peel away superfluous layers like an onion." The trouble is that some components, once in, don't "peel away" that easily, and others, more desirable, disappear almost without provocation when any attempt is made at selective refinement.

The long-delayed ripening of the cool 1980 season gave neither school much choice in the question of early picking of red wine grapes, however, and the freak heat arrived too abruptly to be taken in half measure. Those who subscribed to initial curtailment could do little more than cut the vatting time when juice and skins stayed together, hoping in that way to limit, at least, the corpulence of the year's intense, rather raw tannin. Even those who thought otherwise were still very circumspect in a year such as this, especially as the concentration of sugar and acid had already taken both beyond their control (with rare exceptions 1980 Cabernet Sauvignons are universally richer in both alcohol *and* acid than 1981s.) Varietal flavor, too, was difficult either to moderate or to modify. In cool weather Cabernet Sauvignon retains defensively a harsh pungency, which in milder circumstances softens to the aromas of black currant and eucalyptus that we associate with normal, fully ripened fruit. Concentrated along with everything else, this green taste, a shading of character neither better nor worse in itself, serves to heighten the stark edginess of many 1980s. Like late medieval illuminations, the 1980 Cabernet Sauvignons project little compromise of halftone; their jewel-cut brilliance glows with primary intensity. Even while admiring their chiseled composition and enameled definition, I confess to being somewhat in awe of such severity.

Conventional opinion in California wine country, on the other hand, holds that the 1980 Cabernet Sauvignons are superb and are destined to develop magnificently, no matter how glitteringly hard some of them might presently appear to be. Winemakers, in fact, are pleased about them almost without reservation. They have achieved at last, they feel, the lean structure, the focused flavor, and the defined composition demanded of them. Are they then not entitled to bask in the satisfaction of *quod erat faciendum*?

For those who have learned to suspect any promise to "develop magnificently," let me add that at a recent tasting of a number of the most highly regarded Cabernet Sauvignons of the 1980 vintage, organized by Joe Heitz of Heitz Wine Cellars, the undeniably bold character of the dozen or more wines there was impressively free of the brusque tannic excess with which such a style has been burdened in the past. Though Heitz Cellars' Martha's Vineyard, for example, and for reasons now understood, shows in 1980 little of the ripe eucalyptus aroma and flavor for which it is usually known, it is well shaped, impeccably integrated, and elegant by any definition. (For what it's worth, my own definition of elegance, in wine as in everything else, is the achievement of a desired effect with all appropriate economy.) Other 1980s there that day included Heitz's Bella Oaks Vineyard and Jordan Vineyard's, impenetrably rigid wines, perhaps, but of patrician quality and of admirable proportion. Beringer's Lemmon-Chabot Private Reserve Cabernet Sauvignon, particularly and uncomfortably difficult when first approached, opened up during the hour or two of the tasting to become one of those I liked most, a wine for which I am willing to accept the highest-flown prognostications.

Another much admired 1980, though not among those tasted that day with Joe Heitz, was from Burgess Cellars. Tom Burgess' wines in the past have been marred for me by scale exaggerated to the point of coarseness; but with this vintage he seems to have found himself, bringing to the densely incisive style of 1980 his personal imprint of generosity and flavor, free of the ballast he could well have jettisoned years ago. Impressive, too, for its controlled scale and depth of flavor, is the 1980 Eagle Vineyard of Sebastiani Vineyards, an augury, one might hope, of other splendid things to come. And hardly least of the 1980 Cabernet Sauvignons, Opus One, the Robert Mondavi-Philippe de Rothschild joint endeavor, also manages to combine opulence of scale with the surface gloss that seems to be a hallmark of this particular year.

Over the past year, casually and otherwise, I have met quite a number of 1980s, which, despite the characteristic intensity of the vintage, were nevertheless more forward, or at least more suave, than others. A warmer vineyard, lucky timing, some secret knack —who can say? But Clos du Bois, Fetzer, Heitz Wine Cellars Napa Valley (as opposed to their named vineyard wines), Freemark Abbey, and Louis Martini's Monte Rosso are among those that come to mind. Most others, though, seem to me to need at this stage aeration to unveil their delicacy of flavor, to release texture more varied than first appears, to broach, shall we say, their shell. Caymus Vineyard's Cabernet Sauvignon is an example of what I mean, and so is Joseph Phelps Vineyards' Cabernet Sauvignon (not to be confused with the tightly compact Insignia of the same year). It is only after decanting that the elegant proportions of Sterling's 1980 Cabernet Sauvignon can be appreciated, and the same is true of the smooth integration of Beaulieu Vineyard (though there they are old hands at taking on any style of California vintage and making it work); the appealing balance of Stag's Leap Wine Cellars, the etched delicacy of St. Clement, the otherwise unsuspected charm of Rombauer, the webbed finesse of Inglenook's Limited Cask Reserve, the well-enveloped structure and firm, fresh flavor of Iron Horse Vineyards and the Mendocino clarity of Simi's 1980 Cabernet Sauvignon are worth taking the trouble needed to bring them forward. (Opening a bottle to let it "breathe" is a useless if harmless ritual for this purpose, by the way. The wine must be poured into a decanter or jug preferably, but into the glasses if there is nothing else.)

Not surprisingly—for a conviction that vines must suffer to produce well stems from a mysticism ingrained at all levels of wine culture—California growers and winemakers and nebulous "opinion makers" were concerned that if a drawn-out season had given 1980 Cabernet Sauvignons too much (those late, torrid, dehydrating harvest days were conveniently blotted from consciousness) then it followed that 1981, mild, short, and angst-free, was certain to have given too little. Grapes that ripened so smoothly, they conjectured, would lack structure, definition, and strength of varietal character. (It will be a long time, I fear, before more California winemakers get the message that when the less articulate majority among us choose to buy a bottle of wine, we are not choosing to buy a bunch of pickled varietal flavor.)

In fact, for the more thoughtful of California winemakers, 1981 was a dream. Acidity was lower than in 1980, it is true, but not inconveniently so: Consistently warm days had rarely touched that blistering heat when acids burn out. More importantly, shoots and stems matured at the same easy pace as the grapes; tannins softened and sugars ripened in balance. At first the moderation of the 1981s was held against them. Gently agreeable and easily approached, the wines were thought, for that very reason, I suspect, to have shorter prospect of development, and were therefore ranked by many behind the more obdurate 1980s. (One respected East Coast critic actually lambasted California winemakers for the "lightness" of their 1981 Cabernet Sauvignons. I think he missed the point.)

No two vintages are ever quite the same, of course, but the inevitable comparisons between 1980 and 1981 California Cabernet Sauvignons bring to mind my early coaching as a wine trade student in coming to grips with the 1952s and 1953s of Bordeaux. I was given to understand that 1952 was the tougher of the two vintages; the wines were the more solid, the more concentrated, the more durable, the more masculine. (It was a time when such words could be used unselfconsciously, even in print.) My mentors explained patiently that 1953 wines were more attractive to my untutored palate because they were forward, graceful, feminine. They could not improve, of course, nor even last. Thirty years later it always gives me special satisfaction to notice how many Bordeaux 1952s, admirable in their way, are as unyielding as they ever were, and the extent to which 1953s, with time, seem only to have expanded in grace, charm, and liveliness.

If California winemakers really wanted elegance, focus, and integration, 1981, it seems to me, was surely the year that they could have had it. There was still controversy and hesitation over length of vatting time, of course, though a few more were willing to let juice and skins stay together a day or two longer, justifying themselves with the comment that perhaps in a low-key year the wine would benefit in some way.

Years ago, when the present cooperation between Robert Mondavi and Philippe de Rothschild was as yet no more than a beaded bubble winking at the brim, I had the privilege (and it was a privilege) of playing, for a few days, guide and interpreter to Lucien Sionneau, technical director of Château Mouton-Rothschild, as he quizzed his way through Napa Valley wineries trying to get a fix on what winemakers there were actually doing and in what way it differed from what he might have done in Bordeaux. Though the answers held few surprises for me, the persistence of certain questions made me think. Again and again he asked how long skins and juice had macerated together. Repeatedly he wanted to know how many egg whites were used to fine each barrel. (Egg whites are liquid protein, basically. Tannins attach themselves, and the filmy mesh formed not only draws out the tannin of the wine, giving it a softer, rounder "feel," but in settling helps clear organic particles in suspension, leaving the wine smoother, with a cleaner, purer taste and finish.) I could see that to Sionneau, the raspingly tannic samples drawn for him from barrel after barrel, in winery after winery, were perplexingly out of proportion with the short vatting times reported. His surprise was evident, and he was equally bemused at the low use made of egg white (one or two per barrel, usually in dried form, rather than the five or six common in Bordeaux).

The fear of lengthening vatting time here is particularly curious, really, when all California winemakers must be aware that in Bordeaux it is common practice to leave skins and juice together for three weeks in order to make red wine. Amerine, Berg, and Cruess, in their *Technology of Winemaking*, every California winemaker's bible, say, it is true, that in California "crushed grapes [should be] in the vats usually only about three to four days and rarely more than five days," and many believe that the overly tannic, gritty wines that California's customers rejected were a result of ignoring this basic teaching (and of other sacrileges, of course).

In 1981, at least, a few more were prepared to "shove it all in," and then to their amazement they discovered that, although tannic harshness did indeed increase for a few days, beyond that point something seemed to reverse the process. Perhaps the harsh tannins condensed and fell of their own accord. Perhaps there were softer flavors lurking in the skins that needed time for release, to mask the harsher tannins. Michael Martini, of the Louis M. Martini winery, told me that quite a group of acquainted winemakers tentatively lengthened their vatting time for 1981s, and the result, he says, seems to be wines that have a full round grace without being bigger or ponderous.

It is hard to say how many or which individual winemakers with 1981 Cabernet Sauvignons now on the market took the full risk of long vatting and, where appropriate, of heavier egg white fining. Michael Martini acknowledges the longer vatting and heavier fining of his 1981 Louis Martini La Loma Vineyard Cabernet Sauvignon. But many others, too, either to a lesser extent or on partial lots, vatted longer in 1981 and have succeeded in achieving a graceful purity of style. Only those obsessed with bulk will misunderstand the 1981s. As a group I find them the most consistently stylish Cabernets yet to come from California. If 1980s are intense and aloof, 1981s are charming, captivating, and *truly* elegant.

From every region of California and in every price range I have found few 1981s to be less than delightful, and most, despite their delicacy, seem to have the balance and stamina for long innings too.

It is difficult to list favorites when there are still so many for me to taste, but I have particularly liked Vichon, Neyers, Robert Mondavi, Joseph Phelps' Insignia, Charles LeFranc, Robert Keenan, Stag's Leap Wine Cellars, Clos du Val, Chappellet (which made an outstanding 1980, too), Iron Horse Vineyards, Hacienda, St. Clement, Flora Springs, Tudal, and Louis M. Martini's La Loma Vineyard. The 1981 Silverado Vineyards Cabernet Sauvignon, a first release, is particularly delicious—and it came as no surprise to learn that the winemaker, John Stewart, gave juice and skins a full three weeks' vatting, Bordeaux style.

But both 1980 and 1981 Cabernet Sauvignons in their own way have much to offer, and together they represent an important turning point for California, not just a pair of extraordinary vintages. Shouldn't we all, then, buy a clutch of each? How otherwise shall we have, in the fullness of time, the ineffable satisfaction of pontificating to our children on the mistakes people make when judging which wines are for drinking and for keeping? "Let me show you," we shall say, lighting the cellar stairs to look for a last precious pair of 1980 and 1981 California Cabernet Sauvignons, just to show how right (or wrong) we were, and trying to remember which vintage was supposed to prove what.

California Pinot Noir: The New Frontier

CALIFORNIA PINOT NOIRS have been criticized for lack of color, lack of varietal character, lack of body, and lack of staying power. We are told that we have the wrong clone, the wrong climate, the wrong soil, the wrong yields, the wrong yeasts, and the wrong ideas. We probably use the wrong gum on the labels, too. Such is the prevailing conviction that Pinot Noir and California are at odds with each other, that every example that demonstrates the contrary is dismissed as a fluke, and every winemaker who devotes time and energy to Pinot Noir is regarded as quixotic. But since 1969 the acreage of Pinot Noir planted and bearing grapes in California has quadrupled from some 2,500 to well over 10,000, and that excludes the acreage of Gamay Beaujolais, now accepted as yet another clone of Pinot Noir. Compared with the 24,000 tons crushed in 1978, the 1984 vintage brought in over 32,000 tons of Pinot Noir grapes, enough to provide for 24 million bottles—a rather large number to be wrong about.

Though it is unfair, and perhaps illogical, to compare California Pinot Noirs only with the full-blown wines of the Côte d'Or in Burgundy (there are, after all, light, fragrant Pinot Noir wines made in Switzerland and in the Baden area of southern Germany), most regard the wines of Burgundy as the best that Pinot Noir can produce, so it is inevitable that they provide the standard against which California is measured. Burgundian Pinot Noir— even allowing for differences from Côte de Nuits to Côte de Beaune, from grower to grower, and for lapses in standards in recent years—has a combination of strength and grace that is difficult to match. There are California Pinot Noirs that have the color, scale, and depth but miss the shimmering aroma, simultaneously insistent and delicate. Others that promise well on the nose disappear on the palate.

The most impressive Pinot Noirs I have tasted during my years in California seem to have had some common roots. Most often the winery grew the grapes as opposed to purchasing them; the vineyard was usually young, with the low yields expected from immature plants; there was always a degree of heresy in the wine-making (I have yet to taste a California Pinot Noir worthy of more than a pat on the barrel that has been made by the book); and the wines were aged, and sometimes partially fermented, in French oak barrels. Some of the Pinot Noirs I have enjoyed have come from wineries as geographically diverse and varied in size and style as Burgess and Hacienda, Acacia and David Bruce. Consistency with the grape is elusive, however, and, because there is constant experiment, few winemakers are satisfied and even fewer dogmatic.

Early in 1980, a few samples of Pinot Noir arrived in my office unannounced from a small winery south of Hollister. (Hollister is not what we think of as a wine town in California. It is a serious farming community of the kind where shopkeepers would be puzzled rather than amused by the current big-city fad for "merchandising" jeans and work shirts.) The wines, all of the 1978 vintage, were raw and unusually vigorous, with something of the closed, dark style of young wines from the Côte de Nuits. I had been planning a trip south to Santa Barbara County and was sufficiently impressed to start out a day earlier, allowing time for a detour to meet the man who had made these wines.

Josh Jensen worked in Burgundy in the early 1970s, following two vintages from vineyard to cellar. Convinced he could make similar wines in California, he searched to find a chalky terrain similar to that of the Côte d'Or, set in a corresponding climate. In the Cienega Valley, remote in the Gavilan Mountains of California's central coast, he found outcroppings of the limestone

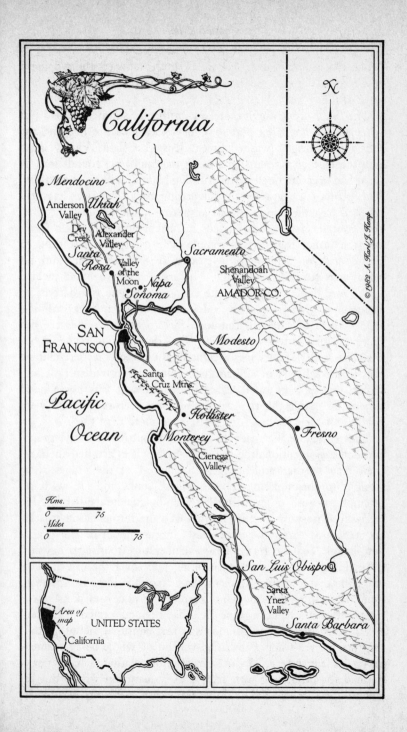

California

Mendocino

Anderson
Valley
Ukiah
Dry
Creek
Alexander
Valley
*Santa
Rosa*
Valley
of the
Moon
Napa
Sonoma

Sacramento

Shenandoah
Valley
AMADOR·CO.

SAN
FRANCISCO

Modesto

Santa
Cruz Mtns.

Pacific

Ocean

Hollister

Monterey

Cienega
Valley

Fresno

Kms.
0   75
Miles
0   75

San Luis Obispo

Santa
Ynez
Valley

Santa Barbara

© 1982 A. Karl/J. Kemp

*Area of
map*
UNITED STATES

California

bench that, some twenty-five miles south, supports the vineyards of Chalone. On two separate knolls he planted about twenty-four acres of Pinot Noir.

The day I drove down there was brilliantly sunny. We had just come to the end of a period of devastating rainstorms, and the hills were a bright, washed green. Jensen's Calera Winery is set into the face of a steep slope, using the multilevel foundations of what had been intended as the crushing plant of a limestone quarry. The plan to use gravity in pulverizing rocks has been cleverly adapted to winemaking. From grapes to must to wine, the flow from one level to another needs no mechanical aid. I felt I was inside a rather busy Aztec temple. We came to a scantling of French oak on which both Jensen's 1978 Pinot Noirs and his 1979s were stowed side by side. The first crop in 1978 had yielded little more than a ton, not quite enough for three full barrels. In 1979 his twenty-four acres had given him seven tons, still less than a third of a ton to the acre. His 1978s in wood were not quite as I had tasted them in San Francisco, though recognizably the same wines. The wine of none of the three barrels resembled that of the other two: all had good color; a Burgundian nose and flavor, but each its own degree of hardness. It was not a good time to be tasting the 1979s (they had just been racked and were tired), but they seemed to promise even more than the 1978s.

Jensen told me he made his wines by putting half the grapes through a conventional de-stalker, where rollers crushed them on their way to the fermenting vat. The rest of the grapes went straight to the tank in whole bunches, stalks and all, with no attempt to crush or even break the individual grape-berries. He introduced no yeast culture but allowed the fermentation to start spontaneously from the wild yeasts in the bloom of the grapes and encouraged the fermentation temperature to rise to a warm 92 °F. He didn't pump the fermenting juice over the cap of skins and stalks that soon floats thick on the surface but, like a Burgundian, punched it down into the wine, keeping the juice and skins working together until all the grape sugar had been converted to alcohol.

His reference to whole bunches at first confused me into thinking that he was using a modified version of whole-berry fermentation, usually referred to as "carbonic maceration," the standard method for producing soft, fruity, early-maturing wines. But his was an open vat, not the kind that traps carbon dioxide as it forms, holding the grapes in anaerobic suspense; and the style of his wines was neither soft nor early maturing. Jensen explained that adding bunches was a way of retaining a proportion of the stalks, a practice that enriches the wine with tannin and toughens it for aging. Most other winemakers who add a proportion of stalks first remove them from the bunches and sometimes chop them before putting them into the fermenting vat. It is a matter of convenience: whole bunches, even whole stalks, would jam the must pipe taking crushed grapes to the fermenting vat. But Jensen felt that stalks added "in the bunch" were less harsh and, more important, that whole bunches in the must released sugar to the yeast more slowly, extending the fermentation and giving a more complex result.

Jensen was trying to follow as closely as possible what he had seen done in Burgundy, but in allowing spontaneous fermentation in California he was taking a risk. Through centuries of making wine and spreading the residue back on the vineyards, Burgundian growers have encouraged certain dominant strains of yeast to develop. Though any number of others might find their way into the fermenting vat, each contributing a thread to the complex pattern of flavor that eventually emerges, the dominant strains take over quite early and bring the fermentation to a predictable conclusion. The University of California at Davis has taken a stand against spontaneous fermentation in favor of introducing known, selected yeast strains because California wine regions are too young to rely on local yeast populations. This policy of meticulous control has been a principle of California winemaking. The consistency and reliability of most California wines spring from this basic, orthodox attention to detail. But, at risk of being labeled a mystic (or worse), I must ask whether there isn't a point beyond which to know more is to understand less. Aristotle advised us to look for precision in all things only so far as the nature of the subject permits. Are not the subtle shades of flavor in Burgundian Pinot Noir attractive to us because they are fleeting, indefinable, and immeasurable? And, if so, how can meticulous control reproduce such mysterious qualities?

The main purpose of my trip had been to visit the Santa Ynez Valley. Since my previous visit four years before, wineries had been opened, vineyards extended, changes made. My first day of visits was illuminated by the enthusiasm of the winemakers. There were richly complex, barrel-fermented Chardonnays, oak-aged Sauvignon Blancs, Sémillons (at Santa Ynez Valley Winery) of a delicacy and crispness I would not have thought possible from this grape, and Cabernet Sauvignons from mature vines that, once released, will end once and for all the prejudiced denigration of this varietal from the central coast. The elegance and balance of the wines were remarkable.

Late in the afternoon, tasting with Tony Austin, then winemaker at Firestone Vineyard, I was shown a 1977 vintage reserve Pinot Noir, to be released the following year, that took me back to my conversation with Josh Jensen. In every way the wine was splendid. It had been made from a second crop of Pinot Noir grapes picked at the end of October in 1977, a gathering of small bunches that had been still green when the main picking had taken place, weeks previously. They gave a ton and a quarter to the acre, with better sugar and acidity than the first crop. About 25 percent of the stalks had been added to the fermenting juice, which had been allowed to reach temperatures in excess of 92°F. Tony Austin told me all this and then added, in a very matter-of-fact way, that the fermentation had been spontaneous. I was delighted (I enjoy piecing together hypotheses) and amazed (Firestone is a substantial and well-controlled winery). Small yield; some stalk; spontaneous, wild-yeast fermentation; warm temperature—and, of course, a year in previously used French oak barrels. It seemed a familiar story. But I had been struck by a new factor: the date of picking.

Pinot Noir matures early, and, in California, where it is usually picked in the first week or two of September, it ripens in the high temperatures of late summer. But experiments a few years ago examined the result of Pinot Noir ripened more slowly at cool temperatures with little variation between day and night. The grapes were enriched with color and tannin, properties inherent in the anthocyanins that were thus intensified in the skins.

I mulled over the significance of cool climate ripening to the late picking at Firestone as I drove to the winery and vineyard of J. Richard Sanford and Michael Benedict. Lying several miles closer to the ocean than do the rest of Santa Ynez's vineyards, Sanford and Benedict enjoys summer temperatures rarely past the mid-seventies and always at least ten degrees cooler than at the vineyards farther up the valley.

The winery, a modest wooden building, stands above the vineyard close to a crest of trees and was guarded, like the Capitol of ancient Rome, by a flock of highly vocal geese. Michael Benedict introduced his wines by explaining that his winemaking began in the vineyard. A third of their 110 acres is planted with Pinot Noir. At present he prunes to control the crop to a maximum ton and a quarter to the acre, as opposed to the three tons to the acre that conventional wisdom allows, but thinks he might eventually extend that to as much as two tons as his vines mature. Restrained yields are essential in a temperate climate to allow the grapes to ripen fully and to give the combination of sugars and acidity that he needs. (Three tons to the acre is not much beyond the limitations imposed for today's *appellations contrôlées* of Burgundy, but it is double the yields common there in the nineteenth century, when Burgundies were richer and more full-bodied than they are today.) After crushing his grapes into open vats of American oak, he adds stalks in proportions that vary from year to year. An evolutionary biologist and botanist who once taught at the University of California at Santa Barbara, Benedict is not overawed by bugs. He introduces selected yeast strains at the start and at a later phase of the fermentation, but makes no effort to incapacitate or restrain the wild yeasts that might be present in the must. The subtleties they introduce, he says, cannot be obtained in any other way. He, too, ferments at warm temperatures, in excess of 92°F, punching down the skins and stalks at regular intervals, but otherwise working to no special theory. "I read a lot, research a lot, and then use the seat-of-the-pants method," he says cheerfully. "You can call me an organic winemaker."

The combination of stalk, wooden fermenting vats, and longer than usual barrel-aging gives Sanford and Benedict Pinot Noirs more tannic astringency when ready for bottling than most other California Pinot Noirs. The winemaker tempers this by fining with egg whites, in line with European practice, using four or five per barrel.

Michael Benedict and I met again very soon after my visit to his winery. His Pinot Noir was one of three presented at the 1980 California Vintners' Barrel Tasting at The Four Seasons in New York City, along with wines from Beaulieu Vineyard and Kenwood Vineyards. Each presented a barrel sample of new-made 1979 and an example of an older vintage from the same vines. The comparison of wines and ideas was instructive.

Beaulieu grows its grapes in the Carneros region, a cool area close to San Francisco Bay between the Napa and Sonoma valleys. For their 1976 wine—one of those shown—they had taken a small yield, barely a ton to the acre. They fermented without stalks, at moderate temperatures, allowing no wild yeast activity. Kenwood's wines, on the other hand, were both made from the same patch of Pinot Noir vines on the steep Jack London Vineyard in the Valley of the Moon in Sonoma County. Again, yield was small—less than one and a half tons to the acre—but the vineyard, with a full-sun exposure, is hot. Robert Kozlowski, the winemaker, is emphatically against wild yeast. He ferments in water-cooled stainless steel at temperatures kept well below 80°F. Afterward, the wine falls bright in redwood tanks and is aged in French oak barrels.

The only factor that *all* these wines had in common was small-yield grapes. The Beaulieu Vineyard 1976 was elegant and mild-mannered; Kenwood's 1977 was big, with a rather voluptuous soft, fruity style; and Sanford and Benedict's 1977, predictably, was harder, with a complex, less direct flavor. The differences of style made sense in terms of what was known about the way in which each wine had been made. The uniformly high quality of the wines seemed to make sense only in terms of sparsely cropped vines. One thing for sure, though: there was nothing wrong with any of them.

Amador County, California

To NOTICE on a wine list that five of the twelve Zinfandels come from Amador County, better known for sleepy gold-rush towns and Saturday night fiddling than for wine, was a signal not to be ignored. Dining at Chez Panisse one recent evening, after a postcard Pacific sunset when the whole sky glowed and for just a few minutes the waters of the bay glittered purple, I ordered a bottle of a 1974 Amador County Zinfandel made at the Mount Veeder Winery. I didn't quite see the connection between the Sierra foothills and the higher reaches of Napa, but the wine was a revelation to me and could not have been more appropriate to the evening: darkly glowing with a rich bouquet and ripe flavor that seemed both to symbolize and to contain the heady cornucopia of California.

Amador County lies east of Sacramento. After twenty-five miles or so of flat valley the foothills rise abruptly at the county border, then Amador climbs in a long narrow wedge to the Sierra heights. It is said that the odd shape, rather like an elephant's trunk, was caused by the county founders' determination to wrest the Carson Pass road from neighboring Calaveras County. It was a lucrative toll, especially in the mother lode country, and any fan of Bret Harte's can imagine how they might have schemed to do it.

At the lower, western end of the county, Route 49, an appropriately numbered highway, meanders through spruced-up mining towns that have forsaken the streams and workings to make fortunes anew from macramé, herb sachets, relics of the forties (the nineteen-forties, that is), and cheerfully preserved inns and saloons. There is reassurance in the neat conical hills, looking for all the world as if Botticelli in a moment of whimsical generosity had scattered another Tuscany in the West, and it is easy to understand why the miners planted their vineyards and orchards here with the confidence of permanent settlers. By 1860 there were already five hundred acres of vines in the county, and the number continued to grow until Prohibition. Many of the miners retired to vineyards and cottages; even the notorious Madame Pantaloons, who mined at Jackson's Gate in men's clothes and boots (with delicate concern for detail), sold her claim in the 1880s and planted a small vineyard nearby. By 1890 there were more than a hundred small wineries flourishing in the hills.

The frost of Prohibition closed down the wineries. One of the few old ones to survive is the D'Agostini Winery near Plymouth. The old building, set back a little from the road, is made from locally hewn oak and stone quarried from a nearby hill. The vats and casks, huge ovals in the German manner with deeply concave fronts, were coopered by the Uhlinger sons, members of the Swiss family that founded the winery in 1856, and by John Davis, one of those men of the West whose origins are always described as mysterious but were probably no more difficult to explain than those of many another new Californian who just cut loose from whatever domestic ties held him east of the Mississippi to seek riches and adventure on the new frontier.

The D'Agostini family bought the winery in 1911 from the Uhlingers and started up again as soon as Prohibition ended. They began with barely twelve acres of vines, but they have gradually purchased and planted more as sales have grown and now have about a hundred. They use only their own grapes and sell most of their wine from the winery door. Twenty years ago, a prospective buyer would taste down the line of barrels until he found exactly the wine he wanted. "That one," he'd say, and they would run off the wine for him.

Those days are long since past, but the winery remains a simple operation with the charm of age and good housekeeping. It has the unusual distinction in California of being one of the few wineries to allow natural yeast fermentation. Normally, the strains of yeast attached to the "bloom" of the grapes that arrive at the crushers in California are so varied that they are unpredictable. A more vigorous, cultured strain is introduced to take over, and in this way the winemaker can be sure of the outcome of his fermentation, secure from off-flavors. But at D'Agostini's, as in Europe, a small quantity of grapes is picked early to make a starter—what in Europe is called a *fond de cuve*—and some of the briskly fermenting juice is then introduced into each new vat as it is filled.

Perhaps it is the almost continuous use of the winery (there was some activity there even during Prohibition), or the fact that the grapes are consistently from the same vineyards, or the isolation of Amador from other vineyard areas, or a combination of all three that makes this possible. D'Agostini tells of the day three or four years ago when the University of California descended on him. "They were in here tasting the wines, and they wanted to know what sort of yeast I was using. I told them none, and they wouldn't believe it. 'It's impossible,' they said. 'The wines taste clean.' You know, they expect natural yeasts to give a strange flavor. They asked if they could come back at crushing time and take away some of the must, and they studied it for about a year. They have a fellow over at Davis who's worked all over Europe on yeasts, and he traced our yeast back to Germany." He shook his head. "Can't think how it got here."

When the wineries shut down during Prohibition, there was a corresponding decline in vineyard acreage. Some demand for Amador grapes continued from home winemakers, permitted by the law, and considerable quantities were shipped to the Basque shepherd communities in Nevada, even as far as Montana. The home winemakers liked the rich style and sturdy sugars of Amador grapes. And it was through this home-winemaking connection that the renaissance of Amador came about.

The catalyst was Charles Myers, a professor of English at Sacramento City College, a keen amateur winemaker now turned professional on a modest scale. Myers had found his way to Amador in the early sixties and was buying grapes from Ken Deaver, the step-grandson of the mysterious John Davis. Darrell Corti, a Sacramento wine merchant, tasted some of the huge Zinfandel wines that Myers produced. By that time, in the late 1960s, the small Sutter Home Winery in Napa was making wines for Corti's own label but was being hard pressed by the rising price of Napa grapes. Corti suggested to Sutter Home's Bob Trinchero that he try Amador County, and together they went to see Ken Deaver, who still cultivated the vines planted by his step-grandfather. The first batch of Zinfandel from the Deaver ranch was fermented by Sutter Home in the fall of 1968, and, when the wine was eventually released, its success was such that Bob Trinchero virtually stopped making any other kind of wine and now specializes in Amador County Zinfandels. Because good news travels fast, other wineries followed. Ken Deaver, a tall, spare man with a wry country humor, is amused at the commotion. Not so many years before, he'd taken grapes on the back of his truck to the wineries in the Napa Valley, and no one would even look at them because they weren't Napa-grown.

I sat in the Deaver kitchen recently, talking with Ken and his son. "We always knew our grapes were good," he said, "but no one seemed interested. We liked to sell to the home winemakers because they would pay a little more for the ton. Otherwise we just hauled them down to the big Central Valley wineries and they paid us Central Valley prices, even though our yield per acre is half what they get down there and the quality is twice as high. The fruit of our Zinfandel even looks different," he went on, "with darker grapes and looser bunches."

In those days there was no question of a grower making a return on the value of his land; no one could think of replanting. All the work was done by the rancher, and he just hoped to have a few more dollars in hand at the end of the year than he had started with. But since then prices for Amador County grapes have risen steeply and now run pretty close to Napa prices. The quality of Amador grapes springs from the soil of the hills: a decayed granite, red with cinnabar and iron. And the style is determined by hot days and cool, breezy nights. The grapes have an unusual combination of high sugar and high acidity, and the wines they give are both robust and zesty. To discuss them in terms of alcohol, acid, and tannin, however, is like describing Nureyev's leaps in terms of muscle dynamics. Amador County wines have a vigor, a strength, and a warmth that is as much the essence of the California foothills as a finely etched red Graves is the essence of the drawing rooms of Bordeaux.

Ken Deaver was trying to remember the age of his vines for me. His acre of Mission was the oldest. These had been the first vines planted in the county and must have been there for "about a hundred twenty years." The Zinfandel went in later, "perhaps in the 1880s," he said.

Mrs. Deaver looked up from the pie she was making to correct him. "Grandpa was eighty-seven when he died in 1961, and he planted those vines when he was sixteen," she said.

Ken Deaver has seventy acres of vines, mostly Zinfandel, but within the last four or five years he has put in some Cabernet Sauvignon. While we sat in the kitchen, we drank a wine from his first Cabernet crop, 1974, made by Charles Myers at his Harbor Winery in Sacramento. It was a big, firm wine with the distinctive varietal taste of Cabernet subtly woven into the Amador style.

There are now about fifty acres of Cabernet Sauvignon planted in the county, all of it since 1969. But Zinfandel still dominates, with nearly nine hundred acres planted, more than half of which were bearing fruit long before the recent revival and probably even long before Prohibition. There are now scatterings of other varieties, too, particularly in the Shenandoah Valley. Shenandoah isn't really a valley at all, just a depression between two ridges; but it was given the name by settlers from Virginia, and it is there, at some 1,800 feet, that the best vineyards are concentrated. Along with Deaver and D'Agostini there must be twenty or thirty growers, some working just an acre or two, and others, like the Monteviña Winery, with almost two hundred.

Cary Gott, the driving force at Monteviña, was one of the first to try his hand at other varietals. He put in Cabernet Sauvignon seven years ago, and he was the first to plant Merlot, Barbera, Sauvignon Blanc, Ruby Cabernet, and even a little Nebbiolo, the grape used to make Barolo in Italy. He is exuberantly enthusiastic about Amador County and likes to experiment. He has tried sun-drying Mission grapes before crushing (like a French *vin de paille*) for a dessert wine; he has made "Zinfandel Nuevo" (Amador's riposte to Beaujolais *primeur*); currently he is experimenting with a sweet Sauvignon Blanc in the style of Sauternes. In his new winery, wines age in small casks, mostly of American oak. His 1977 Special Selection Zinfandel was as fine an example of Amador as you could get. Even his Ruby Cabernet, a hybrid developed by the University of California for the Central Valley and planted in Amador County by Gott, is a full, rich wine that would put some Cabernet Sauvignons of distinguished origin to shame.

With a small vineyard acreage—less than a twentieth of that of Napa—and a total production that can't exceed 150,000 cases a year on present plantings, Amador County wines are unlikely to hit supermarket shelves. But along with the wines of Sutter Home, Harbor Winery, Monteviña, D'Agostini, Ridge, and Carneros Creek, there are Amador County grapes in the blends of Zinfandel of several large California wineries. They are prized for the intense flavor they bring.

I asked Ken Deaver how he felt about Amador's being rediscovered. He looked at me for a moment before replying, "We didn't know we were lost."

California
Johannisberg
Riesling

THOUGH A CYNICAL observer might suppose that the sudden extension of vineyards in California in the early seventies was less a demonstration of confidence than a glimpse of the ingenuity we apply to protect taxable income, none could deny the faith of those who chose to plant Johannisberg Riesling. At the time, few examples of California wine made from this variety had created much of a stir, even though Frank Schoonmaker and Tom Marvel in the 1941 classic *American Wines* had predicted that the grape would produce one of the best American white wines when "given the legal protection it deserves." Perhaps they confused two issues. Whether the description "Riesling" should be restricted by law to wines made solely from the vine variety using that simple, unqualified name in Europe is a matter for debate; whether that same, true Riesling grape, whatever it be called and however much its name be borrowed and abused by varieties at best distant cousins, is able to produce wine of outstanding quality in California's climate is a matter for speculation.

Of course, if we were to believe Frona Eunice Wait, writing back in 1889, the question had already been settled. The quality of California Riesling, she said in an omnibus statement, was recognized "not only in California but [was] conceded by connoisseurs east of the Missouri River and in Europe." Her regard for eastern connoisseurship was no doubt appropriate, but her bounding enthusiasm for all California wines and for everything and everyone remotely connected with their production does give pause to doubt her critical judgment. Her book, *Wines and Vines of California*, praises so broadly and so lavishly the wines, vines, vineyards, hills, and dales of California, with long lists of the winemakers, grape growers, businessmen, and state officials, that I am reminded of the instruction I had from the editor of a small-town paper where I worked as a junior reporter one high school summer. "Put in all the competitors' names," he said tersely, returning my draft account of event winners at the local annual horse show and gymkhana. "We shall sell more papers if they all send copies to their friends and families." I expect that Frona Eunice Wait's book sold pretty well.

Riesling is one of those few grape varieties that have come to impose style on an entire region, or at least define it. And, by establishing criteria, it continues to impose itself even when combined with, or replaced by, similar grapes. Despite the variations of soil, climate, and grapes used, it is Riesling that brings recognizable unity to the cluster of wine districts that border the Rhine and its tributaries in Germany and France, just as Cabernet Sauvignon, present in the wine or not, makes coherent the many facets of Bordeaux, and Chenin Blanc, the confusing abundance of sweet and dry wine of the middle Loire Valley. Though the name Riesling is sometimes qualified—as in Franken Riesling (a synonym for the Sylvaner grape) and in Riesling Italico, grown in the border areas of Italy and Yugoslavia—when used alone in Europe it has only one meaning and refers to only one grape.

In California, that same grape is known in the vineyards as White Riesling, a name occasionally seen on wine labels, too. More commonly, however, wine made from the true Riesling in California (and elsewhere in the United States) is labeled Johannisberg Riesling to distinguish it from wine labeled simply Riesling, the latter sometimes made from Sylvaner grapes, with an obvious allusion to the Franken Riesling synonym, but more often from a blend of various grapes of greater or lesser Riesling association. There is even a California variety grown and sold as Grey Riesling, a local name for what the French call Chauché Gris. It is a respectable wine, but it is not a Riesling. Inevitably, there are many who feel, and with justification, that the qualifying word Johannisberg, obviously connoting the village and *Schloss* of that name on the Rhine, has no place on a California wine label. But the practice of using the word Riesling on blends has now such wide acceptance that it would be quixotic to hope to restrict it to the true Riesling. Attempts to revert to the name White Riesling, and thus avoid use of Johannisberg, have been less than successful. "So how does that make it different from other Rieslings?" is the usual consumer response. "Surely they're all white?" Fortunately, the style of label used in California and the obligation to include some kind of geographic appellation are enough to make the origin clear, and the continued use of the word Johannisberg on California wines is probably a source of greater irritation to purists and to growers of Johannisberg village in Germany than it is of confusion to the American wine drinker.

There are two reasons in particular why the European Riesling has been so successful in the northerly vineyards of the Rhine and Moselle. The breaking of the first tender leaf buds occurs later with Riesling than with many other vine varieties, a protection in regions where dawn frosts are possible and indeed common until May. And the clarity of the Riesling varietal flavor and aroma is emphasized by the effects of long, evenly temperate, northern summer days. Rocky soils and extensive surfaces of river water keep night and day temperatures close together within a range that ripens grapes only moderately rich in sugar, hence with alcohol that does not overwhelm either flavor or charm. At the same time, an absence of heat stress ensures a natural fruit acidity to perk the palate and contribute to the development of bouquet.

California winemakers have always recognized that similar conditions would be necessary if they sought to duplicate a German style of Riesling. But, although growers here look to European wines for style guidance and quality criteria, they know that California wines do not have to be identical to be equal, whether in quality (however we define it) or in pleasure-giving properties (on whatever scale we use). So, most recent efforts in California have been directed toward finding growing conditions for Johannisberg Riesling that will provide sugar and acid in appropriate balance to make a wine that is good in Californian, rather than in European, terms.

Recently I talked about the search for "best" climatic conditions for Johannisberg Riesling with Walter Schug, the wine-maker at Joseph Phelps Vineyards, a man born and raised on the Rhine. We had been discussing how the unusually cool summer in California in 1980 had given the state's Johannisberg Riesling growers their best opportunity for many years. Schug reminded me of the narrow temperature range within which Riesling grapes ripen best. "On hot Napa afternoons," he said, "the vines just shut down. The stomata of the leaves close up to prevent moisture loss as soon as the temperature gets into the mid-nineties; transpiration stops; and the sugar-making function of the leaves ceases as well. In those conditions the vine is stressed and loses its acidity." He thinks the best Johannisberg Riesling grapes will come from high, east-facing slopes where morning sun will get the temperature up to 55°F quickly, allowing the plant to function early in the day, and where, with luck, the vineyard will be protected from the western sun, missing the worst of the afternoon heat.

Idwal Jones, in his delightful book *Vines in the Sun* (1949), recommended "altitude, remoteness and a thin, rocky soil" for Johannisberg Riesling vines in California. He referred specifically to the eastern slopes of the Santa Cruz mountains down the peninsula from San Francisco, where the "white Riesling of Johannisberg is being grown under the green pennons of the redwoods." The very few Johannisberg Rieslings made from Santa Cruz grapes that I have tasted have not been sufficiently impressive to convince me of the area's superiority, though I have heard good things about a striking 1966 and a lighter 1967 produced by Ridge Vineyards in a German Spätlese style, both long since disappeared.

Better evidence of the beneficial effect of high east-facing vine-yards was to be found in Johannisberg Riesling produced in that same late 1960s period by Fred McCrae of Stony Hill and Lee Stewart at his old Souverain Cellars winery above Napa Valley. It could have been a coincidence that Stewart's grapes also came from McCrae's vineyard, but I doubt it. At a time when, to use the word of Walter Schug, California Johannisberg Rieslings were "klutsy," theirs were outstandingly delicate. In those days, according to Schug, most winemakers handled all white grapes identically, so that Riesling, Chardonnay, and Sauvignon, processed with little regard for the subtleties of each variety, inevitably lost whatever distinction they might have had. Today, despite degrees of competence and variations in individual practice, faultless winemaking, at very least, is universal in California. Thus, the measure of a Riesling's quality is more likely to come from the origin of individual batches of grapes and the trouble that a winemaker will have taken in his own vineyard or imposed on his growers. In short, whether the grower and vineyard are now named on the label or not, their importance is unquestionably recognized.

Joseph Phelps owns two Johannisberg Riesling vineyards, one close by the winery, about halfway up the valley and therefore moderately warm, and the other at Yountville, where temperatures are cooler. The winery vineyard often suffers from intense summer afternoon heat that will shut down the vines and wear out the acid. "If I waited for those grapes to reach a sugar level appropriate to Napa, the acidity would by then be so low that the wine would be flat," Schug told me. "But I can let my Yountville grapes hang longer, let them go to higher sugar, and they will still retain better acids than the grapes grown at the winery. They are not so stressed." He handles separately the grapes from these two vineyards, paradoxically making the lighter, crisper wine of the two from the grapes grown in the hotter vineyard because those are the vines he deliberately harvests early.

Robert Gorman, in his *California Premium Wines* (an intelligent and perceptive book that deserved much wider notice than it received when published in 1975), summed up the making of Johannisberg Riesling:

The first [way] is to make a very basic white wine without any elaborate cellar treatment and put it in large (preferably German) oak barrels of 100 gallons or more for anywhere from six months to two years. Most of the older California and German Rieslings were made in this manner. The method still survives in some of the more southerly German wine districts. They are rich, perhaps heavy wines (they have been described as Wagnerian), medium dry and soft, with big earthy and woody flavors. These are good wines for accompanying, say, duckling or rabbit.

The second approach is relatively new in Germany, the result of both a very sophisticated wine technology and some extraordinary vineyard conditions. The objective of this method is to produce Riesling which on the one hand is very crisp and delicate and on the other hand has great intensity of flavor and finesse. Very little, if any, oak is used in this method. The wine is intended to be very fresh and very clean. To this end, the Germans developed temperature controlled fermentation and special centrifuges to render the wine clean and brilliant without the need for excessive filtering. Most of the great Rieslings of the Rheingau and the Moselle regions are made in this manner.

Walter Schug believes these two methods should be complementary rather than mutually exclusive. The control allowed by the use of stainless steel is undeniable, but time in wood—not in French oak, which would introduce a flavor and style at odds with Johannisberg Riesling, but in more neutral German oak—allows the young wine a degree of oxidation necessary for complexity. It also gives the wine a chance to lose its rough edges, and the combination of this acquired complexity and softness contributes to the balance, so that residual sugar to offset the wine's natural acidity is only minimally necessary. Tony Austin, when winemaker at the Firestone Vineyard in the Santa Ynez Valley, agreed. Rieslings that have spent time in wood, he said, gain an extra dimension. He couldn't say why or how, but he believed some mark of the individual cellar or winery was then more likely to be present. His own Johannisberg Rieslings spent a short period in wooden vats specifically to develop a soft blur of fragrance rather than the single, rather floral, note of Riesling character. His 1980 Johannisberg Riesling, with its attractive hint of peach, was a good example of his style in a year when the elements were already in his favor.

In recent years, there has been a move to soften Johannisberg Riesling by holding down the level of alcohol through early harvesting. Alcohol plays a strange role in wine. At moderate levels it warms the mouth and therefore increases the perception of roundness and fullness, its presence helping to balance acidity. But at slightly higher levels the warmth sometimes becomes burn, and then the alcohol might harden rather than soften the wine, reinforcing rather than diminishing the effect of acidity. In California, low-alcohol "soft" wines are made by picking grapes when sugar concentration is still low but acid reasonably high. The presence of that natural acid allows the winemaker to stop fermentation by chilling or by removing the yeast in a centrifuge, leaving a wine at an alcohol level of about 10 percent with about 1 to 2 percent residual sugar to balance the acid.

Richard Arrowood, whose success with both Johannisberg Riesling and Chardonnay at Chateau St. Jean in Sonoma County has earned him wide respect as a winemaker, believes it possible to pick Johannisberg Riesling early and yet attain the varietal character normally present only in fully ripe fruit. There is a point, he says, at which the greenness of immaturity fades, and success depends on recognizing that exact moment to pick before sugar climbs and acid falls. His crisp 1980 Early Harvest Johannisberg Riesling from the Robert Young Vineyards, with slightly less than 10 percent alcohol, was a good example of his theory in practice; but I have to confess that I was more impressed by his two 1980 Johannisberg Rieslings made from normally harvested grapes. The 1980 Kabinett from Robert Young Vineyards, though higher in alcohol, was no less balanced, with superb firmness of style and flavor. Arrowood's 1980 Belle Terre Johannisberg Riesling is decidedly fuller, heavier, richer. It has less elegance than the Robert Young wines, but I prefer it to his 1979 Belle Terre. In the latter, a wonderful bouquet of tropical fruits led to a bony finish that I found inappropriate.

Though not presented specifically as "soft," other Johannisberg Rieslings that I have noticed in this style have included the delightful 1980 of Santa Ynez Valley Winery (labeled, no doubt to the satisfaction of many, White Riesling rather than Johannisberg Riesling), a pale, fresh wine with unmistakable Riesling fragrance; the 1979 Zaca Mesa, which was a little flabby for my taste but full and pleasing; and the 1979 Franciscan Vineyards' Johannisberg Riesling, with a bouquet so perfumed that it was more redolent of Muscat than Riesling.

In 1980, however, growing conditions for Johannisberg Riesling were such that balance came to the wine naturally and early picking was hardly necessary. Low afternoon temperatures left grape acidity intact, and, even when a dramatic heat wave struck northern California at the end of September, its initial effect was to dehydrate the grapes, concentrating everything there—sugar and acid—without changing the equilibrium. Those 1980 Johannisberg Rieslings, with 11 and 12 percent alcohol, were as graceful as any Moselle. Among many that I enjoyed (in addition to those already mentioned) were the 1980 from Raymond Vineyards, with its unexpected suggestion of honey in the aroma, probably a result of some botrytis in the grapes; the Alexander Valley Vineyards' wine, with its tingling, fresh, almost Sauvignon Blanc flavor; Hacienda, a more subdued but equally fragrant wine; Trefethen, with its strikingly intense fruit and slightly hard finish that augured well for keeping; Joseph Phelps, both the aromatic early harvest (bottled, appropriately, in the green glass of the Moselle) and the fuller-flavored regular harvest; Chappellet, with its sprightly, apricot nose, the first of these remarkable 1980s that I tasted; and my favorite (though I apologize for mentioning it because I understand that the couple of hundred cases produced were all sold within California), Flora Springs, a small new Napa Valley winery.

If it was a remarkable year for Johannisberg Rieslings in California, 1980 was not a remarkable year for *Botrytis cinerea*, the fungus that attacks the skin of ripe Riesling grapes and causes them to shrivel rapidly, concentrating both sugar and acid in a way that gives an extraordinary, luscious dessert wine with intense bouquet and flavor. Doubtless there will be late-harvest wines of similar sweetness, but, when the juice is concentrated only through the slow dehydration of grapes left late on the vine, the resulting wines do not capture the honey aroma of botrytis and frequently lose freshness. Too often they have raisin rather than grape fragrance, and, without the glycerine that botrytis brings, they lack the rich viscosity that turns sweet to luscious. For those who had foresight and stout purses (the best of these wines now sell at $25 and $35 a *half* bottle) the 1978s of Joseph Phelps and Chateau St. Jean will provide consolation while we await more propitious conditions. Just a few months ago friends shared with me their last half bottle of Phelps 1975 botrytized Johannisberg Riesling. It was an exquisite, golden wine, in both the literal and metaphorical sense, and we sipped it with a soufflé of ripe persimmons served with whipped almond cream. My diary records only that it was "a successful combination," but I suppose there are times when even I am at a loss for words.

Jerez
de la Frontera

ONE OF THE THINGS about breakfast in England that compensates for cold toast (whoever invented the toast rack?) is a chance to prop *Times* or *Telegraph* against the marmalade jar and digest, along with kedgeree or kidneys, or kippers, or sausages, those solemn accounts of human foible that the Home News pages of both papers provide in abundance. Enjoying a second cup of coffee and regaling myself with more than I deserved to know about my fellow men during a recent trip to London, my eye fell on the headline "Sherry is Top People's Drink." An opinion poll had uncovered the fact that though wine (presumably table wine) had now overtaken sherry by 1 percent as the most popular drink in Britain, sherry still appealed most to mature, "top" people, especially those who lived in the shires of the south and west of England and on the wide flat farms of East Anglia, a region where I spent my entire childhood without ever once feeling warm. (Copenhagen, the only windbreak between the Russian steppes and eastern England, is not very effective for the purpose.)

It was reassuring, in a way, to read that in 1979 England imported more than 20 million imperial gallons of sherry from Spain, compared with less than 4 million gallons consumed by the Spanish themselves and little more than a million gallons imported by the

United States. Of course, some of those British gallons, bottled in Bristol, found their way to American shores, but the figures alone show to what extent Jerez de la Frontera, the center of sherry production in Spain, looks to Britain as its prime market and explain the sherry shippers' optimism for eventual growth of consumption in the States.

But in England sherry is not just something that one consumes. At one level, I suppose, it carries an aura of petty gentility, but, to balance that, sherry has associations of urbanity, of donnish civility, and above all of the well-ordered, albeit old-fashioned, domestic life. In England, sherry is the symbol of hospitality at home. It is as right to offer a guest a glass of sherry as it is wrong, somehow, to order one in a pub. "Will you have some sherry?" is still a common, polite way to propose a casual drink, though it is understood that a guest is equally welcome to a gin and tonic or a glass of beer.

Asked for "cocktails" in England, no matter how deceptively low-key the invitation, one knows to wear polished shoes, collect the family jewels from the vault, and complete a few limbering-up exercises in smart chitchat. But an invitation to "come over for a glass of sherry" promises a relaxed communion of friends, comfortable shoes, and old sweater, an occasion that no one will be using as part of life's strategic game plan. It's a matter of familiarity: the English have been drinking sherry for centuries, and, even if Falstaff's sack differed from the sherry we drink today, there is no doubt we would recognize it.

The name of the wine is a corruption of "Jerez," and was first recorded in English late in the seventeenth century. But as words, particularly then, often circulated for some time before they found their way into print, it is likely to have been in colloquial use long before. Sherry started, and starts, life as a white wine produced in an austere region of Andalusia in southwestern Spain close to the sea and confined between the Guadalquivir and Guadalete rivers. The three sherry towns of Jerez de la Frontera, Puerto de Santa Maria, and Sanlúcar de Barrameda, about twelve miles from each other, form a triangle that encloses much of the best vineyard land.

I said *starts* as a white wine because sherry is as much a result of the art of man as it is a consequence of nature. It is nearly thirty years since I was first sent to Jerez to learn about both. I had a small scholarship from the London Wine Trade Club and a modest inheritance from my grandmother to sustain me. Today's jets swoop down to the south of Spain in a couple of hours, but in the early 1950s propeller planes had to stop for refueling in Bordeaux and Madrid. From Seville there was a long drive, and I eventually arrived after midnight to discover, to my northern amazement, groups of men still drinking and talking at tables in front of the bars and cafés of the Calle Larga as if they intended to remain all night, while streams of people, young and old, crowded the narrow sidewalk. Needless to say, I joined them, and six o'clock seemed to arrive as soon as my head touched the pillow.

When do the Spanish sleep? Not in the afternoon, whatever the popular mythology. In Jerez they drank sherry and nibbled on *tapas* until lunch at three. From five to eight there was often work to do, and from nine until eleven there was more sherry and *tapas* before dinner. Theater and movies started at midnight.

The bitter coffee and sweet rolls of a Spanish breakfast revived and consoled me, and I reported for work at Mackenzie & Co., a small independent sherry shipper now absorbed by Harvey's. Ramiro Fernandez-Gao, the managing director, was waiting for me in the tasting room, in front of him a line of tulip-shaped *copitas*, each with an ounce or two of liquid that ranged from almost colorless to a dark chocolate brown. Before we started to taste together, he explained that when the juice of the Palomino grapes finished fermenting, each butt of wine—in Jerez referred to as *mosto* (grape juice) until a year old—began to acquire a character of its own. Identifying that character, encouraging its development, and successfully blending it to a constant style that could be shipped under a recognized label from year to year without variation was the role of the sherry shipper.

The process starts when the foreman of the *bodega* checks every butt of new wine, drawing a sample with the aid of his *venencia*, a narrow silver cup at the end of a flexible wand of whalebone. Wines that are light, balanced, and clean are distinguished by a short stroke of chalk, a *raya*. Two *rayas* indicate a wine with less promise (between one and two there is a demigrade, *raya y punto*), and three *rayas* a wine that is harsh or inelegant, most often distilled for brandy.

The foreman looks for *flor*, the most important and distinctive influence in the making of sherry. *Flor* is a yeast that grows on the surface of the wine in spring and autumn. Butts are left with generous air space above the wine to encourage it, but the spores are selective and develop most readily on wines with a light, elegant style. In those a veil spreads quickly and soon looks like a layer of lumpy cream. Pliny, almost two thousand years ago, recognized that this velvety growth was not to be confused with the vinegar microbe. On the contrary, *flor* protects the wine from any vinegar attack, diminishes volatile acidity, and greatly increases the nut-like esters and aldehydes that we recognize as the typical sherry fragrance.

Once racked off their heavy lees into other casks, wines classified with one *raya* are again checked for their *flor* growth, essential to the satisfactory development of Fino-type sherry. If the *flor* is strong and the wine delicate, the alcohol is marginally adjusted to the optimum level, between 14.5 and 15.5 percent by volume, the ideal strength to encourage further growth. If the *flor* is weak or the wine less delicate, the alcohol is adjusted beyond 15.5 percent to discourage further growth of *flor*, a move that will direct the wine toward Oloroso type. The *raya* with *flor* is now further distinguished by a small stroke sprouting from the top of the larger one like a primitive palm tree, and the wine becomes known, in fact, as *palma*. Here, then, is the first parting of the ways: *palma* and *raya*, one with *flor*, the other without; the first destined for light Finos, the second, for more full-bodied Olorosos.

As Finos age, they darken from straw to gold and take on a pungent, complex aroma. Olorosos acquire a deep amber color and aromatic flavor. Each, in its natural, unblended state, is quite dry. Sweetness, when required, is added to a blend at the last moment through judicious use of *vinos dulces*, special wines made from Moscatel or Pedro Ximenez grapes. Color, too, is adjusted through the use of minute quantities of wine made from grape juice concentrated in huge copper cauldrons, dark and spicy.

With this basic framework Ramiro Fernandez-Gao introduced me to the twenty or more samples on the tasting bench. They started with a young wine that had barely finished fermentation and could still develop in any direction: perhaps as a young *palma*, eventually becoming a mature Fino; or perhaps a *raya*, with the possibility of becoming an Oloroso of great age. Then came a series of Finos, ending with those that had rounded out with age and acquired the style known as Amontillado. (Amontillado, unfortunately, is a name too often abused. It should describe those Finos that have acquired, with age, something of the round, earthy style of the Montilla wines produced a hundred miles or so northeast of Jerez. But they can acquire that quality along with a depth of flavor and a rich viscosity only in maturity. By its very nature a genuine Amontillado is costly to produce. Inexpensive "commercial" Amontillado blends, with color carefully adjusted and flavor judiciously balanced, might be satisfactory enough, but they can give no idea of what a true, aged Amontillado can be. To those who have never tasted one, it is a revelation.)

As a bridge to the *rayas* and Olorosos, Ramiro had included a *palo cortado*, a rare changeling sherry that combines the aroma of an Amontillado and the body and flavor of an Oloroso. As we tasted Olorosos of increasing age, I could see how their flavor deepened with the years to a level that the palate could not accept, eventually reaching an intensity that seemed to burn. Such wines need the soothing presence of *vino dulce*, or must be used only in small amounts to give complexity to a blend. For the most part we worked with the nose alone, but, as the session was intended to teach, every wine was also tasted, often two or three times to get the differences clearly fixed in my mind. We finished by tasting unblended examples of *vinos dulces* and aged *vino de color*. It was an exhausting morning.

There was to be a reward for my effort. The last big fight of the season was to take place that afternoon in the Seville bull ring. Swept off along the dusty highway without discussion, I had no time to ask myself whether or not a bullfight was something to relish. We ate lunch in Seville at the Hotel Madrid. I have never been back, and I fantasize against all probability that it is still there, unchanged. Built like a Moorish palace, its façade glittering with multicolored tiles on a narrow side street and its cloistered interior a lush, tropical garden, the Madrid at that time was popular with the Spanish movie world. We sipped our sherry under the shady arcade of the patio while actors with somber Byronic faces gestured melodramatically and actresses, softly rustling silk dresses in clouds of perfume, arched their heads gracefully, a posture necessary, perhaps, to support the weight of their extravagant eyelashes. I was young and impressionable, and they seemed to me to be infinitely exotic.

The *corrida* was an exhilarating spectacle, despite its uglier passages. Ramiro kindly explained the language and tradition of the ring, the sequence of moves, the ritual. As the matador played the bull to show his complete control, the band struck up a *paso doble*, and the crowd threw an *olé* of encouragement and admiration at each turn of the cape. For a moment I felt myself part of an audience that had been sitting in that ring (or another) for several thousand years watching bulls, acrobats, and bravura.

We returned to Jerez to dine late at the Fernandez-Gao home, where I made the acquaintance of a typical Jerez *crema*, richer in color and taste than the usual *crème caramel* because the egg whites used for fining the wines leave huge quantities of yolks for cooking, and in Jerez they find their way into just about everything. I suppose cholesterol hadn't been invented.

At seven the next morning I was in the *bodega* and ready to learn about the *solera* system of blending sherry. "The basis of the system," Ramiro explained, "is that a small quantity of suitable young wine, blended with a larger quantity of older wine, will in a short time be absorbed into the style of the older wine. It will be easier to understand," he said, "if you imagine ten butts of sherry blended and aged to a certain required style. It would be very difficult, if not impossible, to replace those butts with wine from later vintages and expect that there would be no appreciable difference."

The problem is avoided by not selling off the ten butts, one at a time, but by selling a butt drawn in small quantities from each of the ten and filling the ullages with quantities drawn from a second rank of ten butts, slightly younger, ready for this very purpose. The second rank in turn is filled from ten other butts, and so on back to selected one-year-old wines chosen for their style to enter the "scales" of this particular system, *palma* or *raya*, as appropriate for Fino or Oloroso. The series of preparatory scales in the system is known collectively as a *criadera*, best translated as "nursery." The final scale, "the row of butts" from which the wine is actually drawn for blending or bottling, is known as the *solera*, or "foundation." On a blackboard Ramiro drew a diagram with scales of butts stacked one upon another, pointing to them as he explained again how sherry would be transferred, a little at a time, from one scale to another as the sherry aged and as the *solera* of the system needed replenishment.

When I seemed to understand the theory, he explained that in practice the different scales of a *criadera* might be widely separated in different sections of the *bodega*; that a *solera* providing the basis for a popular brand of sherry might have several hundred butts in each scale of its *criadera*; and that the final stage, the *solera* itself of a particular system, might be both a source of wine for a blend and the initiating source for the *criadera* of yet another *solera* system, aging some of the wine to an even higher level.

Finos, he told me, present special problems. By law no sherry can be sold before it is three years old, but Finos, to retain their freshness during that period, must be moved constantly and rapidly through a *solera* system to keep the *flor* refreshed. Because the moves are frequent, the quantities each time need to be small so as not to change the style of wine in each butt. And, because the process must continue over such a long time for the wine to conform truly to the required style of the *solera*, a Fino *criadera* needs many scales with many butts in each. There is much labor in producing a mature Fino.

The relationship between sales volume and its demands on the *solera* systems in any *bodega* is crucial. Sudden, large shipments would deplete the *soleras* and *criaderas* too quickly, and, even if quality didn't decline, the styles of each *solera* could suddenly change. Recognizing that, the Spanish appellation law for sherry, unlike any other, restricts a *bodega* to selling no more than 40 percent of its stock in any one year.

Wines drawn from a single *solera*, however, are rarely bottled and shipped without further blending. A *solera* might provide the basis of a particular blend, but added to it will be a proportion of wine from a second *solera*, perhaps, or some young wine not yet part of a *solera*. The formula for making each standard blend for shipment might require the addition of Pedro Ximenez wine to adjust sweetness or *vino de color* to reach a standard hue. My morning ended with some practical work in the tasting room, learning how to use the various *soleras* and other wines to match samples sent from England and Holland for price quotations.

Gradually my days took on a Spanish measure. In free time I explored the narrow streets between the Calle Larga and Alcazar, the old Moorish citadel of Jerez. I roamed the undulating vineyards planted in the improbably white *albariza* soil of Jerez Superior. I walked in blazing sun to visit the town's remote Carthusian monastery. For a short time I was sent to work with another shipper in Puerto de Santa Maria in a *bodega* that specialized in Finos. (While there I lodged in an old hotel, where at three every morning a servant arrived to light a small wood-burning stove in my bath-

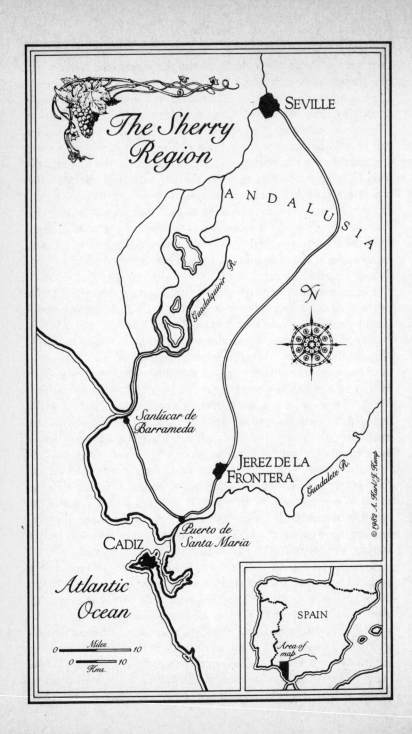

room so that I could have hot water at six. I offered to bathe at night to make life simpler for them, but they wouldn't hear of it.) Closer to the ocean, with cooler temperatures, Puerto de Santa Maria shippers emphasize their Fino and Amontillado sherries, which do well there. But the difference from the Finos of Jerez is barely perceptible when both are compared to the Finos of Sanlúcar de Barrameda, the third of the sherry towns, on the estuary of the Guadalquivir. There the wines have a light, brisk pungency that sets them apart. Manzanillas (as they are called) of Sanlúcar are made from Palomino grapes picked at least two weeks before the general harvest. Partly because of this premature picking and partly the result of cool sea air over the estuary, Manzanilla has unusual zest and fragrance. And then the alcohol of Manzanilla is slightly lower than that of other Fino sherries, an aid, perhaps, to preserving its delicacy and its penetrating bouquet.

Manzanilla was at its best on Juan's jetty at Sanlúcar. Juan is now dead, alas, and the fishing boats unload a mile away. But in those days the fishermen landed their catch on the beach below, and it was understood that the best was reserved for him. While waiting at rickety wooden tables in the salty air, his customers could watch the fish, still palpitating, on their way to the kitchen in his small house across the street. With a bowl of small green olives or a dish of prawns, a platter of fried octopus rings or morsels of swordfish to stave off hunger and a bottle of Manzanilla on ice to generate patience, time passed quickly.

And so it had. My coffee was cold and I had lost half the morning in reverie. It was time to check my host's cellar to see what he had in the way of a decent sherry for lunch. I hoped he would qualify as a top person.

Wine at Its Best

ONE REASON I admire Michael Broadbent's *The Great Vintage Wine Book* is the proof it offers that notes he had taken over many years were entered with discipline into a system that provided for organized retrieval. "There's a note on that wine here somewhere," I bluster as I rummage through files of stained menus, scribbled notebooks and diaries, and well-intentioned but rarely complete three-by-five cards. Compulsive friends urge me to install a computer word processor that would instantly provide chapter and verse on any wine I ever drank with lamb chops, should I need to know. Or on every 1962 wine that was used to precede a 1955, or on every 1955 that was not preceded by a 1962, or on every 1962 that was served with lamb chops, or, indeed, on any combination of wine and wine or wine and food that I might want to recall. If the information is not promptly and correctly recorded in the first place, however, there is no help for it, and that is where most systems break down, including those based on electronic marvels. (But not Michael Broadbent's, obviously.)

I have considered clerical help to copy notes onto my indexed cards, and that would be possible if my handwriting were not so fiendish. But then I would lose what I consider to be the greatest benefit of note-taking: As I transfer an opinion of a wine to the appropriate card, I can't help but see what I thought of it six months, six weeks, or even six days before. On occasion wines that I have noted to be dull will subsequently appear to be quite lively, whereas others that I admired for their style will later impress me (if at all) as clumsy. Regular sessions to bring my cards up to date frequently end with old diaries and notebooks strewn about the room while I look for an original note that will shed light on why an Haut-Brion '67, let's say, was "light, elegant" in February in New York yet "big, full" in May in Colorado Springs. It is a useful exercise in humility, in the unpredictability of wine, and, most of all, in the effect of context. Change an accompanying dish, change the preceding wine, change expectation and atmosphere, and any wine takes on a new personality.

It is because no wine is a constant that I take special care if I want a great bottle, in particular, to show well. A common mistake, I find, apart from fussing it with food thought to be appropriate for the occasion but too often distractingly overelaborate, is to decide that one important bottle deserves another. Instead of a lesser wine preparing its arrival and thereby gracefully confirming its stature, another great wine (and sometimes several) will precede and accompany it. In competition, each wine will almost always throw into relief the flaws of the other rather than illuminate its qualities.

Sometimes, of course, two great wines are brought together deliberately for the sake of comparison or a number of wines of a vintage are poured together to see what common bond the year established. But that is done for intellectual satisfaction rather than sensual pleasure; even the wine one prefers cannot be enjoyed in peace, as it were, because of the claims for attention of so many others. One wine put in the shade of another can hardly be enjoyed properly at all, though it might have had much to offer if served to shine rather than to compete. Many times I have come away from dinners regretting lovely wines dimmed in unfortunate conjugations. Harry Yoxall made the point well in his book *The Enjoyment of Wine*. "It is undesirable to serve several great wines at the same meal, except for some memorable banquet," he said, "just as you do not want a cast of *prime donne* except for grand opera. The great wines are apt to kill each other, as the *prime donne* would doubtless like to."

Conventional wisdom urges that young red wine be served before old, but light before full-bodied. If the younger wine is too big or too vigorous, an older one will seem thin and weary. (Reversing the order won't help: A delicate older wine can make a fine young wine that follows seem coarse.) Bordeaux of a light year, say 1973, makes a following 1967 seem bigger and therefore expands its other qualities, but a vigorous 1975 defeats the 1967 before it has even been tasted. A fine 1950 Bordeaux met after a light 1960 is adequate rebuke to those who insist on 1950s merely middling reputation; the same wine after a 1953 of appropriate stature confirms every prejudice. A first wine, in short, while giving pleasure (what else is any wine for?) should always prepare to enhance the qualities of the second so that they might be more fully appreciated. It should not raise expectations irrelevant to a following wine: It should not show scale before elegance, heady fruit before a complex, discreet bouquet, power before delicacy.

A few weekends ago, unexpectedly in New York, I was invited to join two friends who planned a casual dinner at a steak house off Madison Avenue. One of them had brought two bottles of Carruades de Lafite, freshly decanted: one bottle of the 1966, the other of the 1962 vintage. Bordeaux wines of the 1966 vintage have a spare style that presently can border on the austere. When first poured the Carruades '66 was edgy and tannic. The 1962, poured at the same time, was softly delicate and seemed at first to be faded. Opening up in the glass against a prime rib of beef, the 1966 acquired roundness, and the 1962, darkening as air got to it, released flavor and bouquet that gave at least the illusion of fullness. The evolution of either of those wines alone would have been a source of wonder and pleasure. But the autumnal, nostalgic style of the 1962, a poetic wine, was crushed by the firm, no-nonsense opening of the 1966; and, though we came to appreciate the 1966, its glowing color and bold structure seemed only to intrude on the 1962s fleeting qualities and therefore left an impression of indiscreet bluntness.

There are times, of course, when this style of 1966 can be used to admirable effect in setting off another wine. A few years ago, at a dinner in Bordeaux, the lean quality of the vintage was put to good use by artfully placing a Léoville-Barton '66 to bring out the fullness of a succeeding Ducru-Beaucaillou '64. To indicate how careful one must be, that same Ducru-Beaucaillou '64, admittedly older, appeared to be sharp-edged and pinched when served to me recently, again at a dinner in Bordeaux, because it was immediately preceded by a light young Sauternes served to accompany an opening course of Cavaillon melon.

It is always safe to play down the first of a pair of wines, using it, so to speak, as a curtain raiser for the second (certainly the case when I once offered a Pape-Clément '69, a year of hollow wines in Bordeaux, inexplicably overpraised at the time, before a Gruaud-Larose '64). But sometimes the first red wine of a pair is to accompany a principal course while preparing for a fine bottle with the cheese. Then, even the "lesser" wine must have quality and character enough to support its place at the heart of a meal.

To precede his superb Pétrus '61, Jean-Pierre Moueix, the château's proprietor, served his Trotanoy '62. The wine's big, soft style provided the right balance for roast fillet of beef while preparing us for what was to follow. A Léoville-Barton '67 was recently used in the same way at a dinner in San Francisco. With authority enough to anchor the main course, it had a sufficiently low profile to introduce a rare but fading Langoa-Barton '37. Where the Carruades '66 in New York had established criteria inappropriate to the 1962, the Léoville-Barton '67 was softly agreeable, just substantial enough for a fillet of beef yet with little to catch on to. As a result, the bouquet and flavor of the 1937 appeared stronger than might otherwise have been the case. Though the wine lacked body and, in truth, was beginning to dry out, we, being carefully prepared, were able fully to enjoy what it still had to offer.

I have known wines to be sacrificed, deliberately placed as a buffer between two others. For example, one evening when Château Canon '59, an imposing Saint-Emilion, accompanied the main dish, we were to finish dinner with Château La Lagune '61, a wine I hadn't tasted in years but that my host knew to have been a great favorite of mine when both the wine and I were younger. Shrewdly he introduced between the Canon and the La Lagune a Latour '50, well balanced and lively but uncharacteristically lightweight, thus tactfully moving us into a key in which La Lagune '61 no longer as richly full-blown as it had been in the 1960s, could be better appreciated. The same friend, on another occasion, poured with the cheese Cheval-Blanc '60, elegant and unassertive, in order to modify expectations established by the powerful Lynch-Bages '61 we had been drinking. He then brought dinner to a close with Doisy-Védrines '37, an exquisite but aging Sauternes that would otherwise have been less well appreciated. (He showed the Sauternes off perfectly with nothing more than a slice of ripe pineapple.)

Because our appreciation of any wine changes dramatically in the context of other wines, I am in awe of the temerity with which newsletters in this country constantly publish comparative ranks for wines based on grades awarded to a decimal point, as if some absolute were being measured scientifically. Red wines of discretion, balance, and charm rarely do well in a comparative tasting that includes any that are over-scale, over-tannic, or aggressively made. A wine that stands out in such a lineup is hardly likely to be the most companionable at table. But where Michael Broadbent was content to let us share his changing impressions of wines, explaining his preferences as appropriate, too many newsletter publishers, alas, have confused themselves with the bearer of stone tablets. Jean Delmas of Château Haut-Brion once said (if I do not quote him accurately, I certainly have the sense of his remark), "I make Château Haut-Brion to taste good with food; it is of no concern to me how it tastes with Château Lafite." Amen.

But I shouldn't be so self-righteous. After all, if I accept the advice of my compulsive friends and buy a word processor to store my tasting notes, perhaps it could be programmed to adjust each entry according to context, temper, and tasting order, flash lights when impressions were contradictory, and generally allow for my human fallibility. Then detached from palate, prejudices, and humors, it could rank them to the sixth decimal point in a print-out that would really put it on the line. Perhaps it could be programmed to grill my lamb chops too.

Dessert Wines

Browsing the secondhand bookshops of the Fulham Road one summer, I came across an old copy of T. Earle Welby's *The Cellar Key*, a little book published in the thirties, full of forthright good sense on wine (by which I mean, as we all do when we use such a phrase, that his opinions coincide by and large with my own).

The book was a delight to read; but I was uncomfortable with Welby's assertion that a good dinner, with great red wines, should end with the best of them. It was not that he was prejudiced against dessert wines as such; he felt, rather, that since no dessert wine could rise to a higher plane than the best red wine, to serve one after a suite of fine reds could never be more than an anticlimax. Even so, there is a passage in the book that confirms him to have been capable of appreciating a fine Sauternes. He once served a very old Château d'Yquem to a Scottish visitor of even greater age, a man quite unfamiliar with sweet white wines (which I find hard to believe) but "nobly fanatical about claret." "As the wine took him," said Welby with a questionable excess of lyricism, "he passed into rapture." "I have never cared for sweet wine, but you are right," said the Scot. "This *is* wine." And then, careful of his words in rapture or not, he added, "I will never drink it again. I will keep it as a memory of our evening together." At which T. Earle Welby was both charmed and gratified.

Not that ending dinner with a magnificent red wine was, or is, uncommon. In nineteenth-century England all red wines, more often than not, were kept until *after* dinner, when the ladies had withdrawn and there could be serious drinking. (That is why there still exists in England the curious habit of eating cheese after the sweet course of dinner: a *lady* would no more think of eating cheese than she would of drinking red wine, so the cheese, too, was kept until the men were alone.)

William Younger, in *Gods, Men, and Wines*, gives the menu of a dinner offered sometime in the 1850s by Sir William Hardman to George Meredith and Dante Gabriel Rossetti, among others, at which the *filet de boeuf* and lamb cutlets were accompanied by Amontillado sherry, the chicken Marengo and a strawberry omelet were alike washed down with sparkling hock, and only *after* dinner were those who survived this bizarre presentation rewarded with some decent, mature Chambertin.

The tradition of sitting round the table after dinner with a few bottles of fine red wine can, of course, be quite jolly in a blowsy, Rowlandson sort of way, even though, in Hesketh Pearson's words, "It is many years since the nodding and lolling and snoring of a company of gentlemen at the dinner table was considered an appropriate conclusion of a hearty meal."

As the nineteenth century moved from the plain trencherman fare and plainer drinking of its beginning to the elaborate fantasies of Edwardian gastronomic enterprise of its end, old ideas and new became hopelessly confused by the overriding need to be fashionable rather than sensible. Iced Champagne was served with game; and Claret, making its arrival at the table earlier than before, but obviously not early enough, was drunk with the sweets and dessert. (In 1899, "dessert Claret" was among the wines listed at the then Trocadero restaurant in Shaftesbury Avenue.) Sauternes at that time had other uses: Professor Saintsbury (he of the *Notes on a Cellar-Book*), for example, chose Château d'Yquem 1870 to accompany grilled red mullet.

At Oxford colleges, the practice of drinking red wine after dinner continues: I am sure that a good red Bordeaux is still served, with the nuts and fruit, to the dons of St. Edmund Hall, along with Sauternes, Port, and Madeira, whatever has happened to the pound. To offer a continuation of red wine with dessert to those who prefer it is civilized; to impose it, however, or, worse, to deprive those who might enjoy a small glass of sweet wine at the close of a good dinner is hardly considerate.

Even in Bordeaux, a superb luncheon often rests on the lingering memory of the last of the red wines. I have been surprised to notice how few are the occasions when a fine Sauternes is served (except in the Sauternais itself, of course). Sometimes I have been bewildered by a concluding dry Champagne, served just when the palate needs no further stimulation.

When I have shared with friends and eaten well, those few hauntingly sweet, golden sips of dessert wine are particularly fitting as the evening mellows to post-dinner talk. But in our calorie-conscious age, all sweetness is suspect. Or perhaps it is not our present flight from sweet dishes but the sweet dishes themselves that turn us away from rich, old Vouvray and honeyed Beerenauslesen. "Sweet dishes," thunders Mr. Welby, "are destructive of all wines except the most luscious of Sauternes." The Germans, sensing this, drink their finest sweet wines unaccompanied after the meal; and I have to admit that in many instances carefully plotted combinations of sweet dishes and sweet wines have fallen far short of the memorable experiences they were intended to be.

Just this spring, when the delightful new Muscat wine of the Angelo Papagni winery first appeared in San Francisco, it was served at the end of a dinner party with a feathery confection that seemed to be made of air, cream, and ground hazelnuts in about equal proportions. Most of us were already familiar with the wine and were surprised that it seemed curiously thin and lackluster, despite the minimal sweetening in the hazelnut cream. But the cream itself, coating the mouth, masked both the weight of the wine and its zest.

On the other hand, I remember drinking a glorious Château Filhot 1953 with a summer pudding (an English nursery dish of fresh raspberries and currants, both red and black, pressed firmly into a pudding basin lined with plain bread and left to chill overnight) smothered in the rich, yellow cream of the Loseley herd.

Once back home, I looked through my own old dinner menus and saw that I had been instinctively restrained when serving old Sauternes: orange salad with brown crystal sugar; compote of fresh peaches; ripe figs in raspberry purée; nothing very rich or creamy. But in my notebook there were numerous entries of sweet wines I had enjoyed elsewhere with dishes of much greater variety: a Château d'Yquem 1954 with strawberries Romanoff in New York; the exciting 1973 Edelwein of Freemark Abbey with a freshly made ice of orange and chestnuts at a friend's house in Napa; a delectable Château Suduiraut 1947 with a rich strawberry tart; and, just recently, a young Château Rieussec with a *soufflé au Grand Marnier* at San Francisco's French Club.

Harry Yoxall, in his book *The Enjoyment of Wine*, cautions against serving any fine wine with egg dishes but excepts a sweet white wine with a sweet soufflé, because, he says, "well, because you can." In an old issue of the Wine and Food Society's quarterly I found, over his initials, an account of a dinner at the Dorchester Hotel in London in 1963. The evening concluded with a *soufflé Marie Brizard*, accompanied by a Niersteiner Rohr-Rehbach Riesling und Sylvaner Trockenbeerenauslese, Original Abfullung Dr. Jur. A. Senfter 1953 (when the Germans catch up with California and start to mention on their labels the sugar level of the grapes, the pH of the must, and the fermentation temperature as well, we shall get a really good read for our money). Neither the diners nor the wine were ruffled by the eggs. "Against the mild and well-risen soufflé," wrote Mr. Yoxall, the wine "offered a glorious sweetness, but without any cloying." Obviously the occasion itself —happy, as one deduces from the rest of the account—would have heightened the appreciation of the wine, and one can hardly criticize a wine with a pedigree that long.

The more I read and thought about combinations of sweet wines and sweet dishes, the more I realized that I had paid less attention than I should to the effect of one on the other, inexcusable in one who can spend hours wondering whether a rack of lamb or a simple beef daube would be best for a particular red wine. Only idiots, I reminded myself, take their pleasures frivolously.

So, on my first idle Sunday afternoon, in a spirit of inquiry, I assembled ripe peaches and raspberries, a slightly sweetened but otherwise plain apple mousse, and an apple fool (the mousse stirred with whipped cream). I made a *crème caramel* and bought the best vanilla ice cream I could find, a strawberry tart with thick *crème pâtissière*, a cake smothered in rich dark chocolate, and a rum and chocolate truffle. To match the sweets I brought out one of my last bottles of Château Suduiraut 1967; a Schloss Vollrads Auslese '59; a sweet California wine, a light Muscat of Alexandria bottled by Corti Brothers; and a heavier Moscato di Canelli as well as a Malvasia, both from Cresta Blanca. Fortified dessert wines— Port, Madeira, and cream sherry—are impossible to taste at the same time as table wine–strength wines: they obliterate the lighter wines.

A friend who called unexpectedly froze at the sight of my dining table and declined my invitation to stay and assist. I was somewhat daunted myself, I have to confess, but I remembered Bertie of the Guards, the hero of Ouida's novel *Under Two Flags*, and took heart. Bertie drank Curaçao liberally with his breakfast, and the love of his life, Zuzu (a young lady, evidently French, but of uncertain antecedents, whom he had "translated from a sphere of garret, bread and cheese to a sphere of villa, Champagne and chicken"), prescribed for his three-o'clock-in-the-morning depressions Crème de Bouzy with crushed pineapple, and Parfait Amour, a sticky, purple liqueur that hopefully restored him to that equilibrium necessary to assure a good night's sleep for both of them. Compared with that, mine was hardly a test of fortitude.

I started with Château La Salle of the Christian Brothers. Against the peach and the plain apple mousse it was fresh and clean, lightly fruity, and with an agreeably balanced sweetness. The raspberries subdued its flavor, but the addition of a little cream to the raspberries toned *them* down and restored the flavor of the wine. The ice cream deadened the palate, and I had no taste impression of the wine at all; the eggs in the *crème caramel* robbed the wine of flavor and made it taste thin. The fruit tart with *crème pâtissière* also detracted from the fullness and flavor of the wine, and the sweetness of pastry and glaze made the wine seem dry. The chocolate cake and the rum and chocolate truffle both distorted the wine completely.

I drew breath and a glass of Château Suduiraut 1967. It was exquisite against the peach but, to my surprise, even better against the raspberries. Their sharp flavor made the Sauternes seem more luscious, even though its flavor was toned down. It seemed to finish dry against the apple mousse, on the other hand, and against the apple fool it tasted quite dry and hard. Ice cream stunned the wine, leaving just a thin, dry taste. The *crème caramel* and the fruit tart again made the wine lighter and less flavored. The chocolate in both the cake and the truffle distorted the wine as before.

Schloss Vollrads is a rich, golden wine with a perfume and flavor of ripe fruits and honey. Against the peach it was superb, but the raspberries robbed it of flavor. It was drier against the apple mousse and even more so—with less body and less flavor—against the apple fool. I went back to the peach to make sure there was no taste carry-over from the deadening fool to the *crème caramel*; but again the *crème caramel* and *crème pâtissière* of the strawberry tart subdued this huge wine and made it thin and insignificant. Amazingly, the wine was more powerful than the ice cream, and, though the frozen palate had no reaction at all, a diminished fruity aroma came through. The wine was distorted by the chocolate.

By now I was beginning to feel rather shaky, but I drank a glass of water, walked twice round the apartment, and was ready to continue.

Corti Brothers' Muscat of Alexandria is a delicate wine with only slight sweetness. None of the foods enhanced it in any way: it was best drunk alone. The natural sharpness of the raspberries brought out the slender sweetness of the wine but diminished its flavor, and everything else gave poor exchange for what it took from the wine.

The Moscato di Canelli was more powerful and, in fact, more agreeable with its strong flavor toned down by the raspberries, than it was with the more delicately balanced peach. For the first time the *crème caramel* and fruit tart improved a wine by taming the overbearing flavor. The wine even dominated the chocolate, though tasting rather thin and acid against it.

The even more pungent Malvasia, with a marked Muscatel flavor, also was better with the raspberries than the peach. It was more palatable against the apple fool and considerably toned down against the *crème caramel* and fruit tart. But at this stage, unfortunately, my courage failed, and I cannot say how Malvasia stands up to rum and chocolate truffle, chocolate cake, or vanilla ice cream.

Hot and Cold

SOMEWHERE IN a pantry drawer reserved for broken decanter stoppers, useless corkscrews, candle ends and old corks (they might come in handy), I have a special thermometer with which I could regularly check the temperature of wine in my glass before I drink. I say *could* because I have been uncomfortable with the idea of using it ever since a distinguished French *chroniqueur gastronomique*, now departed, used hers with such startling effect at a Paris luncheon at least twenty years ago. Those assembled were on the point of bringing to their lips glasses of freshly poured young Beaujolais, served at cool cellar temperature, when she leapt to her feet. "Stop!" she cried. Wondering what horror I was being protected from, I put down my glass. She held her own aloft, a thermometer sticking from it, in a pose not unlike Liberty with her torch, and came straight to the point. "The temperature of this wine is only nine degrees centigrade," she said. "We must wait until it reaches ten."

And wait we did, watching in silence while she watched the mercury. Fortunately the room was warm, and it seemed barely a minute or two before she relaxed, smiled and nodded. "Now," she breathed. We smelled and we savored—but the spontaneity of our pleasure was gone, though no one was ill-mannered enough to ask even himself how such pedantry could stop the wine continuing to creep up to eleven degrees, to twelve and to thirteen. It is inevitable that wine will warm in the glass: That is why the *Académie Internationale du Vin*, in their published notes on wine service, advise starting to pour wine slightly below the optimum temperature.

Which brings us to the question: What *is* optimum temperature? Though neither glass nor bottle will stay obligingly on the button, what, at least, should we aim for? There never has been total agreement on the temperature at which wine is best served. In one of Robert Browning's poems, a bishop coos with satisfaction at the chill of his claret, urging a companion to put the decanter back in the ice—to the outrage of Professor Saintsbury. ("Icing good claret at all is barbarous," he said in *Notes on a Cellar Book*, "but the idea of freezing, thawing and freezing again is simply Bolshevik.") Politics aside, keeping wine cool seems to have been an obsession in the nineteenth century. Cyrus Redding, in *Everyman His Own Butler*, published in London in 1852, advised no one to "pour out more wine with his dinner than he intends to take at one sip, and then immediately to reverse his glass." Wineglass coolers filled with the coldest water were set by each place and glasses without a base were sometimes used so that it was impossible to omit reversing them in the water. Apart from the awkwardness of reaching for decanter or bottle for every swallow of wine (it was presumably pulled from and plunged back into the ice repeatedly), I am not sure that I would care to have every "sip" of wine diluted by the drops of cold water clinging to my baseless glass.

Conventionally, there are three "temperatures" at which we serve wine: "room temperature," a misleading term we use to suggest something in the range of 60° to 65° Fahrenheit; "cool" or "cellar temperature," from 50° to 55°; and "cold" or "iced," from 40° to 45°. Instinctively one feels that wine would be at its most refreshing served cool. Rabelais thought it best that way ("drink it fresh if you can" is a rough translation of something he said somewhere), and Keats, of course, preferred his "cool'd a long age." Instead of finding it necessary to justify drinking wine cool, perhaps we should have good reason when we choose to drink it any other way. Instead of asking, "Why do we drink Beaujolais, a red wine, at 'cellar temperature'?" perhaps we should ask, "Why do we drink red Bordeaux at 'room temperature'?"

If we accept a cool 55° as a norm, at least hypothetically, we can ask ourselves why we would serve any wine warmer or colder and establish for ourselves a guide more practical than the printed tables that link temperatures to wine names as if all Cabernet Sauvignons were the same, all Sauternes indistinguishable, one from another, and all red Burgundy of equal maturity. Food eaten directly from the refrigerator lacks flavor, as we all know. Similarly, when we serve a wine at a temperature below the norm we neutralize taste and smell increasingly the colder we go. Wine served below 45° releases almost nothing of its aroma and bouquet, and, in fact, anesthetizes rather than stimulates the taste buds. As a wine's temperature mounts from the norm toward 65°, on the other hand, so aroma and bouquet are increasingly released until, at about 68°, evaporating alcohol begins to dominate, and some of the other volatile compounds present, agreeable when barely perceptible, become more intense and make the bouquet less attractive. Hence the need to keep even red wines cooler than the average American dining room.

Aroma and *bouquet* have precise meaning in relation to wine, and differ from each other. Young wine has *aroma*, uncomplicated odor of the grape and of fermentation—fruity, sometimes floral, universally appealing. *Bouquet* (associations with a mixed bouquet of flowers or of herbs are deliberate) is a result of changes and combinations that take place in the sealed bottle. It is a legacy of time, and was thought, for many years, to be the result of oxidation. Though there is still little agreement on the nature of wine's bouquet, generally it is now accepted that, in table wines anyway, it is a result of reduction, the opposite of what was thought before. During fermentation, usually presented to us with a simplified formula showing only the transformation of sugar into familiar ethyl alcohol and carbon dioxide, there are formed traces of many other alcohols. Since they are in the presence of organic acids of equal diversity, interaction, along with the aromatic mutation of substances otherwise without odor, leads in time to an immeasurable complexity of evanescent compounds that volatilize when wine is poured.

When all the talking is done, capacity to develop bouquet is the real measure of wine's quality: that is the point of aging it at least. Not all wines are suitable, and we say of them that "they do not age well." In time, the grape and fermentation aroma present in such wines fades, and there is nothing to take its place. The capacity to form bouquet is relative to balance and to depth (as opposed to superficiality) in the wine. It does not appear to depend on scale, nor, in particular, does it depend on heavy tannin or on alcoholic strength, though a well-composed wine, one that will lend itself appropriately to aging, will have due proportion of each. Contemporary methods of winemaking, particularly in California, ensure that elements of grape and fermentation aroma persist to a certain extent, even in mature wines, so we need not be surprised to detect varietal characteristics, for example, in red wines ten and fifteen years old. The important issue is that if bouquet is the objective of fine winemaking, then when it exists it should be appreciated fully. That means drinking the wine as close as possible to 65° as other factors allow.

What other factors are there to consider? Don't we just trade the fresh, cool feeling of 55° for the increased satisfaction of taste and smell at 65°, or vice versa? Often that is exactly the exchange we make. Young white wines without bouquet are drunk at cool temperatures that suppress slightly their aroma because the refreshingly cool pleasure we gain seems fair compensation. In the case of a fine, mature white Burgundy, a complex Chardonnay, or an old white Graves we are less willing to sacrifice taste and smell, so we find instead a compromise temperature.

But the direct effect of temperature on the wine is only half the question. We ourselves react physiologically to the temperature of what we drink. For example, we are most sensitive to sweetness in wine when the wine is warmer, and become less so the more it is chilled. An undistinguished white jug wine with coarse aroma and unattractively sweet finish can be rendered at least acceptable if served very cold. A fine old Sauternes, on the other hand, probably much sweeter, but matured in bottle long enough to have acquired a richly complex flavor, should never be served cold, whatever is said about icing sweet wines. One finds a degree of coolness that will balance the desired restraint of sweetness against appropriate opportunity to appreciate fully the wine's bouquet.

White wines that seem either too high or too low in acidity are typically wines that can be served with advantage at temperatures below the norm. If the problem is lack of acidity, flabbiness will be less apparent; and a low temperature, numbing slightly the taste buds, will mask excessive acidity. White wines with good acid balance do not need such assistance, and serving them at temperatures below the norm suppresses taste and smell for no balancing gain, and therefore serves no pleasurable purpose.

Although, at low temperatures, sensitivity to acids and sugar is reduced, it is increased to bitterness and astringency. A red wine that slips down easily at 65° can become hard and astringent to us at 50°. It is this amplification of bitter and astringent elements of red wine at low temperatures that lies behind the conventional wisdom of serving red wines warmer than white. Red Bordeaux, tannic when young, *bouqueté* when mature, has always something to gain from being served at "room temperature." Others, like Beaujolais, low in tannin and drunk for their aroma rather than for bouquet, lose little by being served cool, and thereby gain in their quality as refreshment. Red Burgundy, rarely as tannic as Bordeaux, can be served on the cool side when young, but not when mature bouquet has formed.

Electing to serve a wine at 65°, 55°, or 45° is one thing; getting it there, just right and just when you want it, is another. If the cellar, closet, kitchen corner or boot-box where wine is kept is no cooler than the rest of the house or apartment, some adjustment will always have to be made, even for red wine. In my experience, wine needs to be placed in the refrigerator for at least two hours if it is to be cold, but an hour or an hour and a half is usually enough to make a bottle quite cool, depending on the setting of the refrigerator and the original temperature of the bottle. Red wines to be brought down to 60° from a normal apartment temperature need forty-five minutes in the refrigerator: the "twenty minutes" sometimes recommended does little more than cool the glass.

The quickest way to cool a bottle of wine is to plunge it into a bucket of ice and water, but if the bottle stays too long in the mixture the wine will continue to get colder. Depending on how quickly the bottle will be used and on the temperature of the room there is sometimes more satisfaction to be had if the wine is first allowed to become a little cooler than ideal, and then left out of the bucket while consumed. Since wine is always best within the parameters of 45° to 65°, temperature adjustment need never be a major problem. Twenty minutes of cold air in the freezer is

hardly more severe than twenty minutes in an ice-and-water
bucket, and unless one lives in an igloo, only limited patience is
needed to raise the temperature of a bottle of red wine from "cellar
temperature" to "room temperature." The counsel often given
that a red wine needs to be placed in the dining room three days
before required implies that such a bottle will somehow adjust to
the ambient temperature more gradually than a bottle placed in the
same room three hours before required. The idea that a bottle of
wine might control its own rate of temperature change is from a
metaphysical realm beyond my experience.

Whatever applies to still white wines applies to sparkling white
wines except that, generally speaking, sparkling wines should remain quite cold if bubbles are to be released gradually. A bottle
is therefore best left in its bucket of ice and water. But an older
champagne, especially one that is late-disgorged, is approached as
any other older, fine wine: bouquet and flavor will be stunned if
the wine is too cold. The trade-off is not too difficult to make because older champagnes release their less forceful *mousse* more
slowly anyway, and they have less need to be thoroughly chilled.
In this, as in everything else connected with wine, common sense
and personal preference will prove to be better guides than simplistic rules.

INDEX

ABOUT THE AUTHOR

GERALD ASHER writes a regular column on wine for *Gourmet*. He began his career as a wine merchant in London after training in France, Spain and Germany, but now lives and works as a wine importer and merchant in San Francisco, where he presides every year over the California Vinters' Barrel Tasting, the most distinguished annual American wine event.